CARIBBEAN

Bruce Geddes

WORLD FOOD Caribbean
1st edition – May 2001

Published by Lonely Planet Publications Pty Ltd ABN 36 005 607 983

Lonely Planet Offices
Australia Locked Bag 1, Footscray, Victoria 3011
USA 150 Linden Street, Oakland CA 94607
UK 10a Spring Place, London NW5 3BH
France 1 rue du Dahomey, 75011 Paris

Publishing manager Peter D'Onghia
Series editor Lyndal Hall
Series design & layout Brendan Dempsey
Editor Patrick Witton
Mapping Natasha Velleley

Photography
Many images in this guide are available for licensing from
Lonely Planet Images. email: lpi@lonelyplanet.com.au

Front cover – Rachel from Montego Bay with her shrimp earrings, Jamaica
Back cover – Barbecued corn sprinkled with lime juice, street stalls of Kingston, Jamaica

ISBN 1 86450 348 3

text & maps © Lonely Planet Publications Pty Ltd, 2001
photos © photographers as indicated 2001

Printed by
The Bookmaker International Ltd
Printed in China

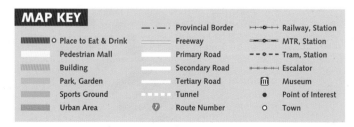

MAP KEY		
○ Place to Eat & Drink	— · — Provincial Border	⊢•⊣ Railway, Station
Pedestrian Mall	Freeway	⊷⊶ MTR, Station
Building	Primary Road	– ○ – Tram, Station
Park, Garden	Secondary Road	⊢•⊣ Escalator
Sports Ground	Tertiary Road	🏛 Museum
Urban Area	Tunnel	● Point of Interest
	Route Number	○ Town

About the Author

Bruce Geddes was born in Windsor, Canada, and educated in Halifax, Guadalajara, Kingston, Bogota, Toronto and London. He is the author of *World Food Mexico* and has found print in the *National Post, IE:Money* and *Business Traveller* magazine. He is also the co-creator (with Robert Plowman and Michael Mabbott) of a situation comedy called *Grey Matter* which has been optioned but will probably never get made and so bears mention here as the only possible source of recognition. Bruce is no stranger to good food – not to mention drink. His current bar stool is located in London, Ontario.

Bruce wishes to thank (in no particular order): Professor John Kirk of Dalhousie University for his continuing insights into Cuba, Tanya Carey and her entire family of Cable Beach (the Bahamas) and her trusty sidekick Greg Walker, Christian Baird the transplanted Trini, Robert Plowman, Erin Ilês, Mike Malouf whose expertise in Jamaican poetry came in handy, Geoff Rector, Kristen Rector along with her little black book, Drew Yamada, Sabrina Di Marco for teaching me the true meaning of 'jump up', Don Alejandro Mangiola whose disgusting habits came in handy for once, Anthony Cooper, Robert Conrad of Martinique Tourism, Barrington Colwater, Judith Simmonds, Dennis Klaus of Willemstad (Curaçao), that bartender in Trinidad, Horacio Zequiera of Havana (Cuba), Carla Woo, Nancy Carr, Kate Austin who is a good photography tutor but not much of a dancer, and Miss Donna Haynes of Kingston (Jamaica). Many thanks also to the LP crew in Melbourne for their patience and good advice. And lastly, to my wonderful family without whose undying patience and support I would be worth dirt.

About the Photographer

Jerry Alexander is a highly credited food & travel photographer with extensive experience working in South-East Asia, particularly Thailand. When he's not travelling around the world – leaving behind a trail of crumbs from eating his props – Jerry lives in California and tends to his vineyard in the Napa Valley.

Jerry wishes to thank: Aida, Rolando and Theresa who opened my eyes and heart to Cuba. Thomas and family for their kindness. In Puerto Rico, Michael, Norma and Lourdes for their help in opening doors and getting me there. Dittos to Tito. In Jamaica, Parchi for her willingness to share her knowledge and the kids for their fun. Rappy for guiding me; Donavan, Michael and Paul for showing me their Jamaica. And Nora and Jerry! In Curaçao, Angelo made it special, Dinah for a treasured few hours. The Avila Beach Hotel, great place, great people!

In St Martin; Steve and Jean Paul for their help and friendship. And all of those I have not mentioned I'm deeply grateful. Thank you!

From the Publisher

This first edition of *World Food Caribbean* was edited by Patrick Witton and designed by Brendan Dempsey of Lonely Planet's Melbourne office. Natasha Velleley mapped, Lara Morcombe and Foong Ling Kong proofed, Lyndal Hall oversaw the book's production and Patrick Witton indexed. Martin Hughes, former series editor, assisted with pre-production.

The language section was compiled by Sabrina Di Marco.

Valerie Tellini, of Lonely Planet Images, coordinated the supply of photographs, Glenn Beanland assessed and Brett Pascoe managed the pre-press work on the images.

Warning & Request

Things change; markets give way to supermarkets, prices go up, good places go bad and not much stays the same. Please tell us if you've discovered changes and help make the next edition even more useful. We value all your feedback, and strive to improve our books accordingly. We have a well-travelled, well-fed team that reads and acknowledges every letter, postcard and email and ensures that every morsel of information finds its way to the appropriate people.

Each correspondent will receive the latest issue of Planet Talk, our quarterly printed newsletter, or Comet, our monthly email newsletter. Subscriptions to both are free. The newsletters might even feature your letter so let us know if you don't want it published.

If you have an interesting anecdote or story to do with your culinary travels, we'd love to hear it. If we publish it in the next edition, we'll send you a free Lonely Planet book of your choice.

Send your correspondence to the nearest Lonely Planet office:

Australia Locked Bag 1, Footscray, Victoria 3011
UK 10a Spring Place, London NW5 3BH
USA 150 Linden St, Oakland CA 94607
France 1 rue du Dahomey, Paris 75011

Or email us at: talk2us@lonelyplanet.com

Contents

Introduction 8

**The Culture of
Caribbean Cuisine** 9
History 11
The Caribbean Today 24
Eating in the Caribbean 29
Etiquette 36

Staples & Specialties 37
Seafood 39
Meat, Poultry & Game 45
Peas & Rice (or Rice & Peas) 47
Vegetables 49
Fruit 51
Herbs, Spices & Other Flavorings 63
Breads & Pastries 64
Desserts & Sweet Snacks 70

Drinks 71
Alcoholic Drinks 72
Non-Alcoholic Drinks 89

Home Cooking & Traditions 103
Utensils 118

Celebrating with Food 119
Festivals 128

Regional Variations 129
The English Islands 130
The Spanish Islands 143
The French Islands 160
The Dutch Islands 165

177 **Shopping & Markets**
179 At the Market
186 Supermarkets & Grocery Stores
186 Street Stalls & Vendors
187 A Caribbean Picnic
190 What to Bring Home

191 **Where to Eat & Drink**
193 Where to Eat
211 Where to Drink
214 The Menu

217 **A Caribbean Banquet**

223 **Fit & Healthy**

229 **Eat Your Words**
230 Caribbean Culinary Dictionary

263 **Recommended Reading**

264 **Photo Credits**

265 **Index**

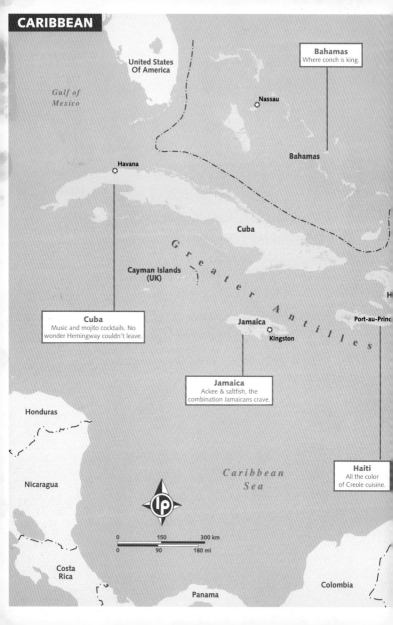

CARIBBEAN

United States Of America

Gulf of Mexico

Bahamas
Where conch is king.

Nassau ✪

Bahamas

Havana ✪

Cuba

Cuba
Music and mojito cocktails. No wonder Hemingway couldn't leave.

Cayman Islands (UK)

Greater Antilles

Jamaica

Kingston ✪

Port-au-Prince

H

Jamaica
Ackee & saltfish, the combination Jamaicans crave.

Honduras

Nicaragua

Caribbean Sea

Haiti
All the color of Creole cuisine.

| 0 | 150 | 300 km |
| 0 | 90 | 180 mi |

Costa Rica

Panama

Colombia

Elevation

3000 m	10000 ft
2000 m	6500 ft
1500 m	5000 ft
1000 m	3000 ft
500 m	1500 ft
0 m	0 ft

Dominican Republic
Baseball and bandera dominicana,
the nation's flagship meal.

*Atlantic
Ocean*

**Turks & Caicos
Islands (UK)**

Puerto Rico
Sofrito, the heart of
Puerto Rico's cuisine.

**Dominican
Republic**
✪
Santo Domingo

**British Virgin
Islands (UK)**

Anguilla (UK)

San Juan ✪
**Puerto Rico
(US)**

St Martin (Fr)
St Barthélemy (Fr)

**Virgin
Islands (US)**

**Sint Maarten
(Neth)**

**Antigua &
Barbuda**

**Netherlands
Antilles (Neth)**

**Guadeloupe
(Fr)**

St Kitts & Nevis

Montserrat (UK)

Dominica

Lesser Antilles

Guadeloupe & Martinique
A piece of Paris in the tropics.

**Martinique
(Fr)**

Fort-de-France ✪

St Lucia

Lesser Antilles

**Aruba
(Neth)**

**Netherlands
Antilles (Neth)**

**St Vincent &
The Grenadines**

Barbados

Curaçao

Bonaire

Willemstad ✪

Grenada

Dutch Islands
Home of
Papiamento cuisine.

Port-of-Spain ✪

Trinidad & Tobago
Where the flavors of India,
Africa and China converge.

**Trindad
& Tobago**

Venezuela

Even the most patriotic Caribbeans will have to admit: you won't come to the islands for the food. You come for the sun, the sand, the music and the perpetual party that occupies the region's spare energy. But once there, whether for a weekend get-away or for work, you *will* notice the food. You will take sweet pleasure from your first taste of fish plucked from the rich, blue Caribbean waters. You'll be refreshed by any of the tropical fruits growing wildly in the verdant mountains of the interior. You'll be tested by killer-spicy pepper sauce, which locals seem to consume with impunity. You will notice just how smooth and mellow rum can be, and how well a thirst can be quenched with an ice-cold local lager.

These discoveries are the same ones made by the people who have been coming to the Caribbean for centuries: from Amerindians to Europeans to slaves to droves of tourists who, every year, plunk their sun-starved bodies down on a Caribbean beach and forget that winter exists.

But you'll have to get off the beach to find the best Caribbean food. You'll have to explore, seek out, ask questions and take chances. Each foray into the Caribbean appetite will both dispel and confirm your perceptions, present new experiences and introduce you to this often overlooked aspect of island culture. For food is embraced on the islands as much as music and sunshine; people hold strong to their culinary traditions despite the needs and influences brought by foreigners.

This book will help you make your own discovery of the culinary offerings presented on the islands. We look at the history and culture of Caribbean cuisine, we look at the way locals approach food and the role it plays in everyday life and at special occasions. Of course, no words can completely replace the taste of a freshly made Puerto Rican **sofrito**, but you'll soon know both where to get it and how to make it (see the recipe in the Regional Variations chapter). Just remember: Caribbean food is based on adventure, so explore, indulge and enjoy.

the **culture** of
caribbean cuisine

The national motto of Jamaica, 'Out of Many, One People' might well apply to the Caribbean as a whole – with a slight modification. Let it instead read: Out of Many, One Cuisine. For despite the diversity of Caribbean peoples and cultures that have produced a multitude of cuisines, there is an undeniable common thread, traceable through history, land, sea and sun.

Distinctive signage at a roadside Rasta stall, Jamaica

The Caribbean is a culture of immigrants and migrants, a place where people have been arriving and leaving since the Arawaks began their northward island-hopping some 2000 years ago. It is a cultural construct that reaches beyond the azure seas and touches nearly every part of the globe. Food plays a major role in this amorphousness. It serves as a bridge to the homeland for the many Caribbeans who have traveled abroad, and as a cultural handle for those who have never set foot on Caribbean soil.

For visitors to the region, the local cuisine will provide the backbone to both the classic and unexpected Caribbean experience. Taste seven-year-old rum in Cuba as the sun sinks into the ocean, or French-style pastries for breakfast in Martinique or **jerk** (meat marinated with a mixture of spices) in a small Jamaican town, and soon you'll hear the music, from driving Dominican meringue to steely Trini calypso. It all comes together to create the Caribbean scenario, one that lingers in your mind – and tastebuds – long after you've left.

History
Amerindians

For nearly 2000 years, the rich soils and abundant waters of the Caribbean were home to the Arawaks and Caribs, collectively known as the Amerindians. The Arawaks were the first to venture north from their homes in the Orinoco River valley in what is present-day Guyana and Venezuela. Paddling dugout canoes (the word 'canoe' was among the first American words to enter the European vocabulary), they made their way to Trinidad and then, island by island, to the Bahamas and west to Jamaica and Cuba. The Caribs followed, waging war on the Arawaks. Later, European settlers spread stories of cannibalism among the Caribs, saying that the wars against the Arawaks were nothing more than hunting expeditions. In reality, human flesh was only eaten in rare rituals. However, this perception offered the European conquerors all the justification they needed to enslave the 'barbarians'.

The Amerindians were excellent fishermen and enjoyed a wide variety of seafood. In fact their catches aren't dissimilar to those that make their way into Caribbean kitchens and dining rooms today. Among the most popular variety were (and are) grouper, sturgeon, shark, lobster, conch, oyster and crab. The Amerindians caught fish in the inland rivers and lakes by poisoning the stream with the juices from local plants in order to sedate (but not kill) the fish. Shellfish were also caught as they scuttled across the shallow coastal waters.

Dinah Veeris from Dinah's Botanic & Historic Garden, Curaçao

CULTURE

Sunset over San Juan Bay, Puerto Rico

Animals such as turtles, iguanas, alligators and frogs also provided sustenance for the Amerindians. They also had a taste for turtle and iguana eggs,
which they ate fresh or preserved by pickling, smoking or drying. Harder to
catch but worth the effort were deer (which the European settlers also had
a taste for), guinea pigs, rabbits and agouti, a rat-like creature. The
Amerindian diet also included ants, termites, caterpillars and grubs.

Apparently the Amerindians dried and preserved their food by cooking
it on a **brabacot** (a wooden framework over a pit of coals). The Spanish
adopted this technique and named it **barbacoa**, from which the word 'barbecue' was adapted (see Barbecue in the Where to Eat & Drink chapter).

OKONOROTE & THE LAND OF WALKING ANIMALS

The Amerindians, had a rich culture of folktales explaining the way the
world was and how things came into existence. One such legend relates
to the time when their ancestors lived in the sky. Among them lived a
famous hunter, Okonorote, who on one search for food stalked a bird for
several days. Finally, he got within range and shot it with his bow and
arrow. The bird fell into a deep pit and Okonorote chased after his kill only
to find another world where animals did not fly but walked on four legs.

Forgetting the meager offerings of the bird, he killed a deer and
brought the meat back to the sky. The rest of the tribe was thrilled and
decided to descend down this pit to make their lives on earth.

And so it continued until a tremendously obese woman blocked the
hole, preventing any more of the tribe from descending. From that point,
the Amerindians occupied the islands, until Christopher Columbus,
another explorer in search of food (in this case spices) arrived in 1492.

A farmer proudly holds tobacco leaves from his crop in Pinar del Río, Cuba

ORIGIN & INFLUENCE

We have chosen to divide the Caribbean islands based on their colonial heritage to provide a broad picture of regional variations that exist in the Caribbean today. But before we begin, it is important to note that all the countries in the region owe at least some of their culinary heritage to Africa. While the food that was brought to the Caribbean from Africa represented a fairly small portion of the diet the slaves left behind, dishes and preparations survived the journey and the centuries of hardships that followed, and are now staples throughout the region. Similarly, the diets of the Amerindians served to keep the earliest settlers alive, and many of their main ingredients also remain staples throughout the Caribbean today.

English Islands
Bermuda, the Bahamas, British Virgin Islands, Turks & Caicos Islands, Cayman Islands, Jamaica, Antigua & Barbuda, Anguilla, St Kitts & Nevis, Montserrat, Dominica, St Lucia, St Vincent & The Grenadines, Barbados, Grenada, Trinidad & Tobago

The English were drawn to the Caribbean by the economic attractions of agricultural production, predominantly in the form of cotton, tobacco and sugarcane plantations. There were no easy colonizations in the Caribbean, but the English seemed to come out somewhat better off than their European counterparts. The English have left behind a legacy of parliamentary democracy, afternoon teas and driving on the left hand side of the road.

An old-style homestead, Kingston, Jamaica

Spanish Islands
Cuba, the Dominican Republic, Puerto Rico

While Spanish ships docked at nearly every island during the long strug-
gle for supremacy, they tactfully concentrated their efforts on the
region's three largest islands: Cuba, the Dominican Republic and Puerto
Rico. The Spanish were also more avid settlers than their rivals, building
bigger cities and convincing more men in the old country that their
future lay across the ocean.

They did not, however, convince many women and as a result, many
citizens of these three countries can count Africans and Amerindians
among their ancestors. This racial mix is also reflected in the foods
enjoyed in each country, although each has their own distinct interpre-
tation of their common culinary legacy.

Long live the Revolution! Old Havana, Cuba

Dutch Islands
Aruba, Bonaire, Curaçao, Sint Maarten

It's possible that the Dutch islands, and Curaçao in particular, is the most
concentrated area of multiculturalism in the world. A wind-swept, dry
and featureless island with no mountains full of gold, nor lands suitable
for sugarcane, coffee or bananas, the islands in the south were virtually
ignored by European settlers for most of the colonial era. The only
resource of any value they could find were the Arawak Indians who
were plucked from their lands to work on other islands in the region.

CULTURE

The city of Willemstad on the island of Curaçao is resplendent with tropically inspired European architecture

French Islands
Martinique, Guadeloupe, St Martin, St Barthélemy, Haiti

The French have left a legacy of contrasts. To one extreme there is St Martin and St Barthélemy, two of the Caribbean's wealthiest islands where French expats relax. On the other extreme is Haiti, the most impoverished country in the western hemisphere, where chaotic and despotic rule has been the norm since slaves rebelled during the French Revolution. Somewhere in the middle sit Guadeloupe and Martinique. Their currency is the French franc and the *drapeau tricolore* flies proudly over Fort Saint-Louis. Nevertheless, like Haiti, the culture owes its roots to Africa.

The azure waters of Sint Maarten

CULTURE

Europeans

Europeans arrived in the Caribbean in 1492, led by Christopher Columbus. His was a discovery borne of appetite, because his exploration was not in search of gold (that was a second prize), but spices. In those days spices were coveted for their preservative qualities. In fact, pound for pound the price of certain spices was even higher than that of gold. Columbus, the Italian, sailed under the flag of Spain. Using Cuba as a base, the Spanish established Santiago de Cuba as their first capital, and it became the trading hub of the Americas, receiving ships packed with settlers from Spain and sending the vessels back filled with silver and gold.

The European settlers took full advantage of the Amerindian diet, even extending their tastebuds to the delicacy, **gru gru worm** (beetle grub).

Taking time out in Havana, Cuba

Corn grew in the arid southern islands and European settlers used it to make cornbread. The Amerindians also introduced them to cassava (also called manioc), which is still a big item in farmer's markets where the hairy, brown root stands in great piles. European settlers were no doubt especially grateful that they did not learn about cassava the hard way, for the juices of the mashed root are extremely poisonous and need to be squeezed from the pulp before it is safe to eat. Other foodstuffs that European settlers grew a taste for included pineapples, guava, papaya, cashews and lima beans.

The European settlers did try to import flavors from home, but these islands did not share the same mild Mediterranean climate as the homeland and so, when Columbus brought wheat seeds on his second voyage to the new world, his attempts to cultivate them failed. A similar fate met subsequent attempts to grow olives for oil and grapes for wine. But not all their initiatives were bungled. Livestock thrived and soon the islands were teeming with pigs, goats, sheep and cattle. Pigs in particular flourished in the Spanish colonies and pork remains the most important meat in Cuba, Puerto Rico and the Dominican Republic. The Spanish introduced limes, oranges, bananas, ginger, cinnamon and rice. It is also believed that the Spanish were responsible for bringing coconuts to the region.

Overleaf – Rachel Harms opts for calm and a strawberry daiquiri despite an impending cyclone Margueritaville bar, Montego Bay, Jamaica

The English came next, followed soon by the French and Dutch. By this time, what little gold there had been was long gone, and agriculture became the economic focus. Enormous plantations were established throughout the islands to grow such crops as cotton, tobacco, sugarcane and bananas.

Old Knip Plantation House, built in the 17th century, Curaçao

As worldwide demand for sugarcane rose, so too did the prosperity of the planters. They wasted no time in spending it, building immense mansions in which they held lavish parties for their neighboring planters. For such occasions they imported fine wines, olive oils and meats from Europe. But for the most part they had to adjust their diets due to the unforgiving heat and humidity. Meats were immediately preserved by way of salting or drying, and rum and beer took the place of wine as the everyday tipple.

The influx of Europeans was disastrous to the Amerindian population. Those that didn't die of diseases new to them were worked to death in mines and fields. Without the large population base of the Aztecs or the geographical range of the Inca, the Arawaks, Caribs and Tainos were all but wiped out. Today, only small pockets survive, most notably in Dominica where a reserve has been established for the Carib people.

Slavery

The crops planted by the European settlers were selected for one reason: trade. Cotton and sugarcane and later fruits like bananas and pineapples were harvested in ships that took them east to Europe and then north to the US. Among these, sugarcane was king.

The Spaniards were the first to plant sugarcane in the Caribbean (in the early 1500s), but the industry did not really take hold until 1630, when the Dutch introduced new planting techniques. At the same time, sugar was emerging as a popular commodity among pastry makers and confectioners in Europe. A boom ensued and nearly all the islands turned their lands into sugarcane plantations, clearing forests wherever possible.

To address the labor shortage, the European settlers brought in slaves from West Africa, who worked the fields and plantation houses, and who today make up the region's largest ethnic group. Today, it is impossible to consider any aspect of Caribbean culture without considering the contributions of the descendants of these early slaves. In music, language and especially food, the ties to West Africa remain strong.

From the early 1500s, a steady stream of men, women and children were taken from their West African homes and brought to the islands to work mines and cash crops. The slave diet changed year on year, paralleling the fluctuations of the price of sugarcane. When the price was high, the planters would seek to squeeze as much profit from their land by planting sugarcane on every available acre. Slaves were fed imported meats and other foods not grown on plantation soil. When the price dropped, slaves were encouraged to grow their own food and were given plots of land to plant such foods as squash, peppers and okra. For the most part, they grew what was already there, such as cassava and peppers, but they also grew plants that had been carried across the ocean on the slave boats. Among these was **ackee**, a bright orange-yellow skinned fruit with soft yellow meat and shiny black seeds that is today part of the national dish of Jamaica, **ackee & saltfish** (see Jamaica in the Regional Variations chapter). Another African import was okra, or **quimbombó** as it is called in Cuba. Preparations in those days were very simple, often employing only one pot or, in the case of corn or meat, nothing more than an open fire. The most common dish was a stew that would include whatever was available.

As more and more of the arable land was turned over to sugarcane production, an increasing amount of the food had to be imported. The islands became dependent on trade for food. Rice was brought from South Carolina, beef jerky from Ireland and salted cod made its way south from the Atlantic coast of Canada (see the boxed text A Codfish Story in the Staples & Specialties chapter). Later, the trend continued as apples were shipped from Washington State and butter made its way from England.

In many ways the diet of the Europeans who claimed the land was similar to that of the slaves who worked it. After all, the cooks in the kitchens of the plantation houses were themselves slaves and the food they prepared was the same food they prepared for their families. There were significant differences, of course, especially in terms of the ingredients that made their way to the table of the plantation owners. The finest cuts of meat were reserved for the plantation owners while the slaves got whatever was left over. Today, many traditional Caribbean dishes call for cuts of meat such as pig's tail, cow's foot, tripe or salt pork. But this is no longer considered second best; many of the region's finest restaurants will serve a pork stew that is a direct descendent of that made in slave kitchens two centuries ago.

Butchers at Havana's public market, Cuba

CULTURE

Indentured Servants

The next major economic event in Caribbean history was also major for food. Abolition began by force in Haiti following the French Revolution. Slave rebellions throughout the region followed, and growing disgust with the practice in England led to emancipation in Jamaica and the English colonies in 1834. Over a half century later, in 1886, the Spanish crown abolished slavery in Cuba. Plantation owners were once again faced with a drastic labor shortage. Beginning in the 1830s, thousands of Chinese and East Indian workers made the long journey to begin new lives working as indentured servants.

Migration was concentrated in the more southern areas, such as in Trinidad. A few years later indentured servants began arriving in Jamaica and Cuba. In all, 380,000 East Indians and 143,000 Chinese made the journey to work the plantations as the slaves had before them. There was one important difference, of course. After a set period, the indentured servant paid off his passage and was released from servitude.

Naturally, both the Chinese and East Indian communities tried to maintain their homeland connections through the food they prepared. They had some success and the culinary influence of both cultures is felt to this day. Most notably, Chinese and East Indian immigrants strengthened the role of rice in the Caribbean. Spices increased in popularity and **roti**, the flatbread that is wrapped around a spicy stew of meat, potatoes and vegetables became a major player on islands such as Trinidad (see Foreign Influences later in this chapter and the recipe in the Caribbean Banquet chapter).

CREOLE IN CONTEXT

Whether you are talking about Martinique specialties or Haitian history, the word Creole will probably come into play. Derived from the Spanish word *criollo* (meaning, native to a locality), Creole can take on a multitude of meanings depending on the context. In the Caribbean, Creole means a native-born person of Spanish or French and African or Amerindian ancestry.

In the realm of Caribbean cuisine, Creole dishes are those that traditionally incorporated local ingredients and Spanish or French cooking techniques. Such dishes, however, have changed beyond recognition over time as other influences came into play. Consequently the term Creole has come to incorporate a range of dishes as diverse as the Caribbean itself.

The Caribbean Today

Over time, others have come to the Caribbean: tourists looking to escape northern winters, the US army, tax dodgers, film stars and the odd disgraced European royal. And Caribbeans themselves have never lost the urge to keep moving. It is not uncommon to find someone who was born on one island living on another. Some go farther, on rafts across the Straits of Florida or on airplanes to Europe to spend a few years in boarding school. New York City's Latin community is mainly made up of migrants from Puerto Rico and the Dominican Republic. Reggae music never would have attained its international status had it not been for the Jamaican community in London. And one of the biggest carnivals in the world, Toronto's annual Caribana would not happen without the strong Caribbean presence in that city.

Today, Caribbean cuisine remains a work in progress. As a major tourist destination, the influence of visitors continues to be a major factor in the way the people approach their food. Moreover, the number of islanders living abroad and then returning with new ideas for food and food preparation ensures that other cuisine styles will continue to have an impact.

Selling guineps on the beach at Bluefield, Jamaica

CULTURE

FOREIGN INFLUENCES

While all Caribbean cuisine is essentially the result of foreign influence, not all of these influences came by way of colonization or slavery. We begin with the Chinese and East Indian, who came initially as indentured laborers bringing with them many of the preparations and ingredients from their homelands.

China

Immigration from China to the Caribbean began in the form of indentured servitude in 1839 (just after the abolition of slavery), but ground to a near halt by the middle of the 20th century. As a result, where Chinese cooking has evolved and become unique in the larger cities of the west, Chinese influence here is caught in a 1950s time warp, as all the wonders of regional cooking (Shantou, Sichuan, etc) were abandoned for bland chow meins and goopy red sauces that westerners demanded at that time. And it's a shame, too, given the fresh ingredients, especially seafood, available in the Caribbean.

Even so, Chinese food has been adapted to the tastes of each of the islands it serves.

Chinatown, Havana, Cuba

For those islands that enjoy spice (Jamaica, Trinidad) the fare is slightly hotter. For others, such as Cuba, there is no kick at all. In all places, the emphasis is on vegetables, including bean sprouts – an ingredient you will not see outside of a Chinese restaurant.

One of the largest Chinese communities is in Trinidad. There are even a few blocks on Charlotte Street in Port of Spain, where Chinese restaurants and grocery stores are concentrated. In supermarkets, you will see shelves of commercially produced sauces (black bean, Hoisin, chile) from Hong Kong that many Chinese in Trinidad use to this day, even if they speak English with as heavy a Caribbean accent as any Rastafarian.

In Cuba, the area of Havana called **barrio chino** is the place to go for Chinese food. Rather than a neighborhood, as the name suggests, it is simply a small side street that has been adorned with a pagoda-topped archway at the entrance. In addition to restaurants, there is an open-air meat market and a few gift shops. Again, the menus are not that distinct from those of Chinese restaurants around the world: chop suey, chow mein and **rolos de primavera** (spring rolls).

Gateway to Havana's Chinatown, Cuba

East Indian

East Indians came to the Caribbean in the same way as the Chinese – as indentured servants. They landed mostly in Trinidad, where today they make up a significant portion of the population. They also went to Jamaica, but today the East Indian population there has shrunk.

Nevertheless, there is East Indian influence in Jamaican cooking. The difference between the East Indian influence in Trinidad and Jamaica is not so much of the food itself, but the degree to which these dishes, ingredients and techniques were incorporated into the existing cuisines. In Jamaica, curry is used widely. Jamaicans will tell you that you can't call a party a proper party unless curried goat has been prepared. In Trinidad, however, the East Indian and African-based cuisines remained relatively separated and restaurants will specialize in one kind of cooking or the other (see Trinidad & Tobago in the Regional Variations chapter). The exception to this culinary separation is curry, which is made with traditional goat, chicken or seafood.

USA

The most prominent modern influence on Caribbean cuisine is the US, and the most prominent forum for this is fast food. Every major chain is represented. Some have been welcomed with open arms such as KFC, whose record for sales at a single store on opening day occurred in the Bahamas. Others, like McDonald's, have had more trouble. When they tried to plant the golden arches in Jamaica, they found another restaurant chain by the name of MacDonald's. Goliath sued David in Jamaican courts but David won. Today, most Jamaican's say "**MAC**Donald's" even when referring to the American chain.

Beyond fast food, it is impossible to escape the US influence. On the English islands, the hotels and resorts cater almost exclusively to American tastes, with the odd curried goat or cracked conch thrown in for local flair. There is, of course, one big exception to this rule: Cuba. Viva la revolución!

Snow cone (sno-cone) stall in Marigot, the capital of St Martin

Mexico

Puerto Rico can boast many Mexican restaurants although it is not clear the route the cuisine took to get here. Most of the restaurants seem to base their menus on northern Mexican cooking – flour tortillas instead of corn, and lots of meat etc – which seems to indicate that Mexican cuisine came to Puerto Rico via the United States.

CULTURE

Eating in the Caribbean

The diversity of Caribbean culture ensures that there is no single way of eating on the islands. Breakfast can range from a pastry and a coffee to a filling meal of eggs, fish, meat (sausage, bacon or ham), potatoes and fruit. On some of the islands it's possible to get a traditional Creole breakfast complete with boiled fish, cassava bread and fresh juice. On Martinique, you will be tempted by the bakeries, their fronts wide open to the street, displaying an array of pastries, breads and sweets. For everyday eating, however, it is safe to say that the lighter, quicker breakfast (sometimes nothing more than a cup of coffee or tea) is the preferred breakfast option.

A typical Cuban breakfast

Outside the major tourist centers (entire islands in some places), you may find it difficult to locate a restaurant that even serves breakfast. You have two choices in this case: go hungry until lunch or improvise. Should you choose the latter, head straight for the local market and pick up a bag full of your favorite fresh fruit. Alternatively, you may find a small bakery that sells pastries and breads – be sure to visit them on the French islands where the **boulangerie** (bakery) tradition is strong. On the English islands, look for **johnnycake**, sweet bread that is served hot with creamy butter (see the recipe later in this chapter and Breads & Pastries in the Staples & Specialties chapter). Or what about combining your fruit and bread by indulging in a freshly baked roll filled with currants, or a pastry made with shredded coconut. For those of you who come from less-fertile lands, take advantage of the variety of fresh fruit available.

The Dutch-influenced architecture of Curaçao

Making a meal of it with friends, Cuba

Lunch is a much more serious affair and in many parts it is still the main meal of the day. But as elsewhere, its prominence is being squeezed by the pressures of the work day. As a result, the long, lazy multi-course lunches are becoming an exception to the rule. By lunchtime, most restaurants are open and waiting for your business. And it is you, the foreigner, they're waiting for. Most Cubans are given lunch in the workplace, paid for by the state. Large factories will have their own cooking facilities and **comedor** (dining room) while others use a catering system.

And so it falls to the evening meal to provide the culinary highlight of the day. Caribbeans tend to eat late. Restaurants in Havana's Vedado district only begin to fill up after 10pm. Even in homes, dinner is not served until after sunset, perhaps in the hope that the heat will not be as strong. Meals at home are big and boisterous; plates of food are laid out with over-sized spoons for heaping portions onto your plate.

In most homes, mothers and grandmothers do the cooking (it seems that Caribbean men are either incapable or unwilling to cook for themselves). It's not unusual to have three generations under the same roof. Recipes are never written down, but learned through years of careful observation. From a very early age, girls are expected to lend a hand in the kitchen. Each generation leaves their mark on family recipes, adjusting them for current taste, and according to availability of ingredients and convenience. Most home cooks these days juggle work, family and play, and simply don't have the time to, say, reduce coconut milk until it thickens to make **rundown** (fish and coconut stew) or to shred cassava, separating the poisonous juices in order to make bread (see Amerindians earlier in this chapter). It still happens, of course, but a trip to the bakery is the more likely source.

Concerning meat dishes, Caribbean cooks are frugal and no part of an animal is spared. This is a holdover from a history where slaves received the cuts of meat the European settlers did not want – from the goat's head to the pig's tail (see Meat, Poultry & Game in the Staples & Specialties chapter).

And when it comes to slaking your thirst Caribbean style, lemonade, fruit juice and beer are the main players. Every major island (and even some of the small ones) brews its own beer, and it's a great adventure to check out how each of the local tipples complements regional foods (see the Drinks chapter).

In fact, beer is the stellar choice when eating out, whether at regular restaurants or roadside shacks where locals crowd to get hearty meals on the cheap. In many places you can't throw a rock without hitting some form of eatery. Look for the signs: smoke billowing from stoves, eager customers shouting orders at indifferent cooks. And once customers are satiated the games begin, with dominoes and socializing continuing long into the night.

Johnnycake

This is the bread eaten for breakfast on many of the English islands. It is heavier and sweeter than most breads, but when johnnycake is served hot with fresh butter, there is nothing better. Don't even bother adding jam or marmalade.

Ingredients
³/₄ cup	vegetable shortening
6 cups	plain flour
	generous pinch of salt
1-3 Tbs	sugar
2 cups	water

Mix the shortening and flour with a dough knife until the there is a lumpy consistency throughout. Stir in the salt and sugar, then add the water a little bit at a time until the dough is the proper consistency for regular bread. Knead it for about 10 minutes, until its smooth, and plop it into a greased bread pan. Bake at 350°F (180°C) until it is tawny and crusty. Serve it right away.

A CARIBBEAN LOVE STORY

Getting away from it all should be easy, but this trip began as a nightmare. After two years together (we had been sharing an apartment for a few months) things between Bruce and I were beginning to unravel.

The day we left, the dog was sick. We were trying to clean up after him as well as do all of our last-minute packing. To top it off, I did not have a bathing suit that fit. Needless to say, we were at each other's throats. I cried all the way to the airport. Doesn't really sound like a loving couple on their way to cruise the Caribbean, does it? We had sunk to rock bottom.

But once we boarded our ship – the aptly named *Inspiration* – we left our troubles behind. With tacky umbrella drinks in hand, we were doing just fine, thank you very much. We started each day with breakfast on the deck, admiring yet another gorgeous view. And ended every evening watching a troupe of Brazilians yell "España!" in unison while they gyrated to techno music in the ship's discotheque.

Then there was the food. The best word I can think of to describe cruise ship food is never-ending. Chocolate buffets. Asian buffets. Pizza buffets. Mexican buffets. On the final night they even offered a buffet of buffets. Every day was an exercise in relaxation and frivolity. We were pampered, overindulged and just plain spoiled rotten.

By the time we arrived in Barbados, we were feeling good. The sun had baked Bruce as brown as a biscuit (as a redhead, I have resigned myself to never achieving a tan), and we were beginning to remember why we were together in the first place.

We spent our only non-cruise ship evening in Barbados, and after five days of buffets, we were determined completely indulge in the native cuisine. So we ventured out on a rollicking cab ride to a buffet-free restaurant.

Camarones (shrimp) with fettuccine & mushrooms, Puerto Rico

A game of volleyball, Montego Bay, Jamaica

Our very tall, very bald Bajan host seated us on an elegant mahogany terrace. The black ocean crawled onto the sand only feet from our table. Small white lights like a million stars lit the terrace. There we were, just the two of us – oh, and a small, striped kitten who lived at the restaurant and had obviously been fed there as well.

If the ambiance was delicious, then the food was breathtaking. Once we were served, we realized why the cat couldn't stay away.

Shark. Sea bass. Black beans. Mangoes. Papaya. We ate every delicious delicacy the island had to offer. Conch fritters with fruit chutney. White and flaky sea bass in a sesame-soy beurre blanc. Wow.

As we ate, neither of us could help slowly savoring each bite, each lick of the lips. We traded bites with movements as rhythmic as the ocean on the powdery sand. Want to try mine? I want you to. Mmmmmm.

Then our dessert arrived – bananas baked to perfection inside a flaky pastry, drizzled with honey and topped with real whipped cream. Oh, baby.

It was while we were dueling over the last honey-covered bites that I looked into Bruce's sparkling blue eyes and understood. Although we had descended into the depths, we had surfaced with a deeper, more enduring relationship. That night in Barbados, I realized I was in love.

I went to the Caribbean with the hope of find a bathing suit that fits, and instead I discovered the man who fits me like a glove. Better than any slinky spandex swimwear, he makes me feel amazing.

Leigh Anne Rose is a happily married writer in Memphis but would gladly trade the muddy Mississippi for the crystal clear Caribbean

Overleaf – Knip Bay, west of Willemstad, Curaçao

Etiquette

The first rule of etiquette in the Caribbean is common sense, the sort of rules your mother tried to teach you as a child apply here: no chewing with your mouth open, no throwing food. Nevertheless, Caribbean meals have a casual air and no one will make you feel as though you are dining with the royal family. People enjoy their food, and enjoy the opportunity to sit, dine and chat with friends and family.

As a guest you will be presented with loads of food. Your host will take a look at you, decide how much you can handle and then proceed to cook four times as much. Nevertheless, your host will look disappointed when you announce that you are full and can't possibly stuff one more morsel down your throat. Just make sure you say it was all delicious and you'll surely be redeemed.

While most things tend to move slower than in western countries, meals are not one of them. People here love to eat. So food is dispatched speedily and devoured before everyone retires to the front porch to shoot the breeze and enjoy the rest of the evening together.

Dining in the Dulce Alberggiare, Old San Juan, Puerto Rico

Etiquette in restaurants depends entirely on the type of place. Upscale establishments will follow the same rules as in North America and Europe. As you move down the ladder, however, the atmosphere changes; diners get a little louder, eating with your hands is more acceptable and beckoning waiters with a sharp 'psst' is the norm. In these places, there are rarely nonsmoking sections (though it never hurts to ask).

staples
& specialties

A diverse history and ethnology has had a major influence on what is eaten across the islands of the Caribbean. However, the sharing of seas and soils, and common links to Africa and the Amerindians, has also created a culinary cohesion. This can be seen – and tasted – everywhere from the markets of Cuba to the beaches of Trinidad.

Seafood

The coral reefs, which once caused so many shipwrecks and are today one of the major tourist attractions of the Caribbean, are also home to an abundance of sea life. Grouper, snapper, **mahi mahi** (dolphin fish), conch, shrimp, lobster, shark, marlin, flying fish, crab and tuna all make their home in these coastal waters.

Historically, European cooks shied away from taking advantage of the sea's bounty. This is not to say they did not eat fish, but the species of choice was the northern cod, which was cheap, plentiful and the easy option for plantation owners when it came to feeding the slaves who worked their fields (see the boxed text A Codfish Story later in this chapter).

Local fishermen have known all along about the delicacies contained in the surrounding seas and seafood was an important part of the Amerindian diet, but only recently has Caribbean seafood received the popularity it deserves. Red snapper is a favorite throughout the islands, coveted for its perfect white flesh and subtle flavor. Chefs have their own secret preparations, but stick with the fresh-fish policy: keep it simple. A delicate grilling and squeeze of lime makes fish sing.

Caribbeans indulge on fish without restraint, and the favored preparation is whole – head and tail included (in fact, the head is the best bit). While lunching on snapper in Port Royal, Jamaica, our novice abilities truly showed. At the end of the meal our plates looked a mess, while our Jamaican host left a skeleton, clean as an x-ray.

As well as enjoying fresh fish, a history of preserving techniques brought by Europeans has left an indelible mark on the seafood diet, with some outstanding results. **Escovitched fish** (**escobeche** on the Spanish islands) can be interpreted in different ways, but generally means that the fish has been pickled with vinegar, lime, and spices.

On the French islands, two dishes immediately spring to mind: **poisson en blaff** and **colombo de poisson**. Made with red snapper or kingfish, poisson en blaff requires marinating the fish in lime, pepper, garlic and salt, then boiling it in a sauce. It is often prepared right on the beach. Colombo de poisson is a curry made with white fish or shark, poached in a broth with onions, coconut cream, lime juice and dark rum. This dish can also be made with lamb and chicken, but the fish version is most popular.

Grouper is a favorite in the Bahamas, where it is caught by spear in the shallow waters. It is a sweet-flesh fish, as is mahi mahi (also called dolphin fish, but no relation to the cute mammals that do flips for sardines). One popular preparation sees grouper filets cut into strips, dipped in a bread-crumb batter and fried, but it is also delicious when baked whole (see the recipe Baked Grouper in the Caribbean Banquet chapter).

Red snapper caught at Knip Bay, Curaçao

SEAFOOD ALFRESCO

It took Ras Creek – with his sunbleached dreadlocks, dazzling smile and sinuous body – about two seconds to talk us into an all-day snorkeling tour, with lunch included.

We nursed placid reef sharks in our arms, hand-fed friendly spotted eagle rays and tickled tiny seahorses. Finally he led us to a glorious coral garden where, to our horror, he proceeded to hunt down our lunch: colorful tropical fish, timid rock lobsters and the luscious Queen conch. We watched through our masks with a mixture of devilish desire and terrible guilt as he caught the innocent sea creatures by hand.

Back at his modest houseboat, there was a feeling of apprehension as Ras Creek cooked up a seafood storm with nothing but a small gas stove. As he slid the conch meat out of its sexy pink shell, he teased us with island tales of this sea creature's powers as an aphrodisiac.

Fresh conch

With the white conch meat cubed and set aside to cure in freshly squeezed lime juice, he tempted us with the scent of fresh fish and lobster that was cooking in a rich coconut curry. Aromatic white rice boiled on the gas stove as he added chopped cilantro (coriander), onion, garlic and bright green peppers for the conch ceviche. It was too much to bear – hunger triumphed. We quenched our thirst with jugs of sweet rum punch as we slowly savored every bite of this melt-in-the-mouth alfresco meal.

Surrounded by the blinding blue Caribbean, infused with its vitality, guilt was replaced with gratitude. Having totally immersed ourselves in this spectacular marine world and truly appreciated its beauty, we ate with utter respect. Sitting in silence on the deck of a rustic old houseboat, barefoot and sunburnt and totally satisfied, it felt like the finest restaurant in the world.

Leigh Robshaw is a Sydney-based freelance travel writer

Shellfish

As with fish, shellfish tastes best when prepared fresh with little aplomb. Lobster, shrimp and crab need no more than a quick dip in boiling water or a moment on a hot grill before being served.

The mighty conch, used by the boy castaways in Golding's *Lord of the Flies* as a symbol of political power, is today one of the most recognizable symbols of the Caribbean. You're no doubt familiar with conch's shape, with its sun-bleached outer shell, spiny body and pearly pink under belly. But for locals, it is the meat inside that is the real treasure. Conch is one shellfish that needs extensive preparation – you need to pound it, and pound it good – otherwise, eating conch is like chewing on a bike tire. Once pounded and marinated in lime juice, it can be prepared in a variety of ways. Bahamians are the biggest eaters of conch: you'll be hard pressed to find a place that *doesn't* serve it in one form or another (see the Bahamas in the Regional Variations chapter). On other islands it is included in the diet but may be called by a different name: in Trinidad it's called **lambis**, and on the Spanish islands, especially in Puerto Rico, look for **carrucho**.

A roadside crab stall, Kingston, Jamaica

Shrimp from Middle Quarters, Jamaica

A CODFISH STORY

It seems odd that the most important species of fish in the history of the Caribbean did not survive in these waters. Nevertheless, the cod, or more specifically salted cod, is an important ingredient in the traditional cuisine of every island in the region. But the story of the cod goes beyond mere sustenance. This flaky white-fleshed fish played a key role not only in the development of Caribbean cooking, but also in the early economic development of the entire Atlantic coast, from Brazil to Newfoundland.

When Europeans first arrived in the Americas, the waters off Canada's Newfoundland and Labrador were teeming with cod. It was said that to catch them, sailors needed only to drop a basket overboard and, when hauled up, it would be stacked full of fat cod.

Before too long, English, French and Portuguese sailors were catching tons of cod salting them and heading back to Europe. It's not that they didn't have cod before. The seas off Scandinavia, the UK and Iceland had been cod-fishing grounds for centuries. But fishing in these waters was complicated by the fact that someone else had already laid claim to them. The waters in the New World, like the lands themselves, were considered a free-for-all, and home to enough cod for everybody. Including the slaves. As sugarcane became the dominant commodity of the Caribbean, the need for slaves increased and so too did the need to keep them fed. Salt cod, which did not spoil in the heat and humidity, was a natural choice. It is also very high in protein, meaning slaves could be kept healthy with a small amount. Moreover, the high salt content replaced that which was lost while working under the blistering sun.

As Mark Kurlansky writes in his book *Cod: A Biography of the Fish that Changed the World,* cod soon supplanted English salted beef as the main source of protein among slaves. The cod merchants were pleased to have the new market, not only for the profits but also because it gave them a place to sell the low-quality cod rejected by European markets.

The ships that brought the cod south to the Caribbean would reload with indigo, cotton, tobacco, coffee and sugar. Others went back east to Europe and then south to Africa to pick up a load of slaves, who were often purchased with the fish.

Whenever you see or hear the word 'saltfish', the fish featured is cod. It is available in markets everywhere and you will likely smell the fishy, salty aroma before you see the stiff gray-white cod, piled in stacks like folding chairs.

To prepare salted cod, you must soak it in cold water for several hours. The resulting flesh is flaky, with a very mild flavor that is best cooked in a stew. In Jamaica, cod is the main player in **ackee & saltfish** (see Jamaica in the Regional Variations chapter).

Ackee & saltfish, Jamaica

On the Spanish islands cod is called **bacalao**, and is used in stews with a simple **sofrito** (see the recipe in the Regional Variations chapter). A similar recipe is popular on the Dutch islands where it is called **bakijow** and is marinated in a vinaigrette with a little pepper thrown in for spice. In Martinique, where it is called **morue**, it's used in many traditional recipes such as **akkras** (fish fritters) and **feroce** (dip made of avocado, cassava flour and peppers). The Puerto Ricans also make a cod fritter called **bacalaitos**.

While the old recipes are still very much a part of the Caribbean culinary scene, the traditional trade routes are not. Cod has virtually disappeared from the Atlantic Coast of Canada and the US, a victim of over fishing and poor management. Today, most saltfish in the world comes from the European Atlantic and Iceland, where the waters are better protected. While it is no longer plentiful or cheap, the taste of the salted cod, despite its origins thousands of miles away, is as distinctive a taste of the region as anything coming from the Caribbean Sea itself.

Meat, Poultry & Game

It is only in the absolute worst of times that a meal in the Caribbean comes without some kind of meat. Even if it's pig's tail or cow's foot and even if the portions are miniscule, there will be meat.

When it comes to cooking meat, the first instinct of Caribbean cooks is to pull out the stewing pots. This tradition can be attributed to a number of factors: firstly, early kitchens were simple and not equipped with much more than a woodfire stove. Secondly, many families only had one pot for cooking, so all the ingredients had to be cooked together. And thirdly, the cuts of meat allocated to the slaves were usually the least tender and therefore required slow cooking in a broth to moisten the meat. One legacy of this tradition is that in restaurants today, your meat will usually come to you well done. When meat is not stewed, it may be fried (pork is often served this way) or battered and deep fried. You don't need to do much research to realize this; the sheer number of fried chicken outlets in the Caribbean is proof enough. But the best way to eat meat is from the grill. From pan chicken in Jamaica to pork ribs in Aruba and kebabs in Martinique, the mere thought of the sizzling meat and the clouds of aromatic smoke is enough to get the gastric juices flowing.

Roast pig in the kitchen of Rolando Perez Batista, Pinar del Río, Cuba

In general, pork is the most prized meat in the Caribbean. Introduced by the Spanish, pigs adapted easily to the new world. In the early days of the colony, Cuba was so overrun with pigs that they were considered a nuisance. However, they are a nuisance no more, in Cuba or anywhere else. Today the pig reigns supreme and is included in everything from the most elaborate feasts to streetside chow-downs.

Beef, on the other hand, did not take as well to Caribbean terrain and until refrigeration, it had to be imported after being salted or dried to make jerk, the dried meat that should not be confused with Jamaican **jerk** (meat marinated with a mixture of spices; see the boxed text The Jerk and recipe in the Regional Variations chapter). As you may well imagine, this was as unappetizing to the settlers as it sounds today and so beef never became an important part of the Caribbean diet. Where it is used today, it is generally

Butchers at Havana's public market, Cuba

imported. On the English islands and especially Jamaica, however, beef plays an important role, and patties and hamburgers are found in nearly every mid-range restaurant.

Chicken has been a part of Caribbean cooking since the arrival of the Europeans, but has gained recent popularity in the face of health concerns over fattier, high-cholesterol meats like pork and goat. Most islands have some version of a chicken stew with a supporting cast of onions, tomatoes, peppers, onions, thyme and other seasonings. An import from the Iberian peninsula, **arroz con pollo** (chicken with rice) is a regular on menus on the Spanish islands while **chicken pelau** is a similar dish you will see in Trinidad and St Vincent. In Barbados, a little lime juice and mustard is added and it's called **fowl down-in-rice**.

Another popular meat is goat, which has a similar taste to lamb, although it is greasier. No party menu in Jamaica is complete without a big steaming pot of goat curry. Often, the head of the goat will be used to make a soup called **mannish water**. Other islands have other versions of goat stews, and in Martinique you will find stews made with lamb.

THE BOLD PALATE

Some meats are a little out of the mainstream and will rarely make it to tourist menus. Nevertheless someone is eating them because many of these animals are finding their way onto the endangered species list. The green turtle, which lays its eggs on the beaches of many of the islands, can only be served at certain times of the year, but when available it's a popular menu item. There is at least one turtle farm (on the Cayman Islands) but its success has yet to be proven. Unfortunately, in most places, the green turtle is not farmed and you should avoid eating this endangered species.

In Dominica, 'mountain chicken' is the name given to the **craupad**, a local species of frog with especially large legs. Dominicans enjoy their mountain chicken stewed or fried. Many islands take advantage of the now-endangered iguana population, which was once a staple for the Amerindians (see the boxed text Lunch of the Iguana in the Regional Variations chapter). However, restrictions have been placed on hunting during the months of March and August.

Broiled crocodile is a Cuban delicacy, and the reptiles are farmed for both hide and flesh. In both Dominica and Trinidad, locals have a taste for opossum, which is caught in the wild, then smoked and stewed. Both the craupad and the opossum can only be hunted at certain times of the year. In fact, the opossum is now an endangered species.

Peas & Rice (or Rice & Peas)

Rice was first introduced to the Caribbean by the Spanish and then reinforced as a part of the daily diet in the 1830s by the indentured servants from East India and China. Rice first found favor in Trinidad and Jamaica as that was where the highest concentration of East Indians and Chinese were based. This versatile grain has since spread throughout the islands and is now a Caribbean staple.

It is difficult to mention rice in a Caribbean culinary context without also mentioning peas. The ever-present side dish of peas & rice is found throughout the islands, although it has various forms and names. The type of rice most often used is long-grain white rice, although more exotic rice such a basmati and jasmine are also used, especially in Trinidad where the large East Indian population demands it.

The peas in this dish can be almost anything. Some will use garbanzos, others go for kidney beans or regular green peas. On the Spanish islands, the dish is called **moros y cristianos** (Moors & Christians) and is made with black beans (see the recipe in the Home Cooking & Traditions chapter). In the Bahamas, there is no coconut water in the peas & rice like there is in Jamaica (where it is called rice & peas). Vegetarians should note that, in some versions, pork is added for a bit of extra flavor. If in doubt, just ask.

STAPLES

Fried pork skins, moros y cristianos and avocado, Bodeguita del Medio, Havana, Cuba

Vegetables

Tubers are cheap, will grow under all sorts of soil and climatic conditions, and are easy to prepare. As a result, they became a mainstay in the diets of the Amerindians as well as plantation workers. Today, few Caribbean meals come without some form of starch, and tubers are the usual choice. Heavy in carbohydrates, tubers are also sleep inducing, and could be the reason why you often see Caribbean workers nodding off at their desk at mid-afternoon. And when coupled with the Caribbean heat, it's a recipe for slumber.

During hard times or at end of the week when the larder was getting a little sparse, tubers were often the only thing available. The custom on the English islands was to cut up the tubers and throw them all into one big pot, let them boil until everything was soft, then add dumplings made of flour and salt. If you were lucky, you could also add a bit of salt beef or pork to help bring up the flavor. As you can imagine, the resulting dish was a bit on the bland side (OK, a lot on the bland side) but was more than adequate to feed a hungry hoard.

Of all the roots, the most popular is the potato, which is most often prepared **a la francesa** (as French fries), but also makes its way into stew or soup pots. In the East Indian homes of Trinidad, the simple potato takes on an entirely different and wonderful flavor when it's prepared as part of a curry.

Cassava (also called yucca), with its brown, fibrous skin and white interior, is eaten throughout the islands, and you'll find it stacked high in most markets. Historically, it has been used to make everything from bread to beer. These days it's most often peeled, sliced and boiled, and served as a side dish. As with potatoes, cooks will also add cassava to a hearty stew.

In Cuba, tubers have taken on greater importance as a staple during food shortages. Malanga, with its rough, brown exterior and reddish, nut-flavored flesh, joins the yucca in markets and kitchens as a popular root vegetable. It too can be boiled but is best when thinly sliced and deep fried. It can also be cooked with milk, nutmeg and sugar for a sweet treat.

Sweet potatoes (**batata** in Puerto Rico) are another common carbo hit. They are served as a plentiful side dish, either fried or boiled with a little butter. Eddoes, which are produced in large quantities in Barbados, are about the size of a large pear and have dark brown skin and white flesh. This tuber is usually boiled with the skin on, after which the flesh easily pops out, ready to be smothered in butter. Dasheens are related to eddoes, and this plant is valued not only for the root, but for the spinach-like leaves that form the basis of **callalloo**, a signature dish in Trinidad (see Trinidad & Tobago in the Regional Variations chapter).

Barbecued corn sprinkled with lime juice, street stalls of Kingston, Jamaica

Papin Market, Kingston, Jamaica

While technically a fruit, one of the largest on earth, the pumpkin receives a similar treatment to many root vegetables: it's boiled. It is also made into fritters, used in soups and as fillings for pastries. Caribbean pumpkins (called **calabaza** on the Spanish islands) have a green and white exterior and sweet orange pulp.

Quimbombó (okra) is a prominent ingredient throughout the Caribbean, a fact not surprising given that it originates from the same area of Africa that the slaves came from, no matter their final destination. You'll find okra in all types of dishes, including salads, soups and stews.

Fruit

Surprisingly, there is not a strong tradition of eating fruits in the Caribbean, despite the fact that the climate and soils are perfect for fruit production. The problem is that for most of its post-Columbus history, all arable land was used for growing sugarcane, cotton and coffee. There have been exceptions: the banana made its home in the Caribbean in the mid 1800s (see Bananas & Plantains later in this chapter). Mango is another tasty resident and is grown today in all its forms from the Bahamas to Trinidad.

Limes are the citrus fruit of choice in the Caribbean. English settlers eagerly took to the small green fruit, as doing so reduced the risk of scurvy. This is why the English are often referred to as Limeys. These days, limes are used to tenderize and flavor meat and seafood. If you spot grapefruit while in Cuba, load up on it! Cuban grapefruit is the best in the world.

The early-morning bustle on the streets of St Ann, Jamaica

When driving in Jamaican cities, look out for dare-devil street vendors who hock their juicy produce on major intersections (at great risk – Jamaicans are notoriously reckless behind the wheel). A must-try item is guinep, a small green fruit that grows in bunches like grapes. To get to the flesh, which is a little tart, peel the skin and suck on the pip (careful not to choke!) until you get all the good stuff off. People in Jamaica eat them like nuts, munching down on one while opening the next. If you've ever eaten fresh lychee, you'll find the guinep similar, both in taste and texture.

Overleaf – A local from St Ann selling guinep, Jamaica

Tomas with bananas, Pinar del Río, Cuba   *Pineapple ready for picking, Jamaica*

The pineapple has been in the Caribbean as long as the Amerindians. When Columbus clamped his eyes on the sweet fruit's prickly exterior (resembling pine cones) he called them **piñas**. The Caribs called them **ananas**, the name by which they are known in France. Papaya, or paw-paw as it is called on the English islands, is a native Caribbean fruit, and is used in juices, fruit salads, ice creams and syrups. Unripe, the papaya can be used like a green mango for curries and chutneys. The papaya leaves can be used to tenderize meat, which is wrapped in the leaves and left overnight. Refreshing watermelon (known here simply as melon) was an African import. It is a common ingredient in fruit salads and makes for delicious, refreshing juice.

Avocados were first introduced to the Caribbean in the mid-17th century. Since then the rich tender fruit has become a firm favorite across the islands. When we asked a friend how Jamaicans like to eat avocados, she simply replied, "we just eat them". You will find them used in salads and sandwiches, as well as eaten straight off the tree. Cooks on the French islands often prepare **feroce**, a dip made of avocado, cassava flour and peppers. You can also add shredded cod as a twist.

More exotic fruits include christophenes, which are also called chayote, a member of the squash family. They have a light green skin and a white interior that can be added to virtually anything because of its subtle taste. Soursop, with its prickly green skin and creamy interior, is a favorite flavor for ice cream. The plum-shaped naseberry (also called sapdilla or sapote) is made into custard and ice cream. Breadfruit is another common fruit rarely seen outside the Caribbean. It is more or less treated like a vegetable: boiled, broiled or baked and served hot with butter. Another much-loved Caribbean fruit is guava, which is enjoyed fresh as well as in jam and jelly (see Dessert & Sweet Snacks later in this chapter).

Ackee is a fruit about the size of a pear. It is related to the mango and has the same red-orange skin that protects a black shiny seed and three yellow pods. The pods themselves are the edible bits of the fruit but they cannot be eaten until the fruit itself splits open to reveal them – otherwise, the ackee is poisonous. In fact, until recently, the US Department of Agriculture completely banned their entry into the United States, much to the ire of the thousands of Jamaicans living in New York. In Jamaica, children are taught from an early age never to pick an ackee until it has split, indicating that it's safe to eat. Ackee is obviously one of the primary ingredients in the Jamaican specialty, **ackee & saltfish** (see Jamaica in the Regional Variations chapter). A Jamaican we dined with compared the ackee to tofu – on its own it is relatively tasteless, but when cooked it takes on the flavor of other foods in the pan. But the tofu comparison only goes so far; unlike tofu, ackee is very rich and high in fat.

Ackee for sale near Montego Bay, Jamaica

Coconuts

Coconut has a way of making its way into many Caribbean dishes – more than you might realize. Its natural sweetness, which is found both in the white flaky meat as well as the 'water' that fills the hollow center, is used to add flavor, body and texture to everything from rice to seafood. It is a staple throughout the islands and is even used as a flavoring in rum drinks like **Cuba Libre** (see the recipe in the Drinks chapter).

Coconut milk is made by mashing the coconut meat (you can use a blender with a little water) then adding boiling water to help separate the milk from the solids. After cooling, the milk is passed through cheesecloth and the solids left in the cloth are discarded. If you let the milk sit for a few hours, a thick cream will rise to the top and is easily skimmed off. Although it is

Cracking open fresh coconuts, Kingston, Jamaica

used less today than in the past, you can also make coconut oil by boiling the milk, then simmering until the water evaporates and you are left with cream on top and oil on the bottom.

Jamaicans use coconut water to cook the rice in peas & rice. You can also enjoy it purely and simply at a roadside stand, where vendors armed with machetes will happily sell you a whole coconut. With a few deft whacks they will remove the top, pop in a straw and hand you the all-contained refreshment. After finishing the drink, ask the seller to split the coconut open so you can get at the cool flesh inside.

For a do-it-yourself refreshment, you can buy your own and use a hammer to crack open the shell. If you're only after the water, use a nail to pierce the nut through the black spots.

Bananas

Although a native of South-East Asia, bananas are now synonymous with the Caribbean landscape and diet. You will see banana palms (they are not technically palms, but herbs) throughout the islands, either covering hillsides with their palm-like leaves or individually on roadsides and in back yards.

The plantain (cooking banana) is larger than other bananas with more distinct edges. These are a much-loved staple throughout the archipelago. In Puerto Rico, they are used in **tostones** (deep-fried slices of flattened plantain), which are sprinkled with salt and served hot. The French islands have a similar version called **banane pesé**. You may also find **arañitas** (literally, little spiders) on certain menus in Puerto Rico. Despite their decidedly unappetizing label, these are shredded plantains deep fried in clumps. It's the way shards of crisp fruit splay in all directions that give this side dish its name. But the most popular Puerto Rican plantain dish is the delightfully named **mofongo** (mashed plantain shaped into a dome, stuffed with meat and vegetables). This dish is always topped with **sofrito** (see the recipe in the Regional Variations chapter).

In Cuba, you might be lucky enough to receive a plate of crisp, deep-fried plantain **mariquitas** (chips), which go splendidly with a daiquiri. Green plantains are also used to make **sopa de plátano verde**, a traditional soup in which the fruit is cooked, ground then added to either chicken or beef broth.

Mofongo served in a paloon (wooden bowl) from the Casa Sica restaurant, Puerto Rico

Fried Plantains

Any Caribbean meal should include a plantain dish. It's simply a must. This recipe is a favorite throughout the Caribbean. You should only need one good sized plantain for every two people you're serving.

The first thing you have to do is choose the right plantain. At the market, look for those that are more brown than yellow, as these will be the sweetest and most tender. If they are not ripe enough, you'll have a tough plantain that will have to be pounded and deep fried, or mashed and made into a soup. And you don't want that.

Then you have to peel it. This is not like peeling a banana! Cut the two ends off and then, with a small sharp knife, make three or four cuts down the length of the plantain, being careful not to cut into the flesh of the fruit. Then carefully separate the sections of peel so your plantain is sitting there butt-naked, ready to be sliced and cooked. You can slice it anyway you like, in discs, on an angle or lengthwise – just make sure that the slices can lay flat in your pan and that none of them are more than a centimetre thick.

Heat a little vegetable oil (olive oil has a mind of its own and will add strong flavor) over a medium flame and gently add the plantain. Cook it until it begins to form a brown crust, then flip it over and do the same to the other side. Drain each slice on a paper towel and sprinkle with a little salt. Serve hot.

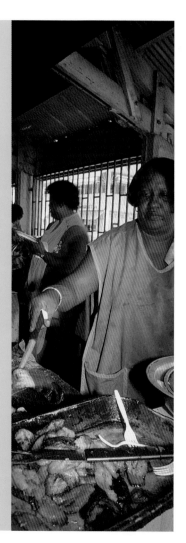

Perhaps the tastiest plantain preparation is to slice the fruit into long flat pieces and then fry them gently in oil over a slow flame until the natural sugars caramelize and the slices form a golden-brown crust. They are then dried on a paper towel and then lightly salted. These can be served as an accompaniment to larger dishes but are also delicious solo.

The plantain's less starchy cousin, the banana, is almost as important in the Caribbean diet. They have long been one of the Caribbean's most successful export crops as they can be cut green from the tree and will be ripe when they arrive at an overseas market.

Those bananas that are not exported are used in juices, dessert recipes such as banana fritters (great with ice cream), or of course eaten fresh. They can be mashed and baked into cakes, breads or pastries, and spun into a milkshake or daiquiri. In Jamaica, green bananas sell alongside the more mature yellow ones and are boiled and served as a side dish.

'Splitting the hands' at the Willemstad floating market, Curaçao

And it's not just the fruit that gets used. The leaves of both the plantain and banana plant are used to wrap **tamales**, a dish more common to Mexico and Central America, where the leaves are wrapped around corn mash that's mixed with meat and vegetables, then steamed until the mash slightly stiffens.

There are many different varieties of banana. At home, if your bananas come from the Caribbean (Central America and parts of South America also export on a major scale), they will most often be the Gros Michel and Cavendish varieties. These tend to be large and highly resilient. On the islands you will see many more banana types, with such names as valery, manicou and robusta. Some are no larger than your finger.

Peppers

Most of the English-speaking world calls them chiles (or chile peppers), on the Spanish islands they are **ají**, but on the English islands they are peppers. This regional misnomer is attributed to Diego Alvarez Chanca, a physician who sailed with Columbus on his second voyage to the new world in 1494. The taste reminded him of black peppercorn (a valuable spice at the time) and so he named this spicy food **pimentón** (pepper). The Spanish have subsequently corrected themselves while the English have learned to distinguish between hot pepper, sweet pepper and black pepper. The larger, sweet peppers (capsicum) are used mostly in stews, so as to add a robust sweetness.

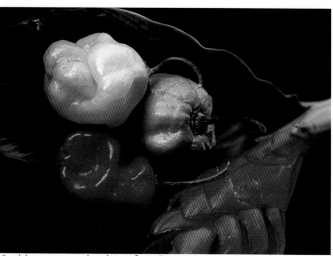

Scotch bonnet peppers and a red ginger flower, Jamaica

Peppers have always been an important part of the Caribbean diet. One early settler found them so plentiful that she compared them with weeds. You will find many varieties of hot pepper in the Caribbean, including the wiri wiri, lady finger and the scotch bonnet – thought to be the spiciest pepper of them all. However, cooks in the Bahamas and Jamaica will tell you that the hottest pepper is the bird pepper, which derives its name from the fact that the only way it seems to grow is when the seeds are eaten by birds and then deposited in the soil, together with natural fertilizers.

But don't be frightened by the likelihood of biting into a local dish and burning your face off. The hottest peppers are rarely hidden in dishes. Instead, they are made into pepper sauce and served as a condiment. Pepper sauce usually consists of pureed peppers with vinegar and salt. Nevertheless you'll find you have many different choices when it comes time to choosing one to buy. They vary in color from a mustard yellow to bright red and, of course, they vary in heat. Many brands include a handy thermometer diagram on the label to help guide you. Remember, when the bottle says that its contents are very hot, believe it! Even if your mouth is made of steel, you will find that even a small dose of the stuff will be felt long afterward. If you still feel like experimenting, be sure to have

Street market, San Juan, Puerto Rico

something handy that will cool your mouth. Water is no good as it simply spreads the heat around and puts you into deeper trouble. The ultimate remedy is a few slices of cucumber, bread or some yogurt.

Hot peppers aren't only used for their spicy properties. In fact, the flavor of even the hottest pepper is a distinctive and terrific complement to what is generally fairly tame food. It goes especially well with broiled meats, fried chicken or stronger types of fish. Many locals will even put a bit on their sandwich, a perfect addition when the sandwich also includes some fresh vegetables to help counter the heat. One rare instance where hot pepper is hidden in the dish is in a tossed salad that is served with a dressing infused with hot pepper. The clash of cool raw vegetables and spicy peppers is sensational.

Flavor, not heat, motivates of the use of peppers in Puerto Rico because the local variety, called **ají**, isn't at all spicy. There are a few common varieties but the most popular looks similar to the fiery scotch bonnet. Having said that, as a bull is to a steer, they could not be more dissimilar in function and taste. The ají is an essential ingredient in **sofrito**, Puerto Rico's favorite dish (see the recipe in the Regional Variations chapter).

Herbs, Spices & Other Flavorings

Spices have played no small part in the history of the islands. Firstly, Columbus came looking for spices when he originally sailed from Spain. More importantly for your taste-buds, however, is that for centuries (even before the arrival of the Europeans) spices were used to preserve meats, with the most famous example being Jamaican **jerk** (see the boxed text The Jerk and recipe in the Regional Variations chapter).

Blue Mountain ginger flower, Jamaica

Herbs & spices still play a key role in the character of Caribbean cuisine and the leading player is thyme, which grows in abundance throughout the islands. Thyme is added to sauces and stews at an early stage of the cooking process to allow the fresh flavor to spread throughout the dish.

Allspice (also known as pimiento or Jamaican pepper) is not technically a spice, but rather a berry that grows on the indigenous pimiento tree. Its flavor is strong and distinctive, so you don't need much allspice to get the pimento point across. Even so, allspice does not mask other flavors, and so makes an excellent part of the seasoning for any stewed meat, and is one of the primary ingredients in Jamaican jerk.

That pinch of oregano (or thyme in many cases) is as much seasoning as you are likely to get in Cuba. In general, the food is very mild and the hot peppers that are so essential to cooking in many of the other islands are not used at all in Cuba.

There are those who claim that Jamaica produces the best ginger in the world, and as a consequence much of it goes to the export market. Locals use it in drinks (tea and wine) as well as in breads and curries. Achiote, the seed of the annatto tree, was used by Amerindians as a body paint and for medicinal purposes. These days achiote is key ingredient in Puerto Rican cooking where it is used for its flavor and as a red coloring. Nutmeg, black pepper, garlic, oregano, basil and chives are also essentials in a Caribbean kitchen. Finally, Caribbean cooks are fond of adding just a wee bit of rum to many of their dishes. After all, happy food is good food.

On the Pan American with plenty of garlic to sell, Cuba

Breads & Pastries

Bread of one kind or another has been a staple in the Caribbean diet since the first people arrived on the island some 2500 years ago. For the Amerindians, the choice was cassava bread, and later cornbread, both of which were easily adopted into the diets of both settlers and slaves.

Making cassava bread is a laborious process. The root has to be peeled first and then scrubbed before the tough meat is grated. The resulting pulp is then placed in a **matapie** (hanging sack) and squeezed. This step is essential; left undrained, cassava is highly poisonous. Once separated from its juice, the pulp is dried in the sun and then made into bread.

Cornbread was also popular in those early days. The Amerindians had already been cultivating the plant and so the European settlers took to it easily. Today, cornbread is not as common as other varieties, but cornmeal is used throughout the region, most notably to make **coo-coo**, a polenta-like dish usually mixed with okra and other vegetables.

Wheat bread did not immediately catch on in the Caribbean, but this was not through lack of effort. Newly arrived Europeans pined for their precious wheat. Unfortunately, bringing wheat from Europe was expensive and shipments were often infested with bugs.

Today, breads and pastries form the foundation of most breakfasts throughout the Caribbean. In Martinique, the island with the strongest ties to Europe, bakeries serve long baguettes, as deliciously French as the ones you will find in Paris (see the French Islands in the Regional Variations chapter).

Martinique's baguettes are an exception, and most breads, whether long loaves or small buns, are somewhat sweet and slightly heavy. This is especially true of those breads that include coconut or other fruits. A quick look at any Caribbean recipe book reveals that sugar is generally added to most breads. On the English islands, **johnnycakes** are a part of most breakfasts (see the recipe in the Culture of Caribbean cuisine chapter). They are loaves made with flour, shortening, sugar and salt, and baked until the crust becomes golden brown. Although heavy, johnnycakes are delicious when served straight out of the oven with butter.

While most bakery items are baked, some Caribbean breads require frying. This includes the sublime **fry bake**, a circular, flatbread that is fried just enough to make the outer dough crispy while the inside remains soft and chewy. Fry bakes can be split and stuffed with virtually anything or enjoyed on their own. When in Jamaica, try a **festival**, a small oblong piece of fried bread perfect for dousing the spice of a fiery jerk.

Meat pies have become common in parts of the Caribbean. The English gave their colonies the beef pasty, a product that has been perfected by the

Jamaicans in the form of the beef patty (see the recipe later in this chapter). The pies of Trinidad are not the 12-inch round variety, but are rolled, small enough to hold in your hand and filled with beef, cheese, potato or sausage. And where you have East Indian communities in the Caribbean, you will always find **roti** (flatbread; see Trinidad & Tobago in the Regional Variations chapter and the recipe in the Caribbean Banquet chapter).

Fresh croissants for breakfast on St Martin

STAPLES

STAPLES

Patties

There are two crucial elements to a great patty: the pastry and the filling. Both must be perfect if you're going to be able to serve them to anyone who has known and loved patties in the past.

Pastry
4 cups	plain flour
1 tsp	salt
³/₄ cup	butter
5 Tbs	cold water

Sift the flour and salt together into a bowl. Rub the butter and mix well, breaking the butter up as you go until the mixture is like breadcrumbs. Add the water to create a smooth dough. Cover and refrigerate for at least 2 hours. By the end, you'll have enough for about 12 patties.

Filling
1lb (500g)	beef, chicken or fish, finely chopped
1	onion, finely chopped
	salt & pepper to taste
	herbs of your choice
1	egg, beaten

The traditional patty was stuffed with a spicy ground beef filling, but recent innovations have seen the patty expand its horizons to also include chicken and fish. Start with about 1 pound of your choice, either ground or finely chopped (if fish, try ground shrimp). Saute it together with the onion, a little salt and pepper and any other herbs whose flavor feels good on your tongue.

Let the mixture cool. Meanwhile, take a bit of dough (something just larger than a golf ball) and shape it into a circle. Spoon some of the mixture in, fold it and seal it tight by brushing with egg. Press the edges with a fork and then bake them at about 400°F (200°C) until the pastry is golden brown (about 15-20 minutes, but check often). Serve hot with some pepper sauce.

Left – Jamaican Patties in Savanna-la-Mar
Overleaf – A farmer delivers fodder to feed his livestock, Pinar del Río, Cuba

Desserts & Sweet Snacks

Desserts here tend to be served warm, as in the case of bread pudding or bananas in rum and cinnamon. Rich, sweet dishes such as flan with caramel sauce or candied guava with cheese are also popular. But the Caribbean dessert of choice has to be rum cake. There are many ways to make it, but the rum should always be dark as this provides the richest flavor. If you're lucky, it will be covered in a sweet icing that is a winning combination with the rummy cake. Most recipes call for overproof rum, which is to say that it is strong! It seems strange, but if you eat enough of it, you will begin to feel drunk – be sure someone else is doing the driving. The roads in the Caribbean are crazy enough.

A quick tête á tête over cake from the Pain de Paris bakery, on the streets of Havana, Cuba

The more time you spend in the Caribbean, the more you appreciate the qualities of a good ice cream. You'll also develop a craving to get a cone-full of your favorite flavor at day's end, for a bit of internal air conditioning. It's just one of the side affects of Caribbean travel. Passions for ice cream run deepest in Cuba. While line-ups for common goods are the norm, the line up for Copelia ice cream, near the Habana Libre Hotel run especially long even when there is ice cream readily available in other parts of the city. In Jamaica, the brand of choice is I-Scream Ice Cream. Depending on where you are, the flavor selection can boggle: from the classic trio of chocolate, vanilla and strawberry to soursop, naseberry and mango. Ice cream is rarely eaten at home, as most people prefer to go out for it.

drinks
of the caribbean

Drinking is both a pleasure and a necessity in the Caribbean, where the unrelenting sun will rob you of your fluids almost as soon as you step outside. While good health would dictate that water is all that is needed, a good time may require something with a little extra kick.

Alcoholic Drinks

The culture of the Caribbean is tightly wedded with booze. Economically, the rum trade has generated billions of dollars for island distillers. Culturally, alcohol fuels the bacchanalian madness known as Carnival (see Carnival in the Celebrating with Food chapter). Socially, cracking the seal on a bottle of rum can herald the beginning of a long, languid evening of conviviality and conversation.

Drinking is everywhere, especially in places populated with tourists unhindered by the prospect of having to show up to work the next day. Having said that, there is also a large temperance faction in the region. Keep this in mind; a bar might not be the most appropriate place to meet local friends after all.

Save for the odd road-side 'don't drink and drive' sign, you'll rarely see warnings about the dangers of excessive drinking, as advertizers enjoy comparatively free reign to extol the virtues of their product. For example, Guinness' slogan, 'Guinness is good for you' is everywhere in the Bahamas. Brewery and rum distillery tours make for an interesting afternoon, even if the marketing guys do nothing more than push drinks on you as though they were tonic.

Wild Sint Maarten Guavaberry Liqueur, only available in Sint Maarten

Beer

The Amerindians, who occupied the Caribbean prior to the arrival of the Europeans, had their own version of beer, and the first English settlers took to it like children to candy. Known as **perino**, this drink was made by tooth-less women who chewed cassava root into a mush before spitting it into a container filled with fresh water. The enzymes in the saliva would start the fermentation process and the end result was a brew that, despite its rather unsavory manufacturing process, did the trick. After the toothless women (and most of the Amerindians) were gone, **mobbie** became the drink of choice. According to a travel writer of the 1600s, mobbie was made from sweet potatoes, which resulted in a malty beverage of reddish hue.

Today, gallons of beer are made in the Caribbean, but thankfully in larger, more sanitary breweries. It doesn't take a connoisseur to be familiar with the most popular brands in the islands – Guinness, Heineken, Budweiser. But true beer aficionados will recognize brands like Red Stripe (Jamaica) and Carib (Trinidad & Tobago) as these have made their way across the ocean to the shelves of foreign stores.

Cuba's Cristal beer, Havana, Cuba

For the most part, beers in the Caribbean tend to be light lagers. The notable exception is Guinness, whose soupy consistency is remarkably pop-ular among locals throughout the English islands. In Jamaica, Guinness is rivaled by the sweet and malty local, Dragon Stout. Part of the reason for stout's popularity is its alleged ability to improve stamina in the sack.

But the undisputed king of beers in the Caribbean is Red Stripe, a full-flavored lager. Like Carib in Trinidad, Red Stripe is a cultural institution in Jamaica, sponsoring sporting events, reggae festivals and maintaining its status with an omnipresent advertising campaign. Red Stripe is even avail-able in vending machines!

Overleaf – A city of contrasts, filled with beautiful and dilapidated buildings, Havana, Cuba

DRINKS

Relaxing with a bottle of ice-cold Medalla, the favored tipple of Puerto Ricans, The Mason de Melquiades restaurant, Puerto Rico

DRINKS

In the Bahamas, be sure to try Kalik, the only local brew. It is a light and refreshing beer, low in alcohol (3.5%), which comes in tall, clear bottles; a perfect companion to the generally greasy Bahamian cuisine. It is bliss to have a couple of Kaliks while reclining in a beach chair under the Caribbean sun. Kalik comes in a light version and something called Kalik Extra Strong, which is by no means as potent as its name suggests. Also, the higher alcohol content doesn't do much for the taste.

While the beer of choice in Puerto Rico seems to be either Heineken or Corona, there are some local brews worth giving a try. Among these is Medalla Light, a gold-labeled, low-alcohol lager that is well suited to an afternoon of beach-side imbibing.

In addition to Heineken, Amstel is a prominent brand in the islands, especially on the Dutch Islands, a fact due in no small part to being brewed in Curaçao. Their regular lager is joined by a relatively new beer called Amstel Bright. Bartenders have been instructed to serve it with a wedge of lime jammed in the neck of the bottle, in the style of Corona, Mexico's popular beach beer. Fortunately, Amstel Bright tastes better.

In Cuba's Holguín Province, Amstel makes the two most common ales, Cristal and Bucanero. Both are widely available and their light, hoppy flavor goes well with the mild Cuban palate that includes dishes such as simple pizzas, roasted chicken or seafood. As such, Cristal and Bucanero tend to be a little weak.

Rum

Certain drinks define the country in which they are produced, such as Russian vodka or French wine. Others are more local: Sherry in Xeres (Spain) or Tequila in Jalisco (Mexico). With rum, the Caribbean has both. On one hand you have a truly global drink available wherever spirits are sold. Yet on the other, there are independent producers, whose skill ensures that the soul of the drink remains forever attached to the estate that produces it.

As the world's largest producer of sugarcane for centuries, it is natural that the Caribbean should give the world rum. For many years, however, it was virtually unknown outside the region. Europe's first rums were made in Barbados in the mid 1600s. They were strong, foul-tasting liquors that gained the nickname 'kill-devil'. The current name is derived from 'rumbullion,' a word used to describe the rumbustious behavior exhibited by those under its spell.

This crude original rum was lethal in excessive doses. Made from a boiled sugar water left to turn sour and then distilled twice, it produced a highly flammable spirit. Soon the concoction became a favorite among slaves and marauding pirates who yo-ho-ho'd their way from port to port, wreaking havoc. In short, 17th-century rum probably enjoyed about as much prestige in polite society as crack cocaine does today.

Despite its lowly status, the colonies of New England (in present-day US) obtained molasses from the Caribbean, which they distilled into rum. Some of that rum went by boat to Africa where it was traded for slaves (and subsequently sent north to English and other European markets). The slave boats brought their human cargo to the Caribbean and picked up more molasses before returning north.

It wasn't that good rum couldn't be made. It was simply more expensive, requiring more time and better ingredients. Wray & Nephew, for example, took home medals in the 10-, 15- and 25-year-old rum classes at the 1862 London exhibition. It eventually developed the Appleton brand, whose V/X label and 21-year-old rums are favored by connoisseurs.

Appleton Estate Jamaica Rum, Jamaica

Around the same time as Wray & Nephew were winning awards for their fine rums, a certain Catalonian wine merchant by the name of Facundo Bacardí, developed a method for making cheap rum more palatable through a process of charcoal filtering. This mellowed the harsh taste and produced a clear distillate with a lighter, more pleasant taste than its brutish antecedents. The Bacardí rum empire was born and soon branched out into other parts of the Caribbean and the rest of the world.

Other estates quickly copied the Bacardí process, and small producers expanded rapidly as the drink caught on in the US and Europe. One of the biggest factors in this growth was the 1898 Spanish-American War, when US troops invented the Cuba Libre by mixing white rum with Coca-Cola and adding a squeeze of lime juice. Soon after, the daiquiri was born when an adventurous bartender at Havana's El Floridita bar experimented with rum, lime juice, sugar and crushed ice.

Sugarcane and rum, Cuba

White rum remains the most popular version, but aged rum can be pure art, especially when aged anywhere from three to 21 years. This is a darker rum (taking on the color of the oak barrel in which it ages) that exhibits a classic mellowness that makes mixing unnecessary. A good seven-year old, or **añejo** rum, for example, needs only to be poured over ice, perhaps with a lime twist. Note, however, that not all dark rums are aged. There are dark or spiced rums that take on their color when caramel or coloring is added after the distillation process. There is nothing wrong with these rums, but they are more appropriate for mixing in cocktails than sipping straight.

Every island produces its own rum and a handful of producers have transcended national boundaries to become favorites around the world. These include Havana Club (Cuba), Appleton (Jamaica), Mount Gay (Barbados) and Bacardí (Puerto Rico & the Bahamas).

Tomas Perez enjoying a glass of rum on his farm in Pinar del Río, Cuba

Of these, Bacardí dominates. Its flagship white-label rum is the world's largest selling spirit and its success has allowed a family-owned company to expand operations into non-rum arenas. The family was once among the most prominent in Cuba, wielding an undeniable presence that is still felt today. In old Havana, the Bacardí Building (Edificio Bacardí) is a splendid art-deco relic of pre-revolution decadence, despite years of neglect. Today, while the lettering still says Bacardí, the building is occupied by other tenants, much more friendly with the present regime.

The Bacardí business was born in Cuba, but left for good in 1961 when the Castro regime seized their property. By this time, however, the company had extensive operations in other countries and business was able to continue. Nevertheless the Bacardí family have yet to forget. The company is an active supporter of the Miami anti-Castro lobby to the point where the Helms-Burton Law (which introduced further measures to tighten the blockade) has been referred to as the Bacardí Bill.

As popular as the Bacardí label may be, it is far from the best rum around. Even the Bacardí's, who make an eight-year-old drop that's meant to be sipped straight, would admit as much. So which of the old rums are the best?

To get the answer we asked Edward Hamilton, also known as the Minister of Rum. His website www.ministryofrum.com and his book *The Complete Guide to Rum* are as good an introduction to the finer rums as you will find. Edward's mailbox is in Puerto Rico, but he spends much of his time on his yacht, *Tafia*, sailing from island to island and tasting as many of the approximately 1500 rums available worldwide as possible.

Not surprisingly, Edward is inundated with questions about which brand is best. "I haven't found any single rum that connoisseurs would like to drink to the exclusion of all others," he writes. He is also quick to point out that the kind of rum he prefers depends on the situation or occasion – pre-meal, post-meal, evening cocktail, happy hour. Nevertheless, he has narrowed the list of his favorites. Among these are the rare **LaFavorite Eight Year Old** from Martinique, which is distilled in very small batches, and Haiti's **Barbancourt Five Star,** which he describes as having "a rich buttery flavor that comes through nicely with a little water or ice." From the Dominican Republic, Edward cites **Bermudez Anniversario**, which has "a rich mature blend with a rich smoky flavor" although he warns you that you'll probably have to go to the Dominican Republic to find this sipping rum. Among the more widely available labels, he recommends **Mount Gay Extra Old** from Barbados, **Appleton Twelve Year Old** from Jamaica (which is actually a blend of dark rums) and **Bacardí Ocho Años**, made in Puerto Rico.

Cocktails & Other Alcoholic Drinks

It's incredible that perfectly normal people, content to drink beer, wine or simple mixes at their local pubs suddenly turn into cocktail slammers as soon as they touch down on the soft sands of the Caribbean. The colorful concoctions demanded by droves of tourists has given rise to a number of fruity drinks, mostly based on rum. These change, from year to year, from place to place and from bartender to bartender. There are, nevertheless, a few stalwarts that have survived the abuse of paper umbrellas and goofy names to become institutions (see the boxed text RUMble Through the Islands later in this chapter).

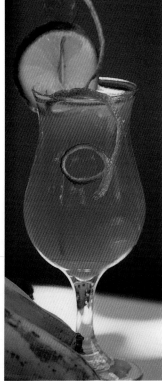

Then there are the gut-wrenching local mixtures that are best left untouched. Take **sky juice** for example, consisting of one part gin, one part coconut juice and a splash of sweet condensed milk. Or the variety of homemade Cuban rum known as **chispa tren** (literally, train sparks), which you can buy on the black market (with reason). In Jamaica, **magnum** is one of many things men will take to increase their virility. While available commercially, those in the know go to independent vendors who bottle the mixture of Irish moss, peanuts, linseed, milk, **malta** (non-alcoholic, beer-like soft drink), wine and nutmeg in recycled plastic containers. Whatever magnum does for bedroom bravado is diminished by the fact that the concoction tastes perfectly awful.

Martinique's national drink is **ti punch**, which is made of rum combined with sugar or sugar syrup and topped with lime juice. **Schaubb** is a local Christmas tipple that's made by immersing orange peel in a bottle of white rum and leaving it for several months.

La Sica – coconut, lemon and passionfruit rum, pineapple and cranberry juice, Casa Sica restaurant, Puerto Rico

DRINKS

A RUMble Through the Islands

The plasma that binds the cellular islands of the Caribbean is, without doubt, rum. Each island has developed their own favorite mixes, depending on the availability of ingredients. This is a guide to national recipes that you can create yourself.

The Bahamas
Cuba Libre

Though technically a child of Cuba, the classic rum and coke combo reaches a new height with this Nassau version.

1½ fl oz (45ml)	añejo rum
1 splash	coconut rum
3-5 fl oz (90-150ml)	Coca-Cola, depending on how much you like rum or the size of your glass.

Pour the ingredients over ice. Add a wedge of lime if you desire.

Bahama Mama

½ fl oz (15ml)	dark rum
½ fl oz (15ml)	coconut liqueur
¼ fl oz (8ml)	151-proof rum
¼ fl oz (8ml)	coffee liqueur
½	lemon, juice
4 fl oz (120ml)	pineapple juice

Combine the ingredients and pour over ice in a highball glass. Garnish with a cherry.

Cuba
Daiquiri

2 fl oz (60ml) white rum
½ fl oz (15ml) lime juice
½ tsp sugar
ice

Mix all the ingredients in a blender until you have a slushy liquid. The classic daiquiri uses only lime juice but it's also fun to experiment with such additions as bananas, strawberries or fresh fruit juice.

El Floridita bar, Havana, Cuba

Mojito

2 fl oz (60ml)	white rum
1/2 fl oz (15ml)	fresh lime juice
2-4 fl oz (60-120ml)	soda water
1/2 tsp	sugar
1	sprig of mint
	crushed ice

Mix the lime juice into the sugar. Add the sprig of mint and crushed ice. Add the rum and top up with soda water. Stir well and serve with a straw.

Curaçao

Not all drinks made with Blue Curaçao are from the island of the same name, in fact beer is the preferred drink here. However, here's a recipe that you'll find in Curaçao bars.

Hurricane Leah

1/2 fl oz (15ml)	light Rum
1/2 fl oz (15ml)	gin
1/2 fl oz (15ml)	vodka
1/2 fl oz (15ml)	tequila
1/2 fl oz (15ml)	Blue Curaçao
1 splash	cherry brandy
3 fl oz (90ml)	lime juice
3 fl oz (90ml)	orange juice

Pour all the ingredients into a large glass over ice and stir.

Jamaica

Jamaican Crawler

1 fl oz (30ml)	light rum
1 fl oz (30ml)	melon liqueur
3 fl oz (90ml)	pineapple juice
1 splash	grenadine

Combine rum, melon liqueur and pineapple juice with ice. Stir well and top with grenadine.

Café Carib

1 fl oz (30ml)	Tia Maria liqueur
1 fl oz (30ml)	dark rum
1 fl oz (30ml)	Caribbean coffee
1 dollop	whipped cream

Pour hot, fresh coffee over the liqueur and rum. Top with whipped cream.

El Floridita bar, Havana, Cuba

Mai Tai (Trader Vic's Original Recipe)

The Mai Tai was invented in California and is most commonly associated with Hawaii, but aficionados insist on Jamaican rum for theirs and so we offer the following recipe:

2 fl oz (60ml)	80–proof Wray & Nephew rum
	juice from half a fresh lime
1 splash	orange Curaçao
1 splash	rock candy syrup
1 splash	French orgeat
1 sprig	fresh mint

Mix all ingredients and pour over crushed ice.

Martinique & Guadeloupe

Ti Punch

2 fl oz (60ml)	white rum
½ fl oz (15ml)	sugar or sugarcane syrup
1	lime, juice
	water (soda or bottled)

Mix the sugar or syrup with the lime juice, add the rum and stir. The water is for chasing this very strong drink.

Planter's Punch

There are many versions of this drink out there, but the essential ingredients are citrus juices, pineapple and, of course, rum.

2 fl oz (60ml)	orange, lime or lemon juice
	or a combination of the three
1 tsp	pineapple juice
2 fl oz (60ml)	light rum
2 splashes	triple sec
1 splash	grenadine

Mix the juices and rum in a tall glass with plenty of ice. Top with the triple sec and grenadine. This is one drink where extravagant garnishes are expected, so go nuts with the fruit and umbrellas.

Puerto Rico

Borinquen

1½ fl oz (45ml)	light rum
1 Tbs	passionfruit syrup
1 fl oz (30ml)	lime juice
1 fl oz (30ml)	orange juice
1 tsp	151-proof rum

Mix all the ingredients in a blender with ice.

Pina Colada

3 fl oz (90ml)	light rum
3 Tbs	coconut milk
3 Tbs	crushed pineapple

Blend at high speed with two cups of crushed ice for a short time. Strain into a collins glass and serve with a straw.

Left to right – a Marti Mix, Tangerine Passion Marguerita and a Strawberry Daiquiri, Margueritaville Bar, Montego Bay

DRINKS

Overleaf – Entertainment at La Bodeguita del Medio, Cuba

Wine

While there is no domestic wine industry to speak of, wine drinkers will be pleased to know that most top-end restaurants maintain extensive wine lists with a wide variety of labels to suit nearly every dish and taste. This is especially true of the islands where tourism and offshore banking are the big industries, such as the Bahamas and the Dutch islands.

Imported bottles of Château d'Yquem Sauternes wine, Grand Case, Sint Maarten

Non-Alcoholic Drinks
Water

Let's start with good old water considering it's probably the most important drink in the Caribbean, especially if you're unaccustomed to the heat. As well as being surrounded by salt water, the islands boast several fresh water sources and tap water is generally fine to drink. Where the water supply is not a natural spring or lake, desalinated water is used. You will probably notice some difference in the taste of desalinated water, but will grow accustomed to it after only a few days. However, bear in mind that a change in environment (including the water you drink) can easily upset your system, so if you're visiting the Caribbean for a short period, it's probably best to stick with bottled water.

There are two options for bottled water: simple purified water and spring water. Most bottled water in the west is (or claims to be) spring water. Purified water is a different story, and the taste is often quite disappointing. Be sure to check the label before you buy to ensure you are getting exactly what you expect. In Spanish-speaking regions, when you ask for water, the server will probably offer a choice of **con gas** (carbonated water) or **natural** (still water).

Blue Mountains of St Andrew, Jamaica

DRINKS

Soft Drinks, Fruit Juices & Sno-Cones

Both Cuba and Jamaica have a thriving local soft-drink industry that competes with the multinational giants. Each offers a version of cola, lemon-lime and orange, all sweet and carbonated. In addition, you can find some exotic flavors that won't be seen beyond the Caribbean, such as Jamaica's Ting, a grapefruit drink, and Cuba's Pineapple Pop. **Kola** is another Caribbean standard made by several different firms. Similar to cola in name only, it is copper colored, intensely sweet and fruity. In the Bahamas, locals enjoy two fruit-based bottled drinks known as Junkanoo and Gombay. Kids love this stuff but it might curl more mature palates.

There are few places on this planet untouched by Coca-Cola, and the Caribbean is no exception. Even in Cuba, where it is referred to as the 'sewer waters of imperialism', Coca-Cola cans are imported from Mexican bottlers who are not restricted by the embargo.

Though fresh fruit abounds in the Caribbean, fresh fruit juices, sadly, do not. And when it does, expect to pay premium. But anything made with papaya or mango, is worth the splurge.

Coconut water is the exception when it comes to expensive juices. For a small price, you'll be able to get chilled coconut from street stalls. The vendor will chop the head off for you and provide a straw to suck the juice out. Similarly cheap are certain health drinks we saw in Trinidad, made from linseed, green fig, peanut, **channa** (chickpeas), carrot or seamoss.

Sno-cones in Old San Juan, Puerto Rico

A sno-cone after school, Old San Juan, Puerto Rico

And finally, one other drink that needs mentioning is the **sno-cone**, which is served from battered trailers, often attached to bicycles, which are pushed through the streets by hot and haggard-looking men. To make a sno-cone, a block of ice is scraped until there are enough shavings to fill a paper cup. Some cherry-flavored syrup (although the definition of cherry is stretched here) is poured over the ice until each glistening crystal has turned red. Sno-cones are ridiculously cheap, so much so that you get the feeling that once the vendors decide to retire, the memory of sno-cones will melt like ice cream in the sun.

Tea & Coffee

Tea is one strong legacy left by the English. Many people on the English islands will have nothing more than a cup of tea for breakfast, adding plenty of cream and sugar to the mix. The standard tea is orange pekoe, but some shops stock specialty teas. Surprisingly, iced tea is not a very popular drink.

CAPTAIN COFFEE – Captain Gabriel Mathieu de Clieu

The oft-told story of coffee's arrival in the Caribbean involves Captain Gabriel Mathieu de Clieu, a French infantry officer who dreamt of building a coffee industry in Martinique. And so in 1720 (with the help of a well-connected lady friend) he connived to procure – some say steal – a tree from the Royal Botanist. His next challenge was to get the plant across the ocean, no easy task in those days. The voyage did not go smoothly. The ship was hit by storms and was captured for a time by Tunisian pirates. With his ship damaged and delayed, the ship's captain imposed water rations. De Clieu was forced to share his own supply with the plant. In the end the tree made it to Martinique where it invoked the scorn of cocoa growers, who regarded it as a threat to chocolate (imbibed in liquid form). As we all know, the plant not only survived but thrived, eventually making its way north to the Greater Antilles, south to Colombia and Brazil, and west to Central America.

DRINKS

Coffee, on the other hand, is popular with locals and tourists alike. As well it should be. The Caribbean produces some of the finest coffee in the world, notably on the islands of the Greater Antilles, a fact often forgotten in a market dominated by Brazilian and Colombian coffee.

Caribbean climatic conditions are perfect for growing coffee: good, low-acid soil on slopes to help drain the soil, adequate rainfall and warmth. One difference between Caribbean coffees and those of Central and South America is altitude. Caribbean coffee is grown much closer to sea level, which may attribute to its sweeter flavor.

Raw coffee beans from the Blue Mountains, Jamaica

DRINKS

CARIBBEAN COFFEE TOUR

For coffee enthusiasts, the Caribbean offers a wide range of brews to savor. Each island's geography and history has an influence on what is put in the percolator, plunger or espresso machine. On one end of the spectrum is Jamaica's Blue Mountain coffee, on the other end are the Bahamas and Trinidad & Tobago, where instant is king. Here is an overview of what to expect in your hunt for a Caribbean caffeine fix.

Cuba

Coffee has been a cash crop in Cuba since the 18th century. Cubans love their coffee as **café cubano**, in a small cup loaded with sugar, and the low-acidity arabica beans grown on the island are perfect for such a brew. You can also, however, easily get a **café con leche** (coffee with milk) for breakfast. The low-acid content of Cuban beans can be attributed to the fact that the arabica beans are grown at low altitude. Sierra Maestra beans, produced in the eastern half of the island, are well known for producing a rich brew.

A farmer from the Pinar del Río region drying his own coffee, Cuba

Dominican Republic

Bani, Barahona, Cibao and Ocoa are regional names to look out for when hunting down Dominican coffee. The most famous is Barahonan coffee, which is more acidic than the others, but still retains a full body. Coffee beans from Bani, Barahona, Cibao and Ocoa are usually dark roasted, bringing out a deep, sweet flavor.

Guadeloupe & Martinique

Martinique was the first Caribbean island to be planted with coffee (see the boxed text Captain Coffee earlier in this chapter). Since then, coffee production has declined on both of these French islands, a result of both natural disasters (frequent hurricanes) and economic instability. This is a great shame since the conditions on both islands are perfect for the production of coffee.

Haiti

Haiti has long tradition of growing coffee, with Haitian Bleu (named for its color) in high demand among gourmet coffee enthusiasts. Most Haitian coffee is low in acidity and best when dark roasted. Nevertheless with such a non-uniform production and grading process, Haitian coffee can certainly be hit and miss. Discerning drinkers will appreciate the fact that Haitian coffee is basically organic being produced without fertilizers or pesticides, but this is more a result of poverty than choice.

Jamaica

The fame of Jamaica's Blue Mountain coffee has shadowed coffee grown in other parts of the country. And rightly so. The Blue Mountain coffee plantations produce some of the finest coffee in the world, the resulting brew is a perfect balance of acidity, sweetness and aroma (see the boxed text Sunday Afternoon, Coffee Country later in this chapter). Beware of other brands that feature the words 'blue' and 'mountain' on their labels as imitators abound.

Puerto Rico

In the late 1960s, the Puerto Rican coffee trade was looking pretty grim. Luckily a few coffee cooperatives continued to produce the country's coffee beans and eventually coffee connoisseurs caught a whiff of what was being brewed on the island. Demand for quality beans has since revived Puerto Rico's coffee industry. Yauco Selecto has become the country's best known premium bean for its heavy body and buttery taste. Lares is another highly regarded coffee producer. Puerto Ricans enjoy their coffee as **café con leche** (coffee with milk).

Trinidad & Tobago

The days of good coffee are long gone for these two islands. There is coffee produced here, but nearly all of it is made into instant coffee, and that is what most of the locals drink. There are, however, efforts being made to turn the tide (see the boxed text A Coffee Crusade in the Shopping & Markets chapter).

The Bahamas

Coffee and Bahamas are two words that should be kept separate. The water on these islands is brackish, not a good start if a coffee is what you are after. Resorts and large hotels generally make coffee with bottled water, but elsewhere the only coffee hit you'll get is instant, with the bad water masked by a good dose of condensed milk. Bottoms up.

DRINKS

SUNDAY AFTERNOON, COFFEE COUNTRY

Craighton House Estate, Jamaica

Getting to the Blue Mountains, Jamaica's fabled coffee country, will make you shake as much as if you swallowed seven consecutive espressos. It involves a steep ascent on a lunar landscape where your obstacles include blind corners, overgrown vegetation and the odd cow or goat. These roads are the reason for off-road vehicles. The average suburban car would be swallowed whole.

Nevertheless, the scenery is striking: birds fly low over hills covered with banana palms. The highest peak, for which the range is named, is shrouded in clouds. It seems incredible, but people live on these mountains, and as you look down into the valleys you can see shacks standing near small plots of vegetables. But the majority of the land, and its rich soils, are given over to coffee trees.

In fact, the other trees growing on the hills (eucalyptus, orange and banana) serve to shade the much smaller coffee trees that grow to about 4 feet (1m) in height and have deep-green, waxy leaves. During a brief flowering period, they produce white blooms with yellow stamens. But more importantly, they produce coffee beans. These begin as small green pellets then grow

DRINKS

Preparing coffee in Cuba

to the size of a marble and turn burgundy, earning them the name 'cherry'. It is at this stage that they are ready to be picked. And so hundreds of workers with burlap sacks strapped across their shoulders head into the mountains to load up on cherries that are ready for processing.

Jamaicans have been growing coffee for nearly 300 years. The first plants (the Arabica species) were brought to the island in 1725 by Jamaica's governor. He felt that they might offer some economic diversity from sugarcane, which was the dominant industry of the day. From this tentative beginning, Jamaica became the world's largest coffee producer and remained so until the middle of the 19th century when Brazil, the current world leader, launched its industry.

Still, there are an estimated 60,000 coffee farmers in Jamaica, most of whom are responsible for a small plot of land and all of whom sell their harvest to one customer: the Jamaican Coffee Industry Board. The JCIB is responsible for selling the beans to the roasters who package it and sell it to you and me.

Mountains situated in the tropics offer the ideal environment for growing coffee. In addition to the limited sunlight ensured by the steep terrain (and compounded by larger trees), the sloping ground removes excess water from the soil. Coffee needs rain, of course, but not too much.

Gregory Arnold at the roasting machine, Craighton House Estate, Jamaica

The Jamaican Mavis Bank Coffee Company sits at the base of one of these valleys. It is a collection of buildings tucked neatly beside the Fall River, which provides water for processing the cherries.

The process begins when the cherries are put through a machine called a pulper, where the fruit surrounding the bean is separated (later to be used as fertilizer) and the beans are washed in an enormous tank of water. Next, the beans are dried in one of two ways: either put through another machine called a dryer or spread out on cement flats called barbecues, where they sit in the hot sun for a full week. Both methods serve to remove the thin skin called the offal from the bean. But our guide, Tristam, insists that the natural method yields a better cup.

Once dried, the beans are then separated according to size into five categories: #1, #B1, #2, #3 and Triage. The smallest bean, #3, is also the sweetest. Hundreds of workers then go through each batch, pulling out the peaberries (hard unusable beans) and separating the light beans from the dark. From there, the beans are packed up and ready for export.

Not all the coffee in the Blue Mountains goes through this process. Many residents will have a few coffee trees themselves amid the thyme, carrots and the odd ganja plant. Once cleaned and dried, the coffee can be roasted at home in a large roasting pot called a **dutchie**, where it is stirred constantly to prevent burning. This is truly special coffee, the kind meant to be enjoyed not out of some tumbler in the front seat of your car, but slowly, deliberately, with friends.

Donovan takes a break from duties at the Craighton House Estate, Jamaica

DRINKS

PASS THE DUTCHIE

For many coffee drinkers coffee is only recognizable in one form: as steaming liquid in a cup. How the coffee ended up in the familiar granulated form that goes into the espresso machine, or percolator is a mystery. Self-proclaimed connoisseurs may grind their own coffee in the hunt for the freshest brew, but will still buy their beans ready roasted and ready for the grinder. Surely the time between the roast and the grind will have an influence on the flavor; a cake roasted yesterday will taste differently today. It must be better go from the roasting stage to the grinder, to the pot. So, if you're hunting the perfect brew why not go one step further and roast the beans yourself?

Roast the beans yourself? Isn't it too complicated? Don't you require custom-built roasters, pressurizers and a sterile environment? Well the short answer is no, and so is the long one. Roasting your own beans is both straightforward and rewarding. A cup of coffee will taste proportionately better the more involved you are in its creation. And imagine the kudos:

"nice coffee" say your caffeine-sated friends.

"Yes, I roasted it myself".

Await looks of stunned incredulity .

So what will you need? Firstly, a desire to reach new caffeine heights. If you're happy with instant because it is 'instant' then close this book right now. There's a good chance that home roasting won't go right the first time. And it may go right, but it could go better: the essence of a bean, its oils, sugars, caffeine levels and other compounds will all alter depending on the roasting environment. You may create something brewable, but you may not appreciate your own creation: too acidic because it was only lightly roasted, too bitter because it was roasted longer ... in any case those who wish to reach coffee nirvana will be rewarded in time.

Concerning equipment, all you will need is a cast-iron skillet (frying pan) with a well-fitted lid, a large spoon, an oven thermometer and a well-ventilated burner. Coffee connoisseurs in the Caribbean use a heavy round-bottomed pot known as a **dutchie** for their coffee roasting requirements. But whatever you call your skillet, it is still a home-style, coffee-roasting must.

So let's get down to business. You'll need about 10oz (300g) of coffee beans in their unroasted form: familiar shape but green in color. Trying to roast more beans at one time is asking for trouble, and roasting less yeilds too little.

Heat the lidded pan to about 500°F (260°C). Open the lid, pour in the beans and shut the lid. Now comes the workout. Start 'shusheling' the

Roasting coffee at home in Pinar del Río, Cuba

beans, that is, moving the beans by shaking the pan back and forth. It may take some time to get the 'shushel' right.

To maintain an even heat, it's best to keep the lid on and let your senses other than sight tell you what is happening. After 4-6 minutes, the aroma of the beans will tell you things are happening. This is the point that you can open the lid and check the state of the beans. Their color will be changing from greenish to yellowish to brown (to dark brown if you cook them for longer).

From here on in you can check them minute by minute, but if they're on the heat, keep shusheling! You will also hear the beans start to pop as the moisture in the beans works its way to the surface. The beans can be taken from the heat at the first pop. But leave them for longer if a darker roast is what you're after. Choosing the right roasting time is where the art of roasting lies. The beans may begin to smoke if a darker roast is being created. For this reason ventilation is a must – aroma is good, but can be overwhelming.

There are no hard and fast rules, as the dutchie, heat source, beans and preferred taste will all have a bearing on the success of the roast. A good thing to remember is that coffee beans are like little bricks: once warm, they stay warm for a while, and even when taken off the heat they'll continue roasting themselves. For this reason it's essential to take them out of the pan before they reach the color you desire.

Place the roasted beans in a large bowl and stir them until they are cool enough to touch with your bare hands. As well as speeding up the cooling process, stirring will help remove particles.

Although the smell of the roasted beans will have you longing for a strong brew. The beans aren't ready for the grinder yet. Spread the beans out on a clean surface, brush or blow away any dust particles and leave them for about 12 hours. This gives the beans a chance to release gasses that would make the coffee sour if it were roasted immediately.

Once 12 hours have passed, it is time to taste your batch of home-roasted coffee. Grind up your custom-roasted beans and fill up your stove-top espresso. Don't skimp on the amount of coffee you use or you'll end up with what Cubans call **café americano**, weak coffee. If you want to make **café con leche**, be sure to heat the milk.

Now for the taste test. For this part of the project, a coffee-friendly environment is paramount. Drinking coffee in the Caribbean is an occasion, not something consumed on the go. Set up your favorite chair and take the phone off the hook. If you want to invite friends over to try your Caribbean custom roast, make sure they're the sort of people that will appreciate your efforts. People who drink 10 styrofoam cups of freeze-dried coffee per day have probably killed their coffee-tasting tastebuds long ago. Be choosy. Be precious. This is unique coffee. Be proud.

home cooking
& traditions

The fact that traditional Caribbean cuisine has survived the onslaught of several million tourists every year is testament to the power of home cooking. Indeed, the very soul of Caribbean society may very well be located in the kitchen where something always seems to be simmering on the stove, filling the rest of the house with an inviting, appetizing aroma.

In the settlement days the kitchen, like much of the rest of the house, was very simple. Most families had to make do with a single source of heat – a stove that burned wood, cane or whatever was available. Utensils were not in great supply; most dishes had to be cooked in a single pot. The kitchen would be located at the back of the house to give the smoke an easy exit. In rural areas you will see smoke emerging from woodfire ovens that are still being used as a heat source.

Today the islands' urban kitchens are fully equipped with stoves, refrigeration and running water. Most will also have a few mod-cons, such as a blender (especially useful for making sauces), a rice cooker and a pressure cooker. But when it comes to basic supplies (pots, pans and the like) most Caribbean kitchens remain uncluttered.

Canned food is kept in cupboards, with fresh fruits and vegetables stored in a separate larder. In the kitchens we visited, there did not seem to be a tremendous amount of food, which reflects how often people visit their local market or grocery store. Certainly, nobody wants to eat fish that is anything less than fresh.

In rural areas, you may see a small plot of land planted with vegetables and herbs outside the house. The kitchens in these areas will be much more simple, although a fridge and stove are normally a part of every house, except in the most extreme poverty.

Cooking is still done almost entirely by women. Girls are expected to learn from their mothers, watching carefully as time-honored family recipes are prepared. They learn not only the proper seasonings and the proper preparation methods, but also the history behind each dish. Caribbean cooks do not traditionally rely on cookbooks but rather memorize recipes. Exact portions are put aside in place of a 'pinch of this' or 'a little bit of that'. The young girls were expected to take it all in and be ready to make a smooth transition from apprentice to head chef of their own brood.

The recipes they learned are the same recipes that locals identify as their favorite national dishes – stews of every description from pig's tail to goat's head, rice dishes such as Cuba's interestingly named **moros y cristianos** (literally, Moors and Christians; see the recipe later in this chapter) or baked sweet breads and pastries.

Carlita in her rustic kitchen preparing coffee, Pinar del Río, Cuba

Not all Cubans have cars and many different forms of transport are utilised, Cuba

Men, on the other hand, rarely enter the kitchen. They are generally inept with pots and pans, except to bang them together during Carnival time. There will be the odd exception, of course, where a man prepares something that has been passed down from his father or grandfather, but on most days, it is the women who provide the family with their hot food.

The situation is changing today. Women still do the cooking, but recipe books are making their way into the Caribbean kitchen. In Cuba, Nitza Villapol almost single handedly displaced the oral tradition with her television show and recipe book, *Cocina al Minuto*. While she overturned tradition, her efforts served to educate the Cuban cook on nutrition, a concept that is only beginning to catch on in other parts of the islands.

Aida Batista preparing tostones, Cuba

THE INIMITABLE NITZA VILLAPOL

Mention her name to any Cuban – whether a chef at a five-star restaurant or someone whose only kitchen experience is with a microwave – and it will be immediately recognized. For nearly half a century, Nitza Villapol was a fixture in the Cuban culinary conscience. Her book *Cocina al Minuto* (One Minute Kitchen) is the first and last word in Cuban cooking and has been reprinted several times since first published in the 1950s. At the Plaza de Armas, used copies are proudly displayed next to the innumerable books by and about Cuba's other great leaders, Fidel, Ché and José Marti. No kitchen would be complete without at least one food-stained copy.

Nitza came on the scene in the early 1950s when her television program, also called *Cocina al Minuto* appeared during the very first years of TV broadcasting in Cuba. From that point, Nitza single-handedly taught Cubans how to cook, how to eat better and how to enjoy the foods that were available to them – in good times and in bad. These broadcasts (sometimes daily, sometimes weekly) ran almost continuously until soon before Nitza's death in 1994.

Her cooking was pure, unadulterated Cuba, traditional yet highly adaptable when conditions required it. The recipes featured on her program would take advantage of seasonal surpluses whilst simultaneously making up for reductions in availability of other produce. During times of severe shortages, recipes would include grapefruit rinds, cactus and banana peels.

Cocina al Minuto is much more than a recipe book. It is a comprehensive guide to dining atmosphere, which Nitza says is "as important as the food itself, from a psychological point of view"; etiquette including everything from eating too fast to the proper way to hold a wine glass; and proper nutrition, which she explains leads to better health, better work and study and better productivity. Throughout the pages of her book she scolds Cubans for relying too much on carbohydrates, though she does concede that "what we eat and who we marry has to be a matter of personal taste, not someone else's."

Nitza was clearly acquainted with the limits of the kitchen in revolutionary Cuban society. And her advice to those concerned rings true "The elements that make up a table do not have to constitute a single set, as long as they are combined and presented with *gusto*". It was this strong, opinionated stance and resourcefulness that endeared her to so many Cubans during their time of hardship. Even those whose ideological differences to the Castro regime forced them north, insisted on bringing with them their much used and beloved copy of *Cocina al Minuto*. After all, as the legendary Ché Guevara said: "homesickness begins with food."

Moros y Cristianos (Black Beans & Rice)

Throughout Latin America, beans have been a staple since before the arrival of Columbus. In Cuba, **frijoles negros** (black beans), whether served alone or mixed with rice to make **moros y cristianos** (literally, Moors and Christians) are the legumes of choice. There are countless versions across the country but this one adds a bit more flavor than most and is best served *beside* rice as opposed to mixed with it. To keep it authentic, you should start with dried beans but using the canned variety will not destroy the dish.

Ingredients

1lb (500g)	dried black beans
1 pinch	dried oregano
4 Tbs	vegetable oil
4-8	cloves of garlic, chopped
1	small bell pepper, seeded and chopped
1	bay leaf
1	small onion (or 1 bunch of green onions)
	hot pepper sauce to taste (this is not Cuban, but something you might like to add)
	salt to taste

Rinse the beans thoroughly. Transfer the beans into a large cooking pot with a little oil, the bay leaf and oregano. Add enough water to easily cover the beans and bring to a boil. Reduce the heat and cook about two hours until the beans are tender. Be sure to check the water level every so often as you will likely have to add more during the process.

When the beans are nearly done, heat a skillet and add the oil, onion, peppers, garlic and hot sauce. You can choose this moment to get innovative: a little cumin, basil or thyme can bring more substance to the flavor. Fresh ground pepper, while not common in Cuba, is another good seasoning. Once the peppers and onions are softened, season the mixture with salt and add the now cooked beans (drain any excess water first). Let the flavors meld by stirring over medium-low heat.

Serves 4

Old and new faces of Cuba

HOME COOKING

AUSTIN CLARKE – Guest Interview

"Food", says Austin Clarke, "is not merely the satisfaction of desire. It soothes the spirit, reinforces friendships, defines one's status. It is an expression of love. It is an aesthetic. It is the greatest link one has to one's original culture."

Austin Clarke and I are talking food. He is drinking a Bombay Martini with a twist, with three green olives on the side. As we chat, he digs his hand into a bowl and pops the odd peanut into his mouth between thoughts. The thoughts run from the philosophical to a few simple truths: "Mashed potatoes done well is a hell of a thing", he says at one point.

In his book *Pig Tails 'n Breadfruit,* Clarke takes us back to his mother's kitchen in the village of St Matthias (or Sin-Matthias as locals called it) in Barbados. The book is full of wonderfully told food anecdotes, and each chapter concludes with a recipe. But these are not the ordinary kind of recipes, where each ingredient is listed with precise measurements and the preparation is presented in a step-by-step fashion. Instead, Clarke relates it the way cooks in the Caribbean have been passing down recipes for generations. He begins the recipe for coo-coo, for example, with: slice up a few okra. Knowing just how many is a matter for the heart.

As Clarke says: "In every self-respecting Bajan household, the woman would not be caught dead with a cookbook. To read a cookbook would suggest that she has not retained what her mother taught her; that she does not know how to cook; that she does not know how to take care of her man; that her mother had neglected to teach her how to 'handle herself' in the kitchen, how 'to do things properly.'"

Austin Clarke left Barbados for university in Canada in the 1950s. His literary efforts, eight novels and five collections of short stories, have brought him international recognition. So why write a food memoir?

Quite by accident, as it turns out. It emerged out a number of columns that appeared in the Sunday edition of *The Nation,* a Bajan daily, in which Clarke discussed certain food-related incidents on the island – one involving a woman so poor she lured a chicken from a neighbor's yard onto her own property, another about the proper way to make **bakes** (Bajan fried bread). Known among friends as a demon in the kitchen, it was suggested he write a recipe book. He initially balked at the idea, but then reconsidered when he came upon the notion to wrap personal anecdotes and memories around his favorite foods.

Not surprisingly, his mother provides his initial gastronomic inspiration. "When I began to look at food, I had to think of my mother and how she had to improvise during the lean times of World War II in order to provide meals of the same delicacy and flavor as we had enjoyed before the war."

"Food was central to our lives. Every day, my mother planned our meal and walked across the street to the shops to buy the food. Once there, depending on what ingredients were available, she might have to substitute and improvise. That journey my mother made and the conversations she had is a chapter in a narrative of her life."

Clarke's mother's voice is heard throughout the book, through direct dialogue: "a little more hot pepper, this time, eh? What you think, boy? You think she could do with a pinch more?" She is also in the voice Clarke adopts as narrator: ingredients become 'ingreasements', and imperative tense is used to gently order the readers. In a passage about souse he says "man, put it in my hand, man!" Likewise exclamatory sentences make for wonderful, rhythmic emphasis "God in heaven! It too sweet, in-true!"

• • •

Food is clearly a part of anyone's culture, but for those living far away from the kitchens and markets of their childhood and adolescence, food takes on a special significance. One of his most poignant memories of those first years away at university was of the day when the campus cafeteria (usually a source of food fit for pigs) served a pilaf, which Clarke and his fellow Bajan immediately identified as **pelau**. Despite the fact that the version served in the cafeteria carried all the institutional qualities, they went back for more again and again. "It was the first and only day in two years I left the dining hall with a full belly," he writes.

Abroad, food takes on new meaning. It is a way of getting back to one's culture, but never fully. The ingredients can echo those from the homeland but are never quite the same, the seasoning is always slightly different. Nevertheless, as anyone who has spent significant time abroad knows, you keep trying. Why do you think there are so many Jamaican restaurants in Brooklyn, New York? Here's a hint: it's not for the Italians.

And even when you go home, you go for the soul food. Barbados, Clarke points out, has changed considerably since the 1940s. Tourism has led to new restaurants where chefs experiment and innovate in order to keep competitive and satisfy the tastes of holiday makers.

Despite this, the old school menus refuse to die. A returning Bajan skips the upscale Bridgetown restaurants, all starch linened and crystal chandeliered as they may be. Instead, says Clarke, "the Bajan who goes home goes to Baxter's Rd at three or four o'clock in the morning to have fried fish."

And when that happens, the lowly fried fish becomes the best thing ever to enter your mouth, for the simple fact that it tastes like home.

Overleaf – Roadside stall in Hado, where the house specialty is peanut soup, Jamaica

!CELEBRACION!

Relaxing before Ano Nuevo

Rolando Perez Batista displays the Ano Nuevo pig, Cuba

December in Cuba is the month of festivities and celebrations and the biggest **fiesta** is **Ano Nuevo** (New Year). For me, the best place to celebrate Ano Nuevo is in the house of my Uncle Tomas in Pinar del Río, the tobacco country east of Havana. The party really starts the day before when my two Uncles, Tomas and Rensol, gather to kill and prepare the pig for the fiesta next day. Between sips of rum and arguments about how to kill the pig faster and with less noise, the men dispatch one of Uncle Tomas' fattest pigs. The jokes come hard and fast during the final step, which requires us to shave the pig. First, we use a knife and hot water but then to get it really smooth, Uncle Tomas uses one of his own disposable razors. I have many childhood memories of Uncle Tomas in his cowboy hat giving the pig a close shave!

In the meantime, the women are preparing the **adobo** (a marinade made of bitter orange, lemon and salt), which will be rubbed on the pig inside and out. The liver is seasoned separately before it is placed back inside the pig and sewn closed. We leave time for the adobe to penetrate for several hours while we dig a shallow hole in the ground and fill it with **carbon**, a type of charcoal made by the neighborhood **carbonero**. While we are working, my cousins take their machetes and return with two **horquetas** (Y-shaped pieces of wood on which a spit can turn).

Ano Nuevo preparations begin

After the pig is impaled on the spit, the hard work begins as it has to be turned slowly, and continuously, by hand. My cousin takes the first turn, and to keep it from getting boring, we place the dominos table next to the pig. Dominos is a very old and traditional game in Cuba played at all the parties. We play for over four hours, the rhythmic slap of the dominos competing against a tirade of good-natured insults. Naturally, the loser of each round of dominos has to turn the pig.

In the house, things are hotting up. Waves of music pound the walls while happy revelers dance as though possessed. In Cuba, music is something that everybody carries in their blood. Everybody dances, little boys and girls sway next to more romantic couples.

My mother shouts from the kitchen, "How much longer for the pig?"

Uncle Tomas tests the skin with his knife and pronounces it ready. The dining table is set outside in the soft, tropical night next to my grandmother's rose garden, so the floral aromas mix with the smell of food arriving from the kitchen: smoky **moros y cristianos** (black beans & rice); **la yucca con mojo** (steaming hot yucca with garlic sauce); **chicharrón** (crispy nuggets of deep-fried pork rinds); **tostones**

Carting the pig

Smiles of anticipation

(deep-fried slices of flattened plantain sprinkled with salt and served hot); delicious **ensaladas mixtas** (mixed salads), composed of tender home-grown lettuce and sweet red tomatoes. And the king of the banquet, the succulent **macho asado** (large spit-roasted pig), its crispy, golden skin contrasting with its soft, white, juicy meat.

Once the main course is devoured, my mother emerges with her masterpiece, **el dulce de coco**, freshly grated coconut meat boiled in a white sugar syrup and served with handmade cheeses.

Time to carve

After dinner, my uncles and I sit on the porch enjoying aromatic Cuban cigars. They tell stories about their glory days as local baseball players and argue about who is a better horse rider until the clock closes in on midnight. My aunt readies the traditional **cubo de agua**, a bucket of water from the last cleaning of the house. As the old year winds down, everyone gathers around with glasses of rum and at the stroke of midnight, everyone kisses and toasts the new year with cries of "Feliz Ano Nuevo!" My aunt throws the cubo de agua out the front door, symbolizing the departure of all that was bad in the past year. The party continues until dawn and we all return to our own houses full of happiness and hope for prosperity in the new year.

*Rolando Perez Batista lives in San Francisco
but left his heart in Havana, Cuba*

The feast of bacchanalian proportions, Cuba

Utensils

The Amerindians used clay to make many of their cooking utensils including the griddle upon which cassava bread was baked, and a pot in which stews were prepared. This one-pot approach survived even after iron was introduced by the Europeans. The primary reason being that slaves were only likely to use one pot, as were their free (yet often poor) descendents.

The utensils of a typical Caribbean kitchen have always been basic. Even in many restaurants, you will not see a sophisticated array of copper pots and pans hanging above the stove, nor will you find a different knife for every kind of cut. There is the odd exception, such as a **dutchie** (large roasting pot for making coffee) but for the most part, you will not find much in the way of specialty utensils.

Tubers and beans spend hours in boiling water before they are ready. With this in mind, many kitchens are equipped with a pressure cooker that saves time, effort and energy without changing the integrity of the dish. For the visitor, this simplicity has one major advantage: replicating your favorite Caribbean dishes at home won't require anything you don't already have (see the Caribbean Banquet chapter).

celebrating
with food

The unexpected appearance of a guest in the house is reason enough to head straight for the kitchen and return with an armload of food and drinks. At the other extreme is Carnival, a celebration in which entire countries head out into the streets for a huge, non-stop party. Somewhere in between these two extremes lie those occasions that call for something special – birthdays, anniversaries, weddings and family reunions.

Musicians, mojitos and traditional Cuban fare Havana, Cuba

Celebrations are not just about food, but you couldn't hold one without spending a few hours in the kitchen to make sure that all your guests are well fed. In fact, at the end of a truly proper celebration there should be plenty of food left over. As a guest, you're likely to be sent home with left-overs to enjoy when you find the space.

While no Caribbean requires a reason to throw a party, certain celebrations require days of planning and are eagerly awaited. Some celebrations are cause for the slaughter of an animal, usually a goat or a pig. At weddings and funerals or milestone birthdays in Jamaica, a fattened goat is the victim. The meat from the goat is used to make a curry, but the head is saved to make **mannish water**, a soup that also includes beans, onions and dumplings. A Jamaican friend tells the story of an Englishman who was invited to celebrate a 50th birthday party and innocently lifted the lid off the simmering soup pot only to find the head of a goat staring right back at him! But don't worry, the head is normally removed from the soup before serving.

With birthday parties, as with most Caribbean celebrations, guests arrive late. If you are told to come at 9pm, look to show up around 11pm. There will be music, perhaps a bit of old-school calypso, ska, reggae or even mod-ern reggae house. In Puerto Rico, the Dominican Republic and Cuba, the music will definitely be some version of salsa or meringue. Later in the

The wedding party descends to the waitng car, Cuba

evening, the furniture will be cleared away and people, whether in couples or in groups, will get up and dance. With some forms of music, the uninitiated will have no trouble catching on. But on the Spanish islands, dancing is a serious skill. Virtually everybody – young and old – is able to dance. And dance well. At first it is intimidating and enough to keep you firmly stuck to your seat sipping rum the rest of the night. But sipping rum will inevitably lead to a foray onto the floor where a sympathetic dancer will take you under their wing and have you boogying with the best of them.

But most social activity is centered around chatter: political arguments, discussions of national sporting heroes (from Trinidad's sprinter, Ato

CARNIVAL

"We don't really eat during Carnival. We drink, we dance, we play music. None of it stops long enough for a meal."

Every island has their own version of Carnival, but all seem to be based in the pre-Lenten festivities that precede a time of privation. For most people, that period of privation is no longer observed, but carnival lives on! It is a time to let go, to forget your troubles and have some serious fun. The mask, which is an integral part of Carnival, is symbolic of the idea that no one cares who you are in these brief, frantic days, as long as you are willing to party.

In the Bahamas, it is called Junkanoo and takes place during the Christmas season. In Cuba, each city has its own Carnival with the largest, the Carnaval de la Habana taking place in Havana at the end of July and lasting a few weeks. During this time street food scales new heights. Makeshift restaurants pop up along the famous Malecón sea wall doling out national favorites such as **lechón asado** (roast pig) under the red and black flag of the revolution. Giant metal beer barrels promote a steady flow of draft poured into brown wax cups. At night, the street is closed to traffic; music booms and giant sparkling floats populated with revelers make their way from one end of the street to the other, cheered on by the crowds.

But the biggest Carnival occurs in Trinidad, where an enormous grandstand is constructed in Port of Spain specifically for viewing the passing parade.

The parade is the center of Carnival. In fact, the parade and the party surrounding it are not distinguished. You can't merely watch, you have to dance, to cheer, to chant with each band as it passes. These bands are well established organizations, formed with the exclusive purpose of creating the most spectacular display and writing the best song. Costumes and floats are highly elaborate, requiring a whole year to make. Soon after one Carnival, bands start working on their carnival

Bolden, to Jamaica's soccer team, Reggae Boyz, as well as the pantheon of Cuban baseball) and extended family updates.

This is especially true at reunions. Caribbean families are usually enormous and widely dispersed. Despite the distance, families remain incredibly close and when the whole crew gets together every few years, it is a major production. Often the family house simply isn't large enough for everyone so the event has to be held in a rented church hall or even outdoors. Needless to say, all the familiar recipes – souse, mannish water, ackee & salt-fish – will be in abundance and consumed amid moans of "they just don't make it like this in the US" or "there's no peas n' rice anywhere like here".

costumes for the next year. Each costume is original; you are not allowed to reuse or recycle. Some of them involve mechanisms that allow the user to have extra arms or legs. The bands that make them operate year-round out of small, out-of-the-way club houses where every detail, every stitch and every piece of colored paper is painstakingly put into place.

The lead up to Carnival begins with a weekend of resting and relaxing, saving up the energy needed for the ensuing festivities. Someone in the neighborhood might make a **braff** (a sort of fish stew) and you'll take your only regular meal for the next 48 hours.

Come Monday or Juve Tuesday (Shrove Tuesday) the party begins in earnest. In the predawn hours, the sounding of a whistle and the banging of a **lapo cabway** (single sheep-skin drum) ushers in the beginning of Carnival. By the time the sun comes up, entire streets have been closed and many people don't bother to go to work. Bosses don't mind; they're out in the streets too! Schools don't even bother opening.

On the street things are heating up, the soca music is non-stop and loud, lead by a bass beat you can feel in the marrow of your bones. Each band's song is repeated over and over until it becomes a hypnotic anthem echoed throughout the streets, accompanied by a sea of brass and percussion. The crowds get tight, and you often find yourself unable to stop dancing, even if you wanted to. You get tired, exhausted even. But you go on, fueled by the energy of the crowd and the knowledge that this sort of thing only happens once a year.

Carnival is a time of happiness and revelry. All the social rules that govern society are thrown out for a few magical days. Strangers dance with strangers, inhibitions are released in this free expression of music and mayhem.

In the end, people rest. The religious go to church, ask for forgiveness and begin their Lenten duties. The streets are cleaned, the bands dismantle their floats and costumes, and as soon as they wake and the ringing in their ears has stopped, they prepare for next year.

Overleaf – Montego Bay birthday party, Jamaica

FAMILY DAY, ST ANN'S CHURCH, TRINIDAD

Sometimes Caribbean's best culinary experiences occur by accident. Such was the case when I happened upon Family Day at St Ann's Catholic Church in Port of Spain, Trinidad. It is an annual event, staged to raise money for the upkeep of church and neighborhood programs. It also serves as a community mixer and non-church members are invited to participate. After the regular Sunday service, tents are set up in the church yard, under which an assortment of used goods are sold: romance novels, ancient household appliances, salt and pepper shakers and other bits of forgotten refuse from the back cupboards and attics of the parishioners. There are games for the kids: a ring toss with rum bottles serving as the target; and a ball throw, where the idea is to knock over a pyramid of empty apple juice cans – the more clang and clatter the better. And then there is the music: big, booming speakers with earth-shaking woofers that produce enough sound to fill an arena.

But most of the activity is centered around the food booths, where groups of ladies sporting T-shirts identifying their affiliation with a particular church group sell homemade food that is kept warm in styrofoam bins. The offerings are eclectic, but reflect the cultural makeup of today's Trinidad. There is a large barbecue where chicken is broiled, coated in a sauce that always includes a little bit of Trini pepper, and served in a box with steamed rice mixed with sauteed carrots and onions. In another tent, a group of ladies prepares cakes and sweets for tea, an English ritual that still occurs in certain sectors of Trinidad society.

Finger foods are provided by East Indian members of the community and include **kachourie** (split-pea fritters) and **saheena** (spinach fritters), served on a paper towel. They also sell **khurma**, a sweet snack made from flour and sugar, which is shaped into long, thin pieces then deep fried and rolled in more sugar. The texture and taste is similar to a plain donut, but the ladies insist that it's not. Finally, the Chinese community is represented with more finger foods including shrimp-filled wontons.

Relations among Trinidad & Tobago's diverse communities are not always harmonious. Indeed, racial tension is a real problem on the islands as the African and East Indian communities vie for political power. Perhaps the politicians have been going about it wrong all along. Maybe they need to just sit down and eat together. Or set up stalls at St Ann's Church.

Port of Spain, Trinidad

Throughout the predominantly Christian Caribbean, Christmas is the most important culinary celebration of the year, followed closely by New Year's. In fact, in many places, celebrating and feasting stretches from Christmas Eve through to New Year's Day. Entire extended families come together from all parts of the island (and quite often from other countries) to enjoy the festive season together. The favored dishes are ham or turkey, both of which are rare treats at other times of the year (see the boxed text Christmas in Martinique later in this chapter).

CHRISTMAS IN MARTINIQUE

In the small towns of Martinique the term 'family' is a broad one. So it is no surprise that a family dinner at Christmas time might involve up to 50 guests. In addition to blood relatives and relatives by marriage, close friends and neighbors are likely to show up. And all of them hungry.

Celebrating Christmas Eve begins with the slaughter of a pig, the most prized meat in traditional Creole cuisine. The animal is chosen carefully for its size and shape. Killing a pig is tricky business and a poor job can result in a lot of wasted meat. For this reason, the butcher is always an honored guest, whether he is family or not.

Inside, the women cook other dishes such as **akkras** (fish fritters), **ragout** (a generic word for stew) or **feroce** (dip made of avocado, cassava flour and peppers). This is Creole cooking where the traditions of France and Africa meet head on.

During the Christmas season in Martinique the drink of choice is **schaubb**, one of a whole slew of drinks made by immersing a variety of fruit or herbs in a bottle of white rum and leaving them to soak for several months. In the case of schaubb, orange peel is added to the rum a few months before Christmas to ensure there is plenty of it when Christmas Eve arrives.

As the hoards arrive, the schaubb begins to flow freely, the cooking aromas drift outside into the streets and the singers in the family (everybody eventually becomes a singer) launch into their favorite **cantiques**. These are songs only heard around Christmas and have religious or seasonal themes – although admittedly with a decidedly festive twist. The singers are accompanied by **ti-bois**, which are in fact not instruments, but anything you can find to bang together – pots and pans, a pencil and a sewing box, hands and a heavy book or a stick and an empty bottle. The celebration extends long into the night with several rounds of eating and drinking. It's Christmas Eve after all!

And what is the traditional way of spending Christmas Day in Martinique? Are you kidding me? You sleep all day long.

Festivals

With all the food that is consumed at celebrations in the Caribbean, it's only natural that food itself gets celebrated from time to time. On a region-wide scale, the best chefs from the best restaurants compete annually in A Taste of the Caribbean, an orgy of gastronomic excellence sponsored by the Caribbean Culinary Federation. This is serious competition where local chefs (usually representing a hotel) must win their way onto the national team in qualifying rounds before moving on to the main event. Bartenders also compete in a separate category.

In Barbados, the Oistin's Fish Festival in April is ostensibly about catching fish, but a whole lot of fish eating goes on as well. In May, the Cayman Islands plays host to a cooking festival of their own, known simply as The Cook Off. In June, the annual Taste of Cayman event takes place. Puerto Rico holds a Festival of Native Dishes in June, with special

Jerk pit in Bluefields, Jamaica

emphasis on food and drink from the best local chefs. In Jamaica, Ocho Rios plays host to the one-day Jamaica Spice Festival in July, where the local cuisine is put on display. Further down the coast, Boston Beach, the birthplace of **jerk** (meat marinated with a mixture of spices) hosted the first annual jerk festival in 1999. The event was so successful that it attracted 20,000 lovers of the spicy meat, twice the number expected. Traffic was nightmarish and many attendees found that the food had run out when they arrived. Organizers

promise to be better prepared in coming years (see the boxed text The Jerk in the Regional Variations chapter). There is even a festival celebrating the yam, in Trelawney, the parish between Montego Bay and Ocho Rios. And then there are all those regattas, when the fabulously wealthy bring their fabulously large boats into port to have a fabulous time, dining and drinking on the foreshore.

regional
variations

It is more than just sea that separates the islands of the Caribbean.
There are variations in history, language, terrain and economy, all
of which continue to have an influence on what is eaten across the
region. Some of the differences are subtle – there's only so much
you can do with peas & rice – but some, such as Gouda in Curaçao,
are far more distinct.

The English Islands

The culinary legacy of the English (some may be grateful to hear) has not been so pronounced. On most of the English islands, the Africans forced to work the plantations far outnumbered the planters themselves and so the African influence is strong. Over the years, each island has developed its own cultural identity and today Jamaicans point to **ackee & saltfish** and reggae for their cultural reference point while the Trini looks to **roti** and Carnival for theirs.

Like elsewhere in the Caribbean, the English islands always make space for starchy side-dishes. However, there is less emphasis on root vegetables and tubers. In their place will be a large dish of macaroni and cheese. This is not, it must be stated, the same sort of macaroni and cheese that comes in a box with a foil-lined package of powdered cheese product. This is the real thing, baked in the oven and packed so tight that it can be cut into slabs and served lasagna style.

When it comes to meat, chicken is the most popular. In some cities, you can't throw a rock without hitting a place that serves fried chicken, roast chicken or, best of all, pan chicken. The best pan chicken is cooked over hot coals in an old oil drum that has been cut in half and designated for a higher calling than transporting crude around the world.

Souse is another English-island favorite. There are many different ways of preparing souse, but the end result is generally a sort of stew with a thick, gravy-like sauce. Fish is the usual main ingredient, but souses can also be made with conch, chicken, pork or tongue. It is a dish with a heritage that stretches back to the days of slavery, when it was a preparation of whatever was left over from the plantation owner's kitchen.

Roast chicken and garbanzo bean salad with fried rice

Jamaica

Among the English islands, Jamaica deserves special attention. Indeed, of all the Caribbean countries it is in Jamaica that a truly national cuisine has developed. When you get to Jamaica, it only takes a trip away from the tourist drags to realize that Jamaicans love to eat. Every city block has a few chimneys where smoke rises continuously throughout the day as a signal that something delicious is under roof.

From a simple roadside shack to the kitchen of a five-star hotel, Jamaican chefs everywhere have successfully blended local foods with tastes from abroad to create some of the most memorable dishes on the islands.

So where to begin? Ask any Jamaican and they will not hesitate with the answer: **ackee & saltfish**. For no other place in the New World grows the ackee that originally arrived from West Africa with Captain Bligh in the HMS *Bounty*. Apparently, what the world's most famously deposed ship's captain lacked in people skills he made up for as an accomplished amateur botanist. To make ackee & saltfish, salted cod is soaked for several hours to reduce the salt content, after which the flaky fish is stewed with the ackee along with onions, peppers and thyme.

If ackee & saltfish is Jamaica's flagship dish, then **patty** is a very close second. Other islands do serve patties, but in Jamaica it's their lifeblood. At one location of Tasty Patty in midtown Kingston, the lunchtime line up is 10 deep, even though it has only one item available (see the recipe in the Staples & Specialties chapter).

Patties consist of flaky, buttery pastry rolled into a circle and folded around a meat filling. Traditionally, the filling is ground beef, which is browned with finely chopped onions and other spices. The patty has evolved to include other fillings such as chicken, cheese, fish or even lobster. It's then baked in an oven and served piping hot with pepper sauce.

Making Jamaican patties, Savanna-la-Mar

REGIONAL VARIATIONS

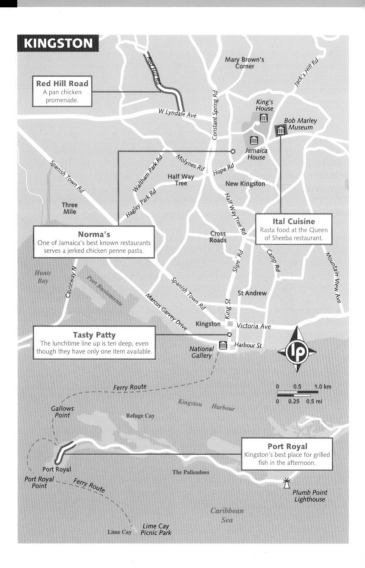

KINGSTON

Red Hill Road
A pan chicken promenade.

Mary Brown's Corner

King's House

Bob Marley Museum

Jamaica House

W Lyndale Ave

Constant Spring Rd

Jack's Hill Rd

Red Hill Rd

Molynes Rd

Hope Rd

Waltham Park Rd

Half Way Tree

New Kingston

Spanish Town Rd

Three Mile

Hagley Park Rd

Half Way Tree Rd

Norma's
One of Jamaica's best known restaurants serves a jerked chicken penne pasta.

Cross Roads

Ital Cuisine
Rasta food at the Queen of Sheeba restaurant.

Camp Rd

Mountain View Ave

Hunts Bay

Causeway N

Port Bustamente

Marcus Garvey Drive

Spanish Town Rd

King St

Slipe Rd

St Andrew

Tasty Patty
The lunchtime line up is ten deep, even though they have only one item available.

Kingston

Victoria Ave

Harbour St

National Gallery

Ferry Route

Kingston Harbour

0   0.5   1.0 km
0   0.25   0.5 mi

Gallows Point

Refuge Cay

Port Royal
Kingston's best place for grilled fish in the afternoon.

Port Royal

The Palisadoes

Plumb Point Lighthouse

Port Royal Point

Ferry Route

Caribbean Sea

Lime Cay
Lime Cay Picnic Park

At some of Jamaica's patty places, you can buy **coco bread**, soft, white bread that is folded before baking and comes to you piping hot. The idea is to split the coco bread and then insert a whole patty. It sounds like a lot of bread and, frankly, it is. A better way to enjoy coco bread is to have a meatloaf patty, where spiced meatloaf is slipped between an unfolded loaf of coco bread.

Jamaicans are also fond of a dish called **rundown**. This is a fish stew made by simmering coconut milk so it reduces, then adding fish (mackerel, snapper or swordfish), chopped onion, thyme and other seasonings. Rundown has become a staple in many upscale restaurants and the version we had at Marguerite's in Montego Bay was wonderfully accented with plantain – a fine example of nouvelle Caribbean cuisine.

Thanks to the East Indian influence, curry spice is an important part of Jamaican cooking, and curried goat is an essential dish at any important event. Likewise, roti is as popular in Jamaica as anywhere.

REGIONAL VARIATIONS

WHAT DID MARLEY EAT FOR BREAKFAST?

To most of the world, Jamaica means reggae music and images of a dreadlocked Bob Marley encased in a thick cloud of smoke as he tokes from an enormous spliff. The music, the hair and the marijuana are, of course, all symbols of Rastafarianism. But just as important is Ital cooking, a culinary philosophy that sets down the guidelines for what a Rastafarian can and cannot eat.

The word Ital means 'vital' and the foods are characterized by their life-giving qualities. Meat, for example is to be avoided as a dead animal does not have vitality. Similarly, foods that are preserved, processed or salted are rejected for their unnatural qualities. Instead, the Rasta diet is dominated by fresh fruit and vegetables, and fresh (not dried) herbs and spices. Herbs, in this case, includes marijuana and Rastafarians will often add a bit of ganja to baked goods and stews. The most ardent among them will not even use utensils that have been forged by a machine, but rather will only eat from clay dishes or cups made from coconut shells.

In practice, the rules of Ital cooking are commonly bent. Indeed, the Queen of Sheeba Restaurant in Kingston, which sits on the grounds of the Bob Marley museum, even serves curried goat! The atmosphere, however, is another story. Ital restaurants rarely have walls, preferring instead the open air where diners eat their **akkra** (fritters with black-eyed peas, onions and pepper) or **Ital stew** (vegetable stew, sometimes with ackee) under huts. You may also notice among the aromas wafting from the kitchen, the distinct smell of burning ganja.

Overleaf – A sunset view of Kingston from the Blue Mountains, Jamaica

THE JERK

Mackey Jerk Centre just outside Ocho Rios, Discovery Bay, Jamaica

The Caribbean islands share many flavors, preparations and ingredients: peas & rice, escovitched fish – these may vary from place to place but in essence they are all pan-Caribbean foods. On the other hand, **jerk** (meat marinated with spices) is pure Jamaican. Locals line up at their favorite jerk pit to get their fill of pork, chicken or seafood and the wonderful mixture of spices that permeates every cell of the meat. And some flavor! Intense, brash, unforgiving, smoky. It tastes like … rebellion.

Jerk was invented by the Maroons, the band of slaves who rebelled against their British masters and won their limited freedom in the 1730s. Limited, because they were confined to a relatively small area of the northeastern part of the country. And for most of Jamaica's colonial history, right up until the 1950s, jerk was virtually unknown outside this area. Once the secret was out, though, there was no stopping it. Today, the jerk pit joins the church and the rum shop as the three fixtures in every small town and village across Jamaica.

The unique blend of spices used to make jerk developed from the need to preserve the meat. Your first bite of jerk may lead you to believe that hot pepper is used by the bowlful. However, the most essential ingredient is allspice. Of course, cooks are not shy about tossing in the odd scotch bonnet pepper – known throughout the world for its fiery flavor.

The intensity of flavor is not only due to the ingredients of the jerk marinade itself, but also from the fact that you must leave the meat in the marinade for a long time. In the case of pork, this means at least 24 hours, but results are better if you can leave it for 48. Chicken requires less time; about 12 hours should do the trick. Purists will tell you that the only way to do real jerk is to cook the pork on slats of still-green pimento wood over a pimento-wood fire. Unless you do it yourself, the only place to get jerk done this way is at Jamaica's Boston Beach, near Portland. You can do it yourself on a backyard or beach barbecue.

Today, jerk is moving into uncharted territory. A fast-food chain called Island Grill offers a jerk burger while Norma's, one of Jamaica's best known restaurants, serves a jerked chicken penne pasta. Given the extent to which Jamaican's love their jerk, this can only be the beginning.

REGIONAL VARIATIONS

Jerk Pork

The key to great jerk is time. You have to plan ahead to make sure that the meat sits in this marinade for at least 24 hours so that all the wonderful flavors have a chance to get well acquainted with the pork. Of all the spices listed, two are especially important: allspice and scotch bonnet (or habanero) pepper. Garlic is important too. So is black pepper. Hell, it's all important.

Ingredients

1 tsp	allspice
1 tsp	dried thyme
1 tsp	chile powder
1 tsp	black pepper
1 tsp	sage
1 tsp	nutmeg
1 tsp	cinnamon
1 tsp	cayenne pepper
	few cloves chopped garlic
1 Tbs	sugar
¼ cup	vegetable oil
¾ cup	white or cider vinegar
3	limes, juice of
1	onion (yellow or white) chopped
	Scotch bonnet peppers (start with one)

Method

In a blender, mix the allspice, dried thyme, chile powder, black pepper, sage, nutmeg, cinnamon and cayenne pepper. Throw in the chopped garlic, sugar, vegetable oil, vinegar, limes, onion (yellow or white) and, of course, as many scotch bonnet peppers as you think you can handle (start with one, you can always change it the next time around or supplement the heat with some pepper sauce). Blend all the ingredients until smooth, adding more lime juice if necessary.

This amount of marinade should do for a small loin cut (about 3-4 pounds to serve at least six), which is a good piece to use because it's tender and about the right leanness. If you are going to use a tougher cut, like a butt or shoulder, be sure to marinate the meat for at least a day and a half. If pork isn't your preferred meat, chicken can be used instead (with less marinating time needed).

Place the meat in a non-metallic dish and dump the marinade on top, spreading it around so that the whole piece is coated. Cover and refrigerate. Then just cook the meat on a rack of pimento wood. A grill will also do the trick. In both cases, be patient: cooking it slowly also allows the smoke to penetrate the meat, adding that extra kick of flavor.

DON'T MISS

- Reggae-inspired cuisine
- Ackee & saltfish – Jamaican to the core
- The many versions of souse
- Fire-in-your-mouth – the huge variety of pepper sauces
- Conch – King of the Bahamas
- Patties – Jamaica's lifeblood
- Blue Mountains coffee – the finest brew on the islands
- Jamaica – home of Jerk, a unique spice combo
- The finest Indian cuisine this side of Delhi

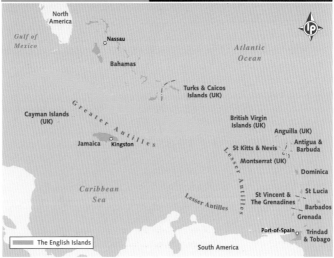

North America

Gulf of Mexico

Nassau

Atlantic Ocean

Bahamas

Turks & Caicos Islands (UK)

Greater Antilles

Cayman Islands (UK)

British Virgin Islands (UK)

Anguilla (UK)

Antigua & Barbuda

St Kitts & Nevis

Jamaica Kingston

Montserrat (UK)

Dominica

Lesser Antilles

Caribbean Sea

Lesser Antilles

St Vincent & The Grenadines

St Lucia

Barbados

Grenada

Port-of-Spain Trinidad & Tobago

The English Islands

South America

REGIONAL VARIATIONS

Trinidad & Tobago

These two islands make up a different sort of Caribbean country. Yes, the history is similar to that of the other English islands, but what makes Trinidad & Tobago different from a culinary perspective is the influence of the East Indian population. Today, the population of Trinidad & Tobago is 40% East Indian, 40% African and 20% other ethnicities including a significant number of Chinese, who like the East Indians, arrived as indentured workers in the 1800s (see Indentured Servants and Foreign Influences in the Culture of Caribbean Cuisine chapter).

As a result, there are really three distinct cuisines in Trinidad & Tobago, but there is very little crossover from one style of cooking to the other. This is not to say that people of African descent don't eat East Indian roti or that people of East Indian descent do not indulge in ackee & saltfish.

Among the most enduring and widespread of the East Indian culinary contributions is **roti**, flatbread wrapped around virtually anything but most often curried beef, lamb, chicken or potatoes, and other vegetables. It is also available in Jamaica, but not to the extent it is in Trinidad (see the recipe in the Caribbean Banquet chapter).

Also look for **doubles**, which are softened curried **channa** (chickpeas) between two pieces of **bara** (small discs of fried bread). These are available everywhere from restaurants to roadside vendors. Be sure to try **phulouri**, a split pea and onion fritter that makes a great vegetarian snack. The East Indian population here has also created a chutney industry. Mango is the most popular but there are others worth trying including those made with peppers.

One of Trinidad & Tobago's signature dishes is the African-influenced **callalloo**, a thick green soup made with okra, onions, spices and the leaves of the dasheen plant, onions, peppers and seasoning. **Coo-coo** (sometimes spelled cou-cou), a polenta-like dish usually mixed with okra and other vegetables, also traces its roots to Africa.

Palms of Trinidad

The Smaller Islands: the Bahamas, Cayman Islands, Turks & Caicos, Antigua & Barbuda, St Kitts & Nevis, Montserrat, Dominica, St Lucia, Barbados, St Vincent & the Grenadines.

After Jamaica and Trinidad & Tobago, the English Islands shrink, both in terms of geography and population. These islands – from the Bahamas to Barbados and much of the Lesser Antilles – are known for their perfect beaches and shallow crystalline waters, both of which serve to attract hundreds of thousands of tourists each year.

While the smaller English islands have been grouped together here for the sake of convenience, it would be a mistake to think they are identical in terms of cuisine. Each of the smaller islands has its specialties. Barbuda, for example, offers visitors venison, a meat that has been hunted and roasted since well before the arrival of the Europeans. In Antigua, locals take saltfish and stew it with vegetables and tomatoes, calling it **duckanoo**. Antigua is also home to the black pineapple, purported to be the sweetest of them all.

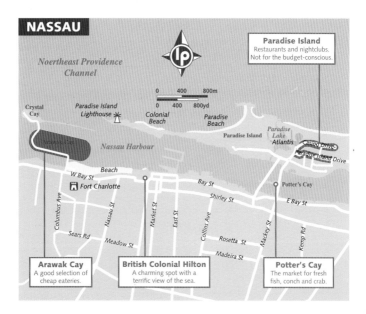

NASSAU

Noertheast Providence Channel

Paradise Island
Restaurants and nightclubs. Not for the budget-conscious.

Crystal Cay

Paradise Island Lighthouse

Colonial Beach

Paradise Beach

Paradise Island

Paradise Lake Atlantis

Casino Drive

Paradise Island Drive

Nassau Harbour

0 400 800m
0 400 800yd

Beach
W Bay St
Fort Charlotte

Bay St

Shirley St

Potter's Cay

E Bay St

Columbus Ave

Nassau St

Market St

East St

Collins Ave

Rosetta St

Mackey St

Kemp Rd

Sears Rd

Meadow St

Madeira St

Arawak Cay
A good selection of cheap eateries.

British Colonial Hilton
A charming spot with a terrific view of the sea.

Potter's Cay
The market for fresh fish, conch and crab.

The Bahamas

An official at the Tourism Ministry claims that no matter how far you go, you'll never find conch the way it is made in the Bahamas. And if you find something similar, she says, you can be sure that the person making it has Bahamian heritage. At Nassau's open air market under the Paradise Island bridge, a chef sums up Bahamian's affinity for this staple: "Bahamian got to have their conch."

Conch (pronounced 'konk') is to the Bahamas as the bull is to Spain, as haggis is to Scotland. Over the years, it has been coveted for its shell, which jewelers in Victorian England carved into cameos worn on the blouses of society ladies. Today, a conch shell is like a stamp in your passport, proof that you have been to the Bahamas.

But it's conch that Bahamians love. Extracting this meat is a skill that invloves striking the shell between the third and fourth space on the helix with a small hammer. A knife is then used to cut the ligament that holds the body in the shell. From there, the meat pulls out easily and is ready to be cleaned and turned into any number of dishes.

Cocktails on the beach, Bahamas

No self-respecting Bahamian restaurant would be caught without conch of some kind on the menu. It can be fried, boiled, broiled or even served raw as conch salad, a sort of ceviche with lime, raw onions and pepper. Conch fritters are popular items in any drinking hole. The conch is prepared by chopping the meat finely then mixing it with seasoning, chopped onion, pepper and a flour-based batter that serves as a bonding agent. The mixture is spooned into hot oil where it is deep fried until golden brown. It comes in servings of six or more, accompanied by a pink sauce that generally consists of mayonnaise, tomato sauce (ketchup), lime juice and a bit of pepper sauce. Cracked conch is a battered and deep-fried version of the national favorite, which is often served with French fries and coleslaw.

ROOTS BY THE SEA

Soufriere Bay, St Mark, Dominica

On a visit to Dominica, my mother, father, brother and I were guided up the mountainside to a parcel of ancestral land called LaCabiere. This was my first visit to my mother's homeland, one so very different than my own North American home. It was not a vacation to the sunny Caribbean Club Med. This was an educational voyage of discovery, and of my Caribbean identity.

We were lead up to LaCabiere by our relative Felton, who not only knew the land but also served as our translator to the ancestors' stories. LaCabiere was a vibrant and rich living history. Now abandoned, this ancestral land in the mountains grows wild with coconut, lime and papaya trees. When my grandfather was a child, LaCabiere served as a plantation where enslaved people could cultivate limes for sale in the city.

The aura here was inviting, rich and dynamic. The birds flew through the trees. Fallen coconuts painted the ground. These dry nuts are considered spoiled in the Caribbean, whereas they are the only coconut North America knows. Felton climbed a coconut tree and brought down a supply. He then held each down against a rock and swiftly sliced the base with a machete. The coconut water was refreshing. We had brought along bottles of local rum and added this to our coconut water. The more mature coconuts were halved and we scooped out the sweet, white jelly-like flesh. While sitting on the ground we drank coconut water with rum, ate coconut flesh and learned of legends.

As we descended the mountainside we joined with our aunts and cousins for a picnic by the beach. There I learned that my cousin Mervin played for the West Indies cricket team and that my cousin Sandra enjoyed dancing in the clubs of London. We were all rooted in LaCabiere yet living global realities. Even the feast of Caribbean classics prepared by Auntie Claudette were common staple foods to all of us. Fried and steamed fish, rice & peas, boiled root vegetables, juices, rum and home-made bread. We knew these foods without having known their lineage.

The picnic went on into the sunset with the family eating and dancing by the sea. As I sat on the smooth rocks of the beach, I glanced up to LaCabiere and realized that this was the home of my culture. The places I had seen and the food I had eaten while on this journey had all confirmed my identity.

Sabrina Di Marco is an author and consultant living in Toronto

The Spanish Islands

No other European country has had such a major impact on the Caribbean way of life than Spain. It shows up in the language, in the architecture of colonial cities like San Juan, Puerto Rico and Santiago de Cuba and, of course, in the food.

The events of the 20th century have had a significant impact on the food served in each of the Spanish islands. As a commonwealth of the US, Puerto Rico has endured a massive influx of US food and chain restaurants. Cuba, on the other hand, has been forced to change its diet due to the US blockade and the subsequent dependence on the Soviet Union to help boost the economy. Cuba is one of the few country's in the world where you won't find a McDonald's. The Dominican Republic, while also heavily influenced by its proximity to the US, as well as the massive numbers of migrants who have gone north, has maintained a greater degree of gastronomic independence than Puerto Rico.

Cuba

As the first and last Spanish colony in the Americas, Cuban culture in general – and cooking in particular – enjoys strong links with the mother country. Havana was, for many years, the most important city on the Spanish islands as all shipments of silver and gold went through its port. Spanish immigrants arrived here first before fanning out to other parts of the empire. Most of these came from southern Spain and today, a number of Cuban dishes trace their roots back to the cuisine of Andalucía.

Cuban food has also been heavily influenced by revolution. The Cuban diet was subjected to a profound shock when relations between Cuba and the US began to fall apart in 1961. The cessation of trade meant that Cuba was suddenly cut off from a traditional source of imports. As Cuban revenue relied heavily on sugarcane, Cuba was forced to find other sources to keep the national larder full. It was then that Fidel Castro declared the revolution Marxist-Leninist and relations between Cuba and the Soviet Union became stronger. New products entered the Cuban culinary lexicon with wheat having the greatest impact. Pasta became a staple, as did pizza and yogurt. While pork remained the most popular meat, there was less of it so chicken and fish took precedence. Beef, which had been common, almost disappeared as did the **manteca** (lard) that Cubans used to cook **guisos** (stews and sauces). Ironically, the diet that was forced upon post-revolutionary Cuba by measures intended to hurt the country, was healthier than the one left behind.

Cubans rely heavily on tubers to meet their caloric needs. This includes malanga, potatoes, sweet potato and yucca. Other starchy foods, such as plantains, bananas and rice also play a big role. When you mix rice with black beans you get **moros y cristianos** (literally, Moors & Christians; see the

REGIONAL VARIATIONS

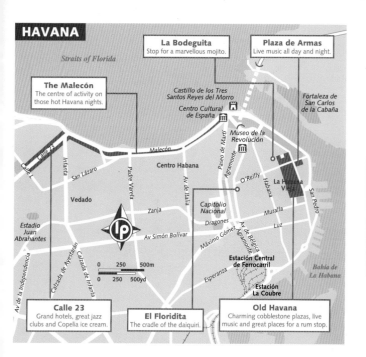

HAVANA

Straits of Florida

La Bodeguita
Stop for a marvellous mojito.

Plaza de Armas
Live music all day and night.

The Malecón
The centre of activity on those hot Havana nights.

Castillo de los Tres Santos Reyes del Morro

Centro Cultural de España

Fortaleza de San Carlos de la Cabaña

Museo de la Revolución

Malecón

Centro Habana

Paseo de Martí

Agramonte

O'Reilly

Habana

La Habana Vieja

San Pedro

Calle 23

Calle L

Infanta

San Lázaro

Padre Varela

Av de Italia

Vedado

Zanja

Capitolio Nacional

Dragones

Muralla

Luz

Av Simón Bolívar

Máximo Gómez

Agramonte

Av de Bélgica

Estadio Juan Abrahantes

Calzada de Ayestarán

Calzada de Infanta

Av de la Independencia

0   250   500m
0   250   500yd

Estación Central de Ferrocarril

Esperanza

Estación La Coubre

Bahía de La Habana

Calle 23
Grand hotels, great jazz clubs and Copelia ice cream.

El Floridita
The cradle of the daiquiri.

Old Havana
Charming cobblestone plazas, live music and great places for a rum stop.

REGIONAL VARIATIONS

recipe in the Home Cooking & Traditions chapter). Most restaurant meals serve this as a side dish, though they can be eaten as a full meal. Although chicken is far more widely available, the meat of choice is pork. Of all Cuba's pork dishes, **lechón asado** is king. The pork leg is roasted and served with a light gravy and some starchy side dishes. Chicken is most often served fried or roasted with a sauce. **Pollo en salsa** (chicken in sauce) is a good example: it includes onions, sweet peppers and a pinch of oregano.

Tortillas, which are simply egg omelets and bear no resemblance to Mexican tortillas, are another common item and perhaps the most substantial breakfast meal on a Cuban menu.

Cubans consume pizza voraciously. And if you're travelling on a budget, it's substantial enough to keep you going. Cuban pizzas tend toward the simple: cheese, tomato sauce and one topping. **Jamón** (ham), **chorizo** (sausage) and **cebolla** (onion) are among the most popular and combinations are rare.

Scattered tables in front of the Catedral de San Cristóbel de la Habana, Havana, Cuba

Pizza is available in restaurants and is also sold from little store fronts (and sometimes houses). While the quality of these is hit and miss, the price can't be beat. Look for the hand-painted signs saying **pizza al momento**. But beware, 'al momento' shouldn't be taken literally. Pizzas here are not pre-made, and along with the dozen or more people queuing for a slice of the action, you might have to wait a while to get yours. But on the plus side, this scenario will present you with one of the best opportunities to meet locals, without having one of them try to flog you a box of cigars.

Picadillo

To look at the recipe, you may be inclined to dismiss picadillo as disassembled meat loaf. However, it is one of those dishes that goes with everything and can be easily adjusted to suit your own taste. No, it's not to be served at a dinner party, but consider it the next time you want something quick and easy to eat in front of the TV.

Picadillo actually has a million different versions. You can experiment with spices and ingredients: capers, hot peppers instead of sweet, celery for texture. We once made a version using a bit of mango chutney from Trinidad. There is really no limit.

Ingredients

1lb (500g)	ground beef (any grade from lean to regular is fine)
2	garlic cloves, minced
1	small onion
1	small green or red sweet pepper
10	green olives, chopped
1 Tbs	unsweetened raisins
	pinch of cumin, oregano and thyme.
⅓ cup	of tomato sauce
	a splash of dry sherry or red wine
	vegetable oil for cooking (optional)
	salt & pepper to taste
1	potato, cubed and boiled

Mix all the ingredients except the oil and potatoes in a bowl and let it sit for at least one hour (refrigerated). In a deep pan, heat some oil (for leaner beef, use a little more, for fattier cuts, you might not need any), add the beef mixture and cook over medium-high heat until the beef is browned. During the cooking process, be sure to break up any clumps. Toss in the potatoes and cook for a few minutes more until the potatoes are heated through. If the mixture appears to be too dry, add a bit more tomato sauce. Season to taste with salt and pepper.
Serves 2

Pizza bases waiting for toppings, Havana, Cuba

PARADISE HAS A WELL-STOCKED HUMIDOR

A story told around cigar circles is that just days before imposing the economic embargo against Cuba, US President John F. Kennedy asked a personal aide to go out to a tobacconist in nearby Georgetown and purchase 1,000 Cuban cigars. The President was about to cut Cuba off, but not before filling up his humidor with his favorite cigar, the tiny but powerful **Petit Upmann**.

This is a story Cubans in the cigar trade love to tell. The US **bloqueo** may have denied Cubans 40 years of normal relations with their rich northern neighbors, but the sanctions would also transform Cuba's beloved **Habano** (cigar) into one of the **yanquis'** few forbidden fruits on earth. It would also give rise to an international cigar industry that markets a product whose primary reason for being is to try to match, or at least come close to, the real McCoys: the **Montecristos**, **Romeo y Julietas**, **Partagás** and **Upmanns** that JFK so jealously stocked. Marketing mantras like "100% Havana seed" and "hand-crafted in the true Havana tradition" today adorn many a box of Dominican, Honduran, Jamaican and Miami cigars.

The Cubans relish this knowledge in much the same way the French gloat about their prowess as vintners to the world. This has always been a country well aware of its ability to produce gems of global significance. Take Son music, Desi Arnez, Bacardí rum, Orlando 'El Duque' Hernández and, of course, the world's most coveted cigar, the **Cohiba**.

No visitor to this island will leave without having had at least a fleeting notion of someone's cigar burning nearby. And it takes little time to figure out that as much as Cuba is about its diminishing colonial grandeur and its modern socialist kitsch, it's also about cigars. This is the place where ashtrays, big ones, are everywhere, and where no one bats an eyelash if you walk into an elevator with a six-inch **Perfecto** protruding from your face.

Even though Cuba's people face increasing economic pressures these days, the cigar remains an important cultural icon and a mainstay in the Cuban economy. Cubans smoke more than 250 million cigars every year, and the Cuban cigar industry produces as many as 100 million cigars that are twisted exclusively for exporting. Even though there are a number of cigar brands produced for local consumption, a large chunk of Cuba's cigar production is earmarked for foreign consumers who eagerly wait for the next batch of **Bolivars**, **Sancho Panzas** and **Hoyo de Monterreys** to turn up at their local tobacconist. Most of the 42 different shapes and sizes of handmade cigars produced for these brands are consumed by connoisseurs from around the world – from Spain to Mexico, France, and as far afield as Japan.

But cigars also play a unique role in the streets of Havana, Varadero, Santiago de Cuba and the increasing number of areas teeming with tourists. Look for tourists and soon after you'll find silver-tongued entrepreneurs pushing cigars. Even though the goods flogged on the street are almost always counterfeit, their origin is usually attributed to a friend, cousin or some **socio** who acquired them straight from the roller's table in a factory just around the corner.

In a country where dollars are vital to acquiring some of the goods available only at tourist dollar stores, the cigar has become the fastest route between a conversation with a tourist and his wallet. The thinking is that the sanctity of Cuba's holiest of products will not be tarnished if a handful of **turistas** are stupid enough to take the bait.

Cigars have had a place in Cuba's history and heritage that goes back long before they became symbols of success and sophistication, and much longer before Fidel Castro, Camilo Cienfuegos and Che Guevara would be seen enjoying them as they marched triumphant into Havana on New Year's Day 1959. Even the packaging art created for brands like **La Gloria Cubana**, **El Rey del Mundo** and **Partagás** hail the cigar as a delicacy with as much cultural clout as the poetry of Cuba's poet laureate and liberator, José Martí. After all, records can be found that suggest tobacco was cultivated and marketed in Cuba as far back as 1557.

And legend has it Christopher Columbus encountered cigars soon after catching sight of the island in 1492. His first impression was that he had come upon something so extremely precious that God himself had put it on earth for Cuba's aborigines to serve to the discoverers of the New World.

This might explain why cigar labels and bands depict celestial nymphs, buxom matrons, trumpeting angels and cheeky cherubs languidly puffing cigars in idyllic pastoral scenes. To Cubans, Paradise has a well-stocked humidor.

Fidel Castro, Cuba's veteran leader and **papá grande**, is said to have given up cigars more than 15 years ago as a gesture to encourage his people, among the world's heaviest smokers, to ease up on their voracious consumption of tobacco. Cigars held a special place in Castro's heart, and he was rumored to actually keep a personal roller to twist his favorite cigars, **Cohiba Panetelas** and **Cohiba Lanceros**. Since quitting, he has been quoted as saying that he still dreams of cigars, and that giving them up was one of the greatest sacrifices he has had to make for the people of Cuba and his beloved **Revolución**.

José Guichard is a public relations executive who lives and works in Toronto, Canada

REGIONAL VARIATIONS

DON'T MISS

- Cuban bars and Cuban cigars
- Lechón asado: Cuba's national pork dish
- Sofrito: the heart of Puerto Rican cuisine
- Mojitos, daiquiris and the world's finest rum
- Moros y cristianos: Cuba's take on peas & rice
- Exploring the history in Old San Juan
- Cold beer and plantains in Puerto Rico
- Paladar restaurants: a glimpse inside the Cuban home

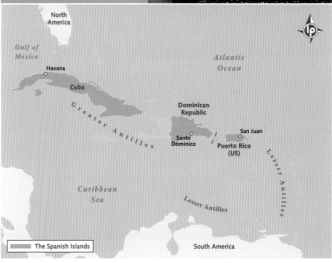

CIGARS – FROM BENCH TO BOX

Tobacco Preparation
Tobacco arrives fresh from the plantation fields and is treated to restore lost moisture. It is then classified and ordered according to type, size, color and texture.

Wrappers
The tobacco stems are stripped, to dissect the **wrapper leaf**, an outer leaf layer used to hold cigars together. The wrapper leaves are then sorted into piles, again according to size, color and texture.

Cigar rolling, Pinar del Río, Cuba

REGIONAL VARIATIONS

Fillers & Binders

The leaves are classified according to the mixtures and specifications of secretly guarded blends. Bundles of the appropriate blends are issued to the **torcedores** (rollers) in amounts sufficient to roll 50 cigars.

Cigar Making

The **torcedores**, seated behind work benches in rows according to skill level, systematically twist loose tobacco leaves into cigars.

A reasonably skilled **torcedor** rolls between 120 and 200 cigars in one eight-hour shift, depending on the size of the cigar. **Lectores** (readers) read-out the daily news or classic works of literature to the **torcedores** as they twist. These works have inspired whimsical brand names such as Montecristo, and Romeo y Julieta.

Row upon row of torcedores

Trimming the wrapper leaf

Trimming the 'foot' of the cigar

Quality Control

Bundles of 50 cigars at a time are collected from the **torcedores** and checked for length, shape, girth, appearance and weight.

Cigar box art

Conditioning Room

The cigars that make it through the rigorous quality assessment are placed in cedar shelves for between three weeks and six months.

With its constant temperature of 65-68°F (18-20°C) and 65-70% humidity, this environment promotes aging and helps to reduce excess moisture.

Color Grading

Color graders select and package cigars in tones ranging from light to dark, and place the best looking 'faces' face-up in the box, so that they'll be the first seen upon opening.

The final product, Pinar del Río, Cuba

Boxes of Cohiba, Montecristo, Romeo y Julieta and Simon Bolivar

REGIONAL VARIATIONS

Banding, Labeling & Finishing

Cigars are dressed with a band according to color. And are then placed in decorative cedar boxes, which are tightly sealed with the all important Government Warranty label.

José Guichard is a public relations executive who lives and works in Toronto, Canada

Unspeakably cool, Pinar del Río, Cuba

Puerto Rico

From the ultra-modern airport to the congested roads to the high-rise apartment buildings and hotels, San Juan, the capital of Puerto Rico, is very much a modern American town. Sometimes it's a stretch to remember that it was only a century ago that Puerto Rico was under Spanish control. It is only when you get to Old San Juan, where brightly colored buildings with detailed iron balconies and old forts give the city a decidedly colonial atmosphere, that you realize this was the domain of Spain (see the boxed text Promenade in Puerto Rico in the Where to Eat & Drink chapter).

Cuisine in Puerto Rico is similarly American. Outside of Old San Juan, you're confronted with every American fast-food chain in existence while the hotels offer the best of haute cuisine. There are, however, vestiges of a more authentic cuisine to be found, and authentic Puerto Rican cuisine

Sofrito

It comes in as many forms as it there are people who prepare it, but sofrito is the single most essential ingredient in Puerto Rican cuisine. It is celebrated in song by salsa-jazz-Latin soul master Mongo Santamaria whose 'Sofrito' is a standard on Latin music compilations. When in Puerto Rico, you can buy some very good sofrito in jars, but you might want to make your own.

Ingredients

2	onions
2-4	cloves garlic
6	chile peppers (called **ají** in Puerto Rico)
4	fresh tomatoes
1	small bunch cilantro (coriander)
1 Tbs	thyme
⅓ cup	lard or oil

Chop the onion and as much garlic as you think your breath will take. Chop the peppers, tomatoes, cilantro and thyme. Traditionally, sofrito is cooked in lard, but you can use oil instead. Saute all the ingredients over medium heat until they are nicely blended. Let the resulting sauce cool then toss it in a blender and puree until smooth.

At this point, you can (and should) use the sofrito as a starting point for virtually anything. Take some **chorizo** sausage, slice it thinly and heat it in a pan over low heat. Once the meat is cooked, add sofrito and cook everything together then serve it on a bed of rice. Try the same method with ham, chicken or shrimp. And sofrito makes a meal magnificent when it is poured over broiled meat or fish.

begins with **sofrito** (see the recipe later in this chapter). It forms the base for almost everything cooked in Puerto Rico: stews, soups and sauces. Cooks use similar preparations in Cuba and the Dominican Republic, but in Puerto Rico it has special meaning. It has inspired a hit song 'Sofrito' by the great conguero, Mongo Santamaria.

Puerto Ricans are very fond of **adobo** seasoning for meats. This is a sort of dry rub of garlic, oregano, salt and pepper. Depending upon the meat, it can be applied up to a day in advance of cooking to allow the flavors to penetrate the flesh. However, you can also simply press the mixture into the flesh before cooking to bring a really nice accent to the natural flavor of the meat. One version even calls for lime juice.

La Mayorquina restaurant, Puerto Rico

REGIONAL VARIATIONS

PUERTO RICO SPACE FOOD

Eating in the Puerto Rican countryside tends to mean plate after plate of rice & peas, goat and plantain – it's delicious when done well but always a bit heavy. So, if you head down the winding forest roads to Arecibo Observatory in Arecibo, you might get more excited about the feather-weight space food on sale in the gift shop than about the fact that you're standing on the site of the world's largest single-dish radio telescope. While the scientists search for signals from extra-terrestrial life, you can browse the range of freeze-dried berries, peaches, even ice-cream sandwiches. And don't worry if you're so full of rice & peas that you can't ever imagine eating again: these astronaut snacks require no refrigeration and keep for about two years.

Dani Valent is a well-travelled writer living in Melbourne, Australia

REGIONAL VARIATIONS

Make sure you go out of your way to get a good **mofongo**, which is popular in both Puerto Rico and the Dominican Republic. This is a deceptively simple stew that is stuffed inside a shell made of deep-fried plantains, and covered with a light sauce. Despite the fact that fish does not traditionally form a part of the mainstream Puerto Rican diet, its preparation has been elevated to an art.

Puerto Ricans are also fond of casseroles, especially those with a foundation of rice. Look for dishes with titles beginning with **arroz con** ... as an indicator.

On the decidedly unhealthy side, try **chicharrón**, which is pork rinds deep fried to a crackly greasy goodness that is too good to pass up. **Chicharrón de pollo** is the same thing with chicken skin, except that a flour batter is used to add volume and texture.

Fried pork rinds. Puerto Rico

The Dominican Republic

As with Puerto Rico, the Dominican Republic is also subject to the influence of the United States. Here, baseball is the most popular sport and US fast-food chains count on hoards of the hungry at lunch.

Chefs in the Dominican Republic do not shy away from spices as much as those in Cuba or Puerto Rico. This is no second Jamaica, but the odd pepper will make its way into the local **sancocho** (a hearty stew with lots of vegetables and meat). Both fresh fish and broiled chicken are also national favorites.

In the Dominican Republic look for **bandera dominicana**. It is something of a national meal that includes a serving of meat or chicken, white rice, beans, plantain, yucca and a slice of avocado. Some restaurants may include a drink or dessert in the price of the meal.

Iglesia de San Jose in Old San Juan, established in 1523 by Dominicans, is the second oldest church in the Western Hemisphere, Puerto Rico

The French Islands

There are moments when the French islands of the Caribbean seem like a piece of Paris plonked in the tropics. At other times baguettes and wine couldn't be further from your mind. Consequently the dining experience across the French islands is one of extremes, with Parisian niceties at one end, and Creole color at the other.

Guadeloupe & Martinique

Both Guadeloupe and Martinique began their modern existence in much the same way as the rest of the Caribbean, where Europeans imported African slaves to work plantations. The Creole cuisine that developed here still determines much of the traditional cuisine on these islands today. However, the relative wealth of Martinique and Guadeloupe, in addition to their status as part of France, has given the culinary atmosphere a distinctly European flair. Breakfast in Martinique, for example, means a trip to your local **boulangerie** (bakery) to buy a baguette and traditional French pastries or French delicacies with a Caribbean twist that include fillings like **coco** (coconut) and **banane** (banana).

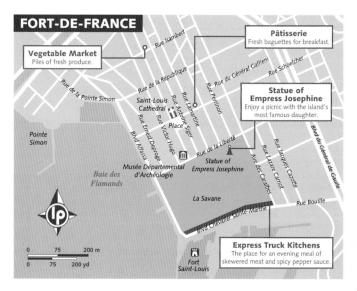

DON'T MISS

- Croissants and Baguettes, fresh and hot from the corner bakery
- Ti-punch – the cocktail that packs a punch
- Feroce – a Martinique tradition
- Ti-malice – the fiery Haitian relish
- Haiti's Barbancourt Five Star Rum
- The color of Creole culture and cuisine

REGIONAL VARIATIONS

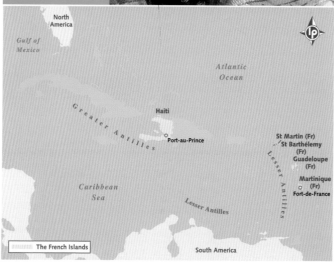

Overleaf – Standing on the roof of a brightly colored intercity bus, Ouest, Haiti

Creole cuisine in Martinique is based principally on fish and seafood, although as with other islands, pork is the most valued meat. Both fish and meat dishes are traditionally spicy, though those restaurants that serve Creole food have put the heat to the side and leave it to the diner to decide how much of a sting they want to add. One-pot stews, consisting of meat or fish, vegetables and seasonings are the norm. One interesting difference from the rest of the region is the popularity of lamb, although within a stew, lamb is usually quite greasy and overdone. Avocados are also a mainstay in the diet and **feroce** (dip made of avocado, cassava flour and peppers) appears regularly on menus. The tradition of frugality of the islands shows up in **pate en pot** (tripe soup).

If you are staying in downtown Fort-de-France, the southeast corner of the Savanne (the city's central park) comes alive after dark when semi-permanent restaurants on wheels set up for evening diners. Here you'll find skewers of meat cooked over coals and served with rice, fries or in a bun with a hot, salty sauce of sauteed onions and thyme.

Martinique and Guadeloupe may be the only Caribbean islands where the locals care about wine. While beer and rum are still more popular, stores will stock a good selection of wines from France and it is common to see people enjoying a glass at a bar.

Funky bar signage, Les Anses-d'Arlets

Haiti

It may seem like a cliche, but Haiti is a land of contrasts. Rich culture, artistic vibrancy and poor people are all inseparable facets of this struggling nation. Haitians generally like their food spicy and **ti-malice** (onion-pepper relish) adds fire and flavor to everything, no matter how bland. Here locals cook on tight budgets and rely on starchy foods – tubers, potatoes and rice – to feed their families. Two Haitian specialties worth sampling are **mayi moulen** (cornmeal mush flavored with peppers and coconut) and **soup jomou** (pumpkin soup), especially if you are vegetarian. The Haitians also make good use of **djon-djon** (local black mushrooms), mixing them with rice for a satisfying meal.

The Dutch Islands
ABC – Aruba, Bonaire and Curaçao

The ABC islands (Aruba, Bonaire and Curaçao) are must-do destinations for avid divers. An abundance of shallows with coral reefs and other odd undersea formations ensure that the familiar white and red divers' flag is never out of sight. Those looking for a food experience should stick to Curaçao. Bonaire is simply too small to offer much variety and Aruba, frankly, resembles any suburban strip mall with an abundance of hotels and chain restaurants. Certainly there is good food to be had on Aruba, but you will not find the same degree of variety, nor authenticity, as you will on Curaçao.

The capital of Curaçao, Willemstad, is one of the most impressive capital cities in the Caribbean, where tourism melds nicely with local commercial concerns (oil, gambling and offshore banking are big industries). Outdoor cafes and restaurants are common and buzz with drinkers and diners from lunchtime to early evening. A constant, pleasant breeze means that the oppressive heat that has you running for air-conditioned shelter on most islands is not a factor.

When you decide to leave Willemstad for a day to sun yourself on one of the many small, charming beaches along Curaçao's rocky coast, or to explore the starkly beautiful Christoffel National Park, you will not have

The beach frontage of the Avila Beach Hotel, Willemstad, Curaçao

any difficulty finding restaurants. For something lighter, look for eateries called **snak**.

It's an odd choice for a national food, but natives of Curaçao have chosen the okra as their very own. This small, conical, green vegetable, which is popular in Creole cooking everywhere from New Orleans to Venezuela, has a special status as the principal ingredient in **yambo** (also spelled **giambo**), a green soup that also includes salt pork, onions, celery and sometimes fish. Although yambo is principally celebration food, you can get a steaming bowl any day of the week at the old market in downtown Willemstad. A hearty mixture with a texture that can only be described as slimy – the result of the pureed okra. Don't let this put you off.

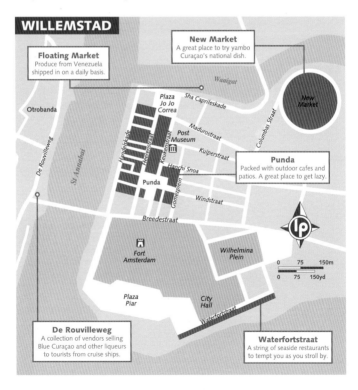

WILLEMSTAD

New Market
A great place to try yambo Curaçao's national dish.

Floating Market
Produce from Venezuela shipped in on a daily basis.

Waaigat

Otrobanda

Plaza Jo Jo Correa

Sha Caprileskade

New Market

Columbus Straat

Madurostraat

Post Museum

Kulperstraat

Punda
Packed with outdoor cafes and patios. A great place to get lazy.

Hanchi Snoa

De Rouvilleweg

St Annabai

Handelskade

Heerenstraat

Keukenstraat

Gomezplein

Punda

Windstraat

Breedestraat

Fort Amsterdam

Wilhelmina Plein

0   75   150m
0   75   150yd

Plaza Piar

City Hall

Waterfortstraat

De Rouvilleweg
A collection of vendors selling Blue Curaçao and other liqueurs to tourists from cruise ships.

Waterfortstraat
A string of seaside restaurants to tempt you as you stroll by.

LUNCH OF THE IGUANA

The world's menus are rarely inundated with this little critter, but in Westpunt, Curaçao, at a roadside eatery called Jaanchi's, iguana has been served up since the restaurant opened its doors in 1936.

Westpunt, as the name suggests, is a small town on the western tip of the island. To get there, you must pass through Christoffel National Park, a stunning natural preserve where cacti grow on the pocked landscape and the sea pounds and shapes the shoreline into dozens of inlets. Inside the park, the law protects iguanas and every other form of life, but once outside the confines of the park, it's open season on the little green dragons.

And so they are hunted for their flesh by bands of boys, who prowl the dry, rocky landscape of the western tip armed with pellets and slingshots. They are Jaanchi's main suppliers.

Today at Jaanchi's you can eat iguana in a soup or stew, both made with onion, pepper, tomato and seasonings. The meat comes in cross sections of the iguana's body, which means that it is quite bony.

First time diners will only get a sample of iguana. "Sometimes they think they want to eat it, but when it comes down to it, they are turned off" says Jaanchi. "I give them a small piece to try, because I don't like to waste it."

Nevertheless demand for tender iguana flesh is high, not only for its taste but also due to the widespread belief that iguana flesh has a positive affect on your sex life, both in terms of desire *and* performance. In fact, there was a time on Curaçao when doctors prescribed iguana as a cure for any number of strength-sapping maladies.

Yambo is the most popular, but by no means the only soup you will find on the Dutch islands. **Sopi di banana** (banana soup) is especially worth a try, and peanut soup, reminiscent of Thai or Indonesian dishes, is another favorite. As in much of the Caribbean, many soups begin with salted meat: pig's tail or other cuts of pork, beef or fish and the resulting broth can be a bit salty. One exception, however, is **sopi di yuwana** (iguana soup), which is made only with the freshest meat, usually caught not far from the restaurants serving it (see the boxed text Lunch of the Iguana later in this chapter). Cactus soup is another dish unique to the Dutch islands, where the climate is such that cactus thrives in the dry, rocky soils. One recipe book (in fact the only one we could find exclusively devoted to the cuisine of the Dutch islands) even lists a recipe for **sopi di binja** (wine soup) a sort of toddy that is made with lots of prunes, sugar, red wine and cinnamon.

Overleaf – The fruit and vegetable market in downtown Willemstad, Curaçao

Curaçao is a long, arid, and predominantly flat island

Venezuelan influence is strong here. The floating market, which is the best place to buy fresh produce on the island, is a collection of boats that make the brief journey from Venezuela to the Willemstad harbor. Nearly every snack bar has a small display case filled with **empanas** (pastry turnovers with meat or fish filling). **Arepas** (cornflour dough shaped into discs and baked) are available but are more common in Venezuela and Colombia. On their own, they are quite bland but can be tasty when toasted over an open flame and spread with fresh butter. They can also be sliced, toasted and stuffed with any kind of sandwich filling.

The Dutch influence is most evident in the variety and quality of cheese available. Gouda is the 'house' cheese, but many others including cheddar, ricotta and Edam are widely available. The hard outer shell of an Edam ball is used to make **keshi yená** (literally, filled cheese; spiced meat stewed with vegetables and dried fruits and turned into a casserole). This is baked with the Edam shell on top. Just before serving, the whole dish is inverted and dumped so that the shell serves as the serving platter.

The Dutch established their colorful settlement in 1634, Curaçao

Of course, cheese is not consumed simply to get to the shell. **Bolita di keshi** (cheese balls) are a popular appetizer, as are **empanas di keshi** (cheese-filled turnovers). In grocery stores, you will find a selection of cheeses that will not be matched in any other Caribbean island.

But foreign influence doesn't end there. The Dutch connection brought a number of dishes from Indonesia and there are even a few Indonesian restaurants on the island. One dish in particular, **nasi goreng** (spicy fried rice with chicken and chopped vegetables) has made its way onto a number of non-Indonesian menus.

Fruit and vegetable market in downtown Willemstad, Curaçao

REGIONAL VARIATIONS

DON'T MISS

- Yambo – a taste of history
- Curaçao cocktails
- The multicultural melting pot of Curaçao
- Amstel beer on Aruban beaches
- Cheese in the European tradition
- Indonesian restaurants – for something completely different
- Strange soups – iguana, cactus or banana?
- Papiamento cuisine and culture

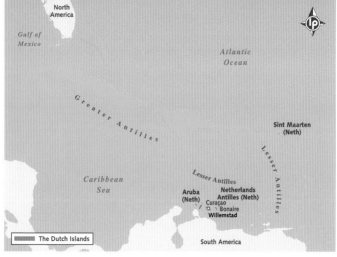

The Dutch Islands

THE HERBALIST – DINAH VEERIS

Food as Medicine

The beauty of the Caribbean makes it hard to realize that this was, at the time of slavery, a place of extreme hardship. Slaves from Africa were not only worked to exhaustion, they rarely received medical treatment from plantation owners when they fell ill. Because of this, people looked to nature for help. The African slaves had an extensive understanding of plant-based medicine. Of course some remedies could only be found in Africa, so the slaves soon found alternatives in the flora of the islands, and adopted Amerindian medicinal traditions.

Herbal medicine was the domain of women, whose knowledge of what plants to use and how to use them was handed down from grandmother to mother to daughter. Using the right plant they could heal such ailments as sinus problems, rashes, digestion and glandular disorders. Of course with the Caribbean being such a different environment to Africa, many remedies were discovered through trial and error. However over time a new 'school' of herbal medicine evolved that used African traditions and New World ingredients.

Western medicine is now commonplace in the Caribbean, and herbal medicine has turned from being the primary healer to an alternative practice. There is, however, herbal medicine still being practiced on the islands. In fact Caribbean herbal medicine is gaining a following as people look for alternative treatments, just as Chinese medicine is gaining acceptance in other countries. One of the major exponents of Caribbean herbal medicine is Dinah Veeris, a herbalist who is based on the Dutch island of Curaçao. As well as running her practice and frequently giving lectures both nationally and internationally, Dinah manages her shop, Dinah's Botanic & Historic Garden, where she sells remedies for everything from kidney stones to 'love potion'.

Dinah has an extensive knowledge of plant species and their powers, but of course it takes more skill than knowing what plant does what. She knows exactly how to prepare each plant to achieve maximum benefit: when to pick plants (they are more effective if picked during daylight); what other foods you should take the medicine with; how to prepare medicinal teas; how much to use. As this type of medicine requires dealing directly with nature, it is far more involved that just dealing out doses. When Dinah prescribes medicine, it is based on the individual. She will prepare remedies based not only on the ailment, but on the general condition of each patient. And her success rate? Based on the growing demand on her skills, hers is a healthy vocation.

Love Potions & Prophecies

Throughout history and across cultures, people have tried to find ways to understand or even control love. This desirous quest has led to some rather strange treatments, but when it comes to love, people are willing to try anything. If you are lacking love, or wanting more, here are some remedial recommendations courtesy of Dinah's Botanic & Historic Garden:

- The karawarah drink was used by the Amerindians as an aphrodisiac and also to open the vision. For maximum effect, they drank the karawarah liquor from a shell on a full moon. When the Spaniards arrived in the Caribbean they heard about the power of the karawarah drink and planted a lot of karawarah trees, so they could also reap the benefits.

- The leaves of the timetica tree can be used to see whether a romance is worth pursuing. When a woman wanted to know if her love for someone was reciprocated, she would put a leaf in a book and leave it there for three weeks. On the fourth week she would reopen the book. If there were roots growing from the leaves, she knew that the love was there. If there was no growth, the love was dead.

MI TA TUMA PIDA KESHI CU ESEI, SI SEÑOR TA GUSTA*

A trip to the islands of Aruba, Bonaire and Curaçao will likely be your first introduction to Papiamento, the beautiful fusion language of the islanders. Based on Portuguese and Spanish Papiamento wasn't codified until 1989 meaning that while there is one official spelling for every word, many islanders continue to use their own version.

While you could enjoy yourself and eat well without understanding the language (English, Spanish and Dutch are widely spoken), knowing a few words in Papiamento will be useful when wandering from place to place trying to decide on a midday snack or light meal. Most of the smaller places outside of the tourist loop list their offerings in Papiamento on chalk boards or on signs above the counter.

bakijow	cod
balchi di pisca	fish balls
bolita di keshi	cheese balls
empanas di keshi	cheese-filled turnovers
karni	meat (similar to the Spanish *carne*)
keshi yená	(literally, filled cheese; spiced meat stewed with vegetables and dried fruits and turned into a casserole inside an Edam shell)
keshi	cheese (similar to the Spanish *queso*)
krokechi	croquettes

*I'll have a piece of cheese with that, if you please.

Seafood on the Dutch islands is no less popular than it is anywhere else in the Caribbean. Red snapper is a popular fish, and is delicious when soaked in a lime and garlic marinade before being dredged in flour, fried and then covered with a sauce of onion, peppers, garlic and tomato. **Bakijow** (cod) is the choice for **balchi di pisca** (fish balls). These are deep-fried fritters made by mashing together cod with boiled potatoes, tomato, sweet pepper, onion and garlic before an egg is thrown in as a binding agent.

You can have your food as spicy as you want it in Curaçao. Not much pepper is used in the actual preparation of most local dishes, but pepper sauce is always available. Also look for the spicy relish of chopped cabbage marinated in lime and hot pepper, which is reminiscent of the Korean specialty, *kim chi*.

shopping
& markets

Even if you don't have access to a kitchen, a Caribbean market trip is essential. There you will see, smell and hear the beginnings of countless home-cooked meals. The colors alone – fruit, vegetables and bottled mixtures with various purposes (from seasoning to improving your sex life) – offer a feast for your eyes as well as your stomach. A beautiful squash? Believe it!

Dried, salted mackerel in Willemstad's floating fruit and vegetable market, Curaçao

After you get over the visual experience, you will notice that each market in the region offers the basics for each island's particular brand of cooking. Most of it will be fruits and vegetables, although you'll also see butcher's counters adorned with cuts of meat, these are more earthy than the clinically packaged cuts found in western butcher shops. However, the majority of markets of this sort are too make-shift to have anything so permanent as a refrigeration system. Stalls are put together with scraps of wood or upturned crates that look as if they were salvaged from a shipwreck.

The biggest markets are in the major cities. Farmers from the countryside truck in their goods each morning and either sell them to a vendor or stick around to sell them direct to the public. Many grocery store managers also make their purchases here then resell them with a mark-up. As a result, the difference in price between a market and a grocery store can be substantial.

At the Market

The history of markets in the Caribbean goes back to early colonial days when slaves were allowed to grow some excess foods in their own gardens and then take them to market in the nearest town on Sunday. This could be quite a lengthy and difficult journey. If you've ever driven the roads that cover the mountains of rural Jamaica you know that they are a challenge even with the aid of modern engineering.

Much of the selling was done by women, a fact that remains the case today on the English and French islands, but not as much in the better organized marketplaces of Cuba and Puerto Rico. Female sellers were called **higglers**, a name that survives today in its verb form: to higgle is to bargain. A vendor at a Jamaican marketplace expects to barter and may initiate it without a moment's hesitation. In Puerto Rico, however, the prices are fixed and trying to bargain is only a waste of everyone's time. Learning who higgles and who doesn't is part of the adventure and unfortunately, there are no hard and fast rules. You should give it a try (no one will hold it against you) but know when to give it up and pay the listed price.

One shopping highlight is Martinique's **marché de legumes** (vegetable market) in Fort-de-France. In terms of attractions it rivals the decapitated statue of Josephine Bonaparte, the island's most famous daughter. Outside on the Rue Isambert side, you will see stalls with piles of fresh produce: onions, peppers, tomatoes, squashes, pineapples, bananas and plantains. Inside this crowded marketplace is sold a strange assortment of homemade, and mostly alcoholic, concoctions. The base for these is rum (or some form of cane liquor) flavored by soaking such ingredients as coconut, cinnamon, peppers, herbs, pineapple chunks and orange peel.

Other bottles contain perfume scented with flowers. One place sells cans of **aerosol de amor** (literally, love aerosol), guaranteed to make that special someone fall under your spell. There are vendors selling giant bouquets of flowers, aromatic spices and candles with the images of saints embedded in the wax. There are enormous Creole women, dressed in layers of skirts and aprons, squatting on low stools with their legs spread wide as the sails of a downwind sloop, selling chunks of raw cocoa.

Under a bridge on the east side of Nassau (the Bahamas) sits the Potter's Cay Market, a collection of stalls where fish, fruit and vegetables are sold. The fish are brought in by independent fishermen, whose small boats do not venture far from the Bahamian shores and by larger commercial concerns, whose haul is caught over a number of days and frozen on board before being brought to shore. However, this is no major fisheries industry; this is a purely local operation where the catch is sold direct to the public. Once unloaded, the fish is scaled, gutted and cleaned in the open air (a process that attracts swarms of flies) and then sold at the nearby booths.

Overleaf – Local market in the small village of Middle Quarters, Jamaica

MARKETS OF THE CARIBBEAN

Whether to buy a mango, to snap a photo or two, or just to bask in the whirl of activity, sooner or later most visitors to the Caribbean find their way to a local market. It doesn't take long to realise that each market is unique and adds its own colorful piece to the Caribbean kaleidoscope.

In Puerto Rico, the small indoor Plaza del Mercado in San Juan offers a glimpse of the past. Perfumed with the heady fragrance of tuberose (a tall slender plant with large very fragrant white lily-like flowers) that is said to bring good luck. Plaza del Mercado offers its bounty simply, with stall owners enticing shoppers with samples of ripe mango or traditional jellied candies called orange or guava paste that come wrapped in corn husks.

Jamaica's Montego market, off the main tourist path, is a bustling mecca complete with saucy **higglers** (sellers). Gorgeous locals dressed to the hilt in peacock-hued calico dresses, they compete at charming the dollars out of your pockets with their cries.

Guadeloupe and Martinique's sun-dappled markets are home to vendors that wear intricate madras head-ties. They smilingly address each buyer as **doudou** (sweetie) and seduce them into sampling and then purchasing more **poudre de colombo** (cumin-scented curry powder) or plump pods of fresh vanilla.

No avid photographer can resist the lure of Curaçao's floating market, where Venezuelan schooners dock and sailors set out their country's lush produce for local customers used to the bounty of a more arid clime. Only die-hard tourists, however, will make their way to downtown Marshe to view local produce and sample tasty dishes like **carne stoba** (densely flavorful beef stew) or a plate of **quiambo** (okra stew) also known as yambo or gumbo.

The Pétionville market in Haiti is where women from Kenscoff, situated in the southern hills, sell the tiny strawberries that grow at high altitudes. But most visitors are too busy searching the displays of local art to find treasure with which to dazzle the folks at home than seeking out produce bargains.

There's turmeric-hued pepper sauce to be had in Grenada's Georgetown market, monkey pots for cooling water in the market in Saint Lucia, trays of tubers known as ground provisions in Barbados and Indian-inspired chutneys in the local markets of Trinidad. For a true market lover the bustle of a Caribbean market; the ring of hawker's cries and colorful flurry of activity creates only one problem – where to pack all of the gorgeous things you've purchased?

Jessica B. Harris is a food historian and author who lives in New York City

Conch caught by divers and crab scooped up from the beach are in abundance at Potter's Cay Market, but you can also find grouper, snapper and even barracuda (teeth included). You can buy your conch still in the shell or ask the vendor to pull the meat out, a task which is difficult in the hands of a novice but over in a matter of seconds when done by these seasoned experts (see the Bahamas in the Regional Variations chapter).

The fruits available are mostly grown locally, either on New Providence or one of the outer islands. There are green and yellow bananas, plantains and thyme (one of most popular herbs in Bahamian and indeed, Caribbean cooking), bottles of crushed tomatoes and piles of ripe red ones, chunks of cassava, plums, mangoes, a hot variety of chile called **finger pepper**, onions, sweet peppers, regular limes and tarter key limes.

As you walk south (away from the water), the booths turn to small-scale eateries. Around noon they start to fill up with locals as well as the odd tourist looking for something a little more authentic. These are not simply places to eat, but centers of social activity with groups of men and women lingering over broiled conch and conch salad, washing it down with swigs of beer. In these places conch is broiled in foil with onions, sweet peppers and tomatoes and served with **malta**, a non-alcoholic beer-like soft drink. Preparations for the lunch meal begin in the morning in anticipation of the midday rush and continue until sundown, or whenever the last people leave.

Nassau's market is not the only one to combine shopping and eating. Many major markets include an area where small kitchens maintain a hot grill or a huge pot of some sort of stew. Both takeaway service and sit-down, cafeteria-style service is available. Yet Nassau's is one of the few we visited where people actually seemed to make a social event out of the midday market meal. The others were more utilitarian, much like a food court in a modern office complex.

Fresh, ripe fruta bomba (papaya) at Havana's public market, Cuba

The food area in Puerto Rico's Rio Piedras Market, just outside of downtown San Juan is a good example. It is totally cordoned off from the fresh food stalls, and completely tiled in shiny white giving it a sterile atmosphere that makes you want to linger about as much as you'd want to linger in a morgue.

The rest of the Rio Piedras Market is equally clean and neatly organized, with vendors sitting calmly at their stalls and shoppers browsing leisurely. At least on weekdays they browse leisurely. On weekends, things get a little busier, a little noisier, and the vendors run themselves ragged, filling as many orders as possible before their customers lose patience and move on to the next stall. Here is where you will find the best of Puerto Rican food. With a few exceptions, everything sold here is grown or produced on the island and anything you make from these ingredients will, by definition, be Puerto Rican.

Tubers, or root vegetables, are prominent. Though you won't find many root vegetables such as yucca or malanga on the menus of Puerto Rican restaurants, these starchy foods still have a place in the home where they are generally boiled and served with butter. The same places sell **batata** (yams) and potatoes (one of the imported items).

Here in the Rio Piedras Market there are a number of other stalls that sell such items as musical instruments (including the **güero**, made from a hollowed-out gourd that you tap with a stick to get a hollow sound), lottery tickets, trinkets and herbal remedies to cure everything from slight indigestion to impotence.

As part of measures aimed at stimulating the economy, the Cuban government agreed to allow farmers to sell their products on a free market basis at special markets called **mercados agropecuarios** (farmers' markets). All products sold at these markets are priced in dollars and so, not surprisingly, the best stocked among the mercados agropecuarios are those in Miramar, the area of Havana where diplomats and more privileged Cubans (politicos or those with access to dollars) reside. The products for sale are all locally produced and include what you would expect to see at any other market in the Caribbean: onions, avocado, tomatoes, beans, plantains, tubers and fruits including extra large **fruta bomba** – a Cuban expression for papaya.

Meat (mostly pork) is also available with the cuts displayed in the open air for your approval and purchase. Cured meats, hams and sausages are also sold. Compared with the rest of the region, Cuba's farmers' markets are clean and well organized. Prices are listed clearly on homemade signs and if you have a problem, you can take it to the **Area de Protección del Consumidor**, the market's very own complaints department.

Selling Otaheite apples, also called ambarella at the Montego Bay Central Market, Jamaica

Supermarkets & Grocery Stores

The Caribbean has yet to catch on to the growing trend of supermarkets that not only sell food but everything from school supplies to pharmaceuticals. Consequently, visitors are thankful that the Caribbean tropical scenery is not blighted with the 10-acre warehouses that pass for supermarkets in other parts of the globe.

Given its proximity to the coast of Florida, a great deal of the food you will find in grocery stores comes from the US. Other consumer goods come from the UK. The Caribbean has always been an importer of food, and most of the islands are just too small to have any comprehensive food industry of their own. As a result, products in Caribbean supermarkets make their way there from every part of the world.

Trinidad's supermarkets, for example, are stocked with a plethora of goods that reflect the island's ethnic makeup. You will find black-bean sauce from China, curry paste from India, breakfast cereal from the UK and sardines from Canada. This, even in one of the few Caribbean countries to have something of a food industry.

Buying food is a challenge in Cuba, for both foreigners and locals. You'll notice that food stores aren't plentiful, or well stocked. As the country struggles to keep afloat, dollars are being spent elsewhere and consumer goods are not a priority. Fruit and vegetables are available, but tend to be in areas where vendors can count on customers with dollars.

On the French islands, grocery stores are fully stocked with continental items, from canned broth to fine cheese, foie gras and wine.

Street Stalls & Vendors

Informal markets, if you can even call them markets, are easily found in the Caribbean, especially in the countries where the Euro-American influence is weaker. They can be rickety wooden stalls piled with limes, a stack of mangoes in the back of rusted pick-up trucks, bananas in baskets attached to the back wheel of bicycles or even coconuts on blankets laid out on the corner of busy intersections. Most will sell only one product.

Sometimes the market comes to you! Busy intersections in urban centers are often crowded with vendors wandering through the rows of stopped cars holding aloft bags of onions, tomatoes or limes. If you're in the mood for a quick, healthy snack, look for plums or **guineps**, small green fruits that grow in bunches and have a sour-sweet flavor. You eat guineps by breaking the skin with a gentle pinch then sucking the tart, somewhat slimy fruit off the pip. Just don't forget to put those fruit-smeared hands back on the steering wheel.

A Caribbean Picnic

We suggest two ways of picnicking in the Caribbean. The first assumes that you have access to some sort of barbecue (loosely defined as anything that grills). In these cases, get some meat, get some vegetables, get some skewers and make up as many kebabs as your hungry crew can stomach.

When direct heat is not available, we recommend a trip to the bakery to buy some sweet, flaky pastries. Look for places selling hearty meat pies, patties or sausage rolls. We found some bakeries in Trinidad that specialized in such items, and what began as a search for a snack ended up in a full-on meal. The bakeries on the French islands open early in the morning when the shelves are packed with freshly baked goods. By noon, they are nearly empty and with reason. When still warm, the baguette is absolutely sublime all on its own. After a few hours, it is still very edible, but something of the magic is definitely missing.

Any decent-sized market should have a nice selection of cold meats or cheese and other snacking goodies that you can pack for your excursion. Different islands will have different takes on this: In Curaçao, for example, there are a number of quality cheeses to choose from (see the Dutch Islands in the Regional Variations chapter).

Al fresco dining, Havana, Cuba

Swimming at Cojimar beach, Havana, Cuba

The other option is to buy some fast food from a small, local restaurant. A place where full meals are served including lots of peas & rice, plantain and coleslaw (such as in Jamaica or Martinique) this is the best way to get a lot of variety without a lot of effort on your part. Just be sure to bring your own containers as in many places, the ones you get will be flimsy and might not survive the trip.

You may be tempted to head straight for the beach with your picnic, but finding a quality public beach where you can set up your spread is not always easy. Plus, there is that annoying crunch that inevitably accompanies eating too close to sand.

Most of the islands have natural preserves or parks that make a better choice for your picnic. Pick up a map from any tourist office and go. Not only will there be less sand in your food, but you will have the opportunity to have a look at some of the Caribbean.

Lourdes Queiros cleans up while the plantains are frying at The Melody restaurant, Pinones, Puerto Rico

What to Bring Home

If it were only legal, we would have brought back buckets of fresh fish, calling ahead to have a neighbor light the barbecue and be ready to cook before we'd even unpacked our bags. Alas, the best of the Caribbean can only be enjoyed on the islands.

You will, however, find plenty of packaged goods that are worth lugging home. Start with a few bottles of pepper sauce, perfect for adding a Caribbean taste to dishes. You will soon find that your favorite dishes just don't have the same kick as they do when you add a few drops of pepper. Most brands of pepper sauce available outside the Caribbean are made with the lowest tolerance in mind and are to Caribbean pepper sauces what water is to gasoline.

There are literally thousands of brands available, especially on the English islands. While it would have taken a massive effort (and bowels of titanium) to try them all, we can safely recommend anything made with scotch bonnet peppers. These have a yellowish tinge and a delicious burn that you can feel in your ears. Try it with absolutely anything, especially broiled meats, stews and even egg dishes such as quiche.

In Trinidad, look for mango-based chutneys that are spiced with tamarind or pepper. Good ones include Mango Kuchela, Mango Chuchar and Shadou Beni Chutney (don't worry, the ingredients are listed in English on the side). Use them to accompany meats or as a topping for a good cheddar cheese and fresh bread. Trinidad is also home to Mr Gouda, a large food processing company that specializes in local fare. Mr Gouda's products are canned and so will never match up to the quality of home-made versions, but if you're craving **channa** (chickpea stew) or **callaloo** (soup made with okra, onions, spices and dasheen leaves), you will have to rely on his offerings. Check out Mr Gouda's Creole seasoning, a bottled puree of chives, thyme, celery, vinegar, garlic and pepper.

In Jamaica, you'll find an incredible assortment of bottled jerk marinades, and given the scarcity of the scotch bonnet pepper outside of the Caribbean (and Mexico), you better grab a few bottles if you've developed an addiction. Of course bottled jerk marinade won't match the fresh version, but when this is not available, the commercial variety will evoke some memories.

where to
eat & drink

When the pangs of hunger hit, you won't have far to go for satisfaction. Restaurants and eateries of every type abound in the
Caribbean, ranging from the most simple outdoor operations, with
an open grill and a casual atmosphere, to some of the finest upscale
restaurants, maintained by legions of waitstaff. Some of these cater
to a customer's home-town tastes while others bring the best of
Caribbean cooking to your plate.

The Mason de Melquiades restaurant, Puerto Rico

The high concentration of restaurants in the region is a result of both the prominence of tourism and the fact that Caribbeans eat out regularly. Both lunch and dinner are much more convenient (and not much more expensive) in a nearby restaurant than at home, save for the upscale restaurants. In families where both partners are working all day and have little time to cook a substantial meal, the only way to get the food you grew up with is to go out for it.

Where to Eat
Upscale Restaurants

Eating well on the islands is not difficult. It can, however, be expensive. A dinner for two in an upscale restaurant with wine and tip can easily free you of US$200. Most of these places are associated with a particular resort or hotel and are almost exclusively patronized by tourists. Some are exquisitely good and well worth the money, both in terms of food innovations and service. However, many inevitably compromise quality when their kitchens are expected to serve a few thousand meals each night.

For classic ambience, head to one of the smaller restaurants close to the water's edge. Be charmed by the experience of dining in a colonial setting, in one of the old buildings in San Juan or Havana, for example. Their high ceilings and small, intimate rooms provide the perfect setting for lengthy meals finished off with robust after-dinner rums.

Preparations underway for a strictly invitation only banquet at the Avila Beach Hotel, Curaçao

In most places, the dress code is relaxed and most establishments understand that you're not likely to have packed a three-piece suit or evening gown. Nevertheless, you should plan on wearing long pants at the very least; T-shirts with 'Life's-a-Beach' slogans are frowned upon. In areas where tourism is not the primary industry, more formal dress may be the norm. In San Juan, for example, how you dress is very important and those not appropriately attired should not expect much attention from a maitre d'.

But back to the food. If your budget only permits one or two nights of upscale dining indulgence, choose wisely. Head to a place that serves nouvelle Caribbean cuisine, a fusion of traditional Caribbean ingredients or cooking methods with contemporary concepts. Be aware, however, that many places claim to have nouvelle Caribbean cuisine, but the emphasis is more on the nouvelle and less on the Caribbean. Look for menus that strike that elusive balance between the traditional and the adventurous. You might see dishes like **island coconut lobsters** for which local lobsters are simmered in a coconut cream sauce and spiked with a shot of coconut rum; or a **mahi mahi niçoise salad**, where a fresh filet of dolphin fish is pan fried and served with niçoise salad. There are back-to-the-roots soups such as pea or pumpkin bisque. In Jamaica, the well-known Kingston restaurant, Norma's, created the **jerked chicken penne pasta**. The same place serves a deliciously light smoked marlin salad. Most high-end restaurants display a menu outside, allowing you to peruse before punishing the purse-strings.

The Blue Lagoon restaurant, Port Antonio, Jamaica

Pubs & Mid-range Restaurants

Mid-range restaurants generally boast varied menus. Unfortunately, the quality of these places peaks and troughs, with some surprisingly good and others just dismal. Mid-range restaurants are for either local or tourist tastes, but not both. To find the former, look for clumps of locals noshing and imbibing like regulars.

Ambience is always an elusive concept, but when looking for the best dining vistas, choose somewhere with an outdoor patio, either overlooking the sea or overlooking the city (as a number of Havana restaurants do). Some look as though they raided a garage sale while others feature simple, unpretentious decor; the odd painting or poster, unobtrusive lighting and music played at a pleasant level.

The former English colonies feature pubs, which were established to
serve colonialists desperate for
bangers & mash whilst residing on
conquered shores. In the Bahamas,
where independence was only
recently granted and where offshore
banking thrives, there's a fairly large
British presence and therefore a
number of pubs. Those in downtown Nassau are not unlike their

The Mason de Melquiades, Puerto Rico

English counterparts except that their limited menus do feature Bahamian standards such as conch fritters and grouper fingers as well as British pub standards. Many of these pubs are colored with video games, big screen televisions, posters and bar towels advertising beers that are not available. The Nassau pubs are situated on the wharf, providing a panorama of classic images as gigantic cruise ships dock.

In Martinique, expect light fare to be light: sandwiches, pastries and other finger foods are the norm. One caveat about eating out in Martinique: many places in downtown Fort-de-France close before 6pm. Hotels and upscale restaurants may extend their hours but if you're travel-ing on a budget, make the midday meal your largest (and have it a little later) and then go searching for a snack later on.

In Cuba, sandwiches are also the norm, but look for a place that serves a good pizza when you want something fast, filling and cheap. Puerto Rico will give you the usual bar menu of chicken wings, nachos, and various fried snacks, along with burgers and double-decker sandwiches. The Dutch islands might feature these along with a few island specialties – **yambo** (a green soup that includes salt pork, onions, celery and sometimes fish), **empanas** (pastry turnovers with meat or fish filling) or a homemade stew.

EATING OUT IN CUBA

Guests of the Cuban Hotel Nacional have included Frank Sinatra and Ava Gardner

Open mindedness is essential to overseas travel. This is especially true in Cuba, where the tourism industry is undergoing a reawakening after more than three decades of official dormancy. To give you an idea of the explosiveness of this growth, consider the fact that in 1990, some 350,000 foreigners visited Cuba. By 1999, that number had reached 1.6 million. But the changes have been more drastic than these numbers reflect. In 1989, the Cuban economy was supported by the Soviet Union. When the USSR collapsed, so too did its subsidies to Cuba.

In desperation, Cuba turned to the industry that had at one time been considered a symbol of decadence: tourism. The government has undertaken a massive effort to build up the meager tourism infrastructure. English replaced Russian as the second language in schools. Numerous joint ventures were formed with foreign companies to help build hotels, resorts and restaurants. The growth has been phenomenal, but there have been growing pains. This is evident in the erratic service – beer served in a brandy snifter, meat ravioli with no meat, and pizzas you can order with ham or onions but not ham *and* onions.

The authentic Cuban experience is certainly an elusive one for dollar-paying tourists. While you can find restaurants everywhere that serve traditional Cuban food, much of the Cuban population itself is shut out of this experience.

One reason for this circumstantial segregation is that Cubans employed by the state (almost everyone) are served lunch at the workplace. Also, without access to dollars, many Cubans are left to feed themselves via a ration system or at peso-paying establishments. Here, while the food is very cheap, availability and quality are issues. Still, one of the best pizzas we had in Cuba came from this kind of operation.

Paladares

Almost all restaurants in Cuba are owned and operated by one of the state-owned hospitality companies. Since the 1990s, this arrangement began to change when the government decided to allow locals to open **paladares** (house-based restaurants). This initiative has been a terrific success. Paladares offer some of the best food in Cuba with such home-style dishes **pollo asado** (roast chicken) or **lechón** (pork), seafoods and lots of sides. The service is generally several levels above that of the big restaurants. Plus, if you choose the right place, the atmosphere can be exquisite. It was in one paladar that we cracked open a bottle of rum and shared it with the hosts. Although tempted to talk politics, the better part of discretion kept us off the subject. Instead, we relied on that old conversational stalwart: the weather. While in most instances, this is a deathly boring way to chew the fat, in this case the chat was livened by the fact that our hosts had experienced several hurricanes. While we bleated about weather-induced subway delays, one woman told us how she had watched her roof fly away. Another told of receding flood waters leaving a dead cow on the third floor of a nearby hotel.

Unfortunately, paladares open and close with chaotic irregularity. Guides published only months ago may be horribly out of date. Asking around is the best bet, otherwise you may be left searching for hours and be left vulnerable to cabbies and hustlers. The desperate quest for dollars means that the streets of Havana and other tourist areas are full of **jineteros**, the hustlers that are simply everywhere waiting to 'help' you out in return for a commission. In short, be prepared for anything. Blame Castro or blame the CIA, these are the realities of eating out in Cuba.

The interior of La Gringo Vieja, a paladares restaurant, Havana, Cuba

Overleaf – Vegetable stall at Havana's public market, Cuba

CIGAR ETIQUETTE

A cigar by any other name is just that, a cigar. Right? Well, don't count your **panetelas** (5 inch cigar model) yet. Because it really depends on who you ask.

The cigar **cognoscenti** (connoisseur), for example, may tell you that the last time they savored a Montecristo No. 2 from their humidor it tasted heady and robust, with an enticing yet ambered aroma, and a complex, rich finish. The cigar, they continue, had a pronounced taste with a slightly vegetal, spicy and acidulous character.

The one you tasted – or so you thought – was pretty good, a little strong, but pretty good. Spicy? Maybe. Then you had a chance to observe the complex ritual that goes into the cutting of the cigar, the twirling of it as it is lit (with a sulphur-free, wooden match), the measured puffs, and the masterful tact involved in keeping the ash from falling into an ashtray until it grows to almost two inches in length. Cigar lovers live by these rituals, and they claim the smoking experience is enriched if they are adhered to with officious precision.

Zino Davidoff, the famous Russian emigre and cigar czar who is credited with bringing the noble art and elegance of cigar smoking to the world, insisted that a cigar should be treated like a delicate wine. It should be looked at, admired, sniffed ever so lightly, and savored with meticulous and humble care. A cigar, he said, should be puffed lightly no more than once every 60 seconds. The rest of the burning life of a cigar is to be allotted to appreciating its construction and aroma, and, of course, to the relaxation and spiritual well-being of its smoker.

This may be difficult to justify, especially when a **Habano** (cigar) of average size and quality can easily cost you around US$25. But common sense should tell you a few things if you want to enjoy your cigar and at

Cuban cigars are completely hand rolled and packed in cedar boxes

Cigar's Place, Grand Case, Sint Maarten

the same time manage to annoy as few people as possible.

Ask questions. Tobacconists love to talk about cigars, and are used to answering what may sound like stupid questions. If you encounter a snob who seems annoyed by your questions, chances are his cigars will be more expensive than those of his friendlier competitor down the street. Here are a few cigar tips to get you started:

Don't bite off the head of the cigar à la Clint Eastwood in *The Good The Bad and The Ugly*. There are a variety of cigar cutters at various prices that will allow you to cut, punch, poke or trim the head of your cigar to give you a generous and firm draw.

Try to use a sulphur-free, wooden match and twirl the cigar slightly over the flame to ensure it is evenly lit. Lighters can spoil a good cigar by dousing it with gas or lighter fluid fumes.

Don't over-draw and try to maintain a sizeable ash. This allows the cigar to burn cooler than it would if you puff on it too often or if the embers are constantly exposed.

Be discreet and respectful of others. People will be more offended by cigars than by their ugly cousin, the cigarette, so make sure people are aware that you're lighting up. If they still complain, hey, you warned them.

Find a friend to share in the experience. Having a friend smoking with you may give you the opportunity to use phrases like "heady and robust". Besides, there's safety in numbers.

Enjoy yourself. Look at your cigar, admire it, and give thanks that you have this moment to enjoy something so simple yet so noble and sublime.

José Guichard is a public relations executive who lives and works in Toronto, Canada

Lighting-up in Cuba

WHERE TO EAT & DRINK

Fast Food & Cheap Eateries

Economists might scoff, but Caribbean travel opened our eyes to the primary forces of globalization: the hamburger and fried chicken. Every major global fast-food chain is represented, from McDonald's to Burger King to KFC. And their presence scores the landscape. Consequently, the outskirts of Oranjestad in Aruba resemble a suburban mall rather than an exotic Euro-Caribbean locale.

But residents on the English islands mustered little resistance against the onslaught considering fried chicken is a traditional dish. In Nassau, locals brag that when the first Kentucky Fried Chicken opened, it racked up world-record patronage in its first year. KFC dominates the fast-food scene in other islands, adopting a no-fear approach by leasing its franchises, even in areas that other American chains wouldn't waste the concrete on.

*La Fonda el Jibarito restaurant,
San Juan, Puerto Rico*

By far the best fast-food experience is found at small, independent, often barely noticeable shacks – keep your eyes peeled for shanty-town structures with a few tables and a straggly collection of chairs. The best of these wait for discovery in Jamaica where they are called **joints** or **shacks**. Don't be surprised if lunch consists of a plate overflowing with mashed potatoes, potato salad, stewed pork, cow's foot, fried chicken drumsticks, fresh tomatoes and peas & rice. Any normal-sized appetite will be challenged by half as much. But dig in, go for your life and the locals will love you. These eateries – there are hundreds of them throughout Jamaica – are usually tucked away on a side street, relying on word-of-mouth as opposed to location to ensure a steady stream of customers.

In the rural back blocks of Curaçao, hand-written signs are scrawled with the word **snak** announcing an eatery serving local specialties (see the boxed text Mi Ta Tuma Pida Keshi ... in the Regional Variations chapter). As on other islands, these little pit-stops double as bars and in some the local patrons don't care for the food when there's tipples to be had. For those more interested in getting a meal, expect a menu full of stews, sandwiches and soups.

Open-air cafe in Marigot, St Martin

PROMENADE IN PUERTO RICO

The Paseo de la Princesa, a pleasant walkway by the bay in Old San Juan, Puerto Rico

There is a carnival-like atmosphere on Puerto Rico's Paseo de la Princesa, a promenade that runs below the moss-covered walls that protected San Juan from the English during the colonial period. It may be the crowds of people who stroll up and down the paseo: couples, families or old men in *guayabera* shirts smoking cigars. It may be the smell of pizza or **alcapurrias**, a snack of yucca dough wrapped around beef or seafood and fried until golden.

Sweet food is another feature of the promenade. There are vendors selling **algodón** (cotton candy), fruit shakes, **churros** (donut-like ribbed strips that can be stuffed with a chocolate, vanilla or strawberry filling), **manzanas** (candy apples). More traditional Puerto Rican sugary treats are also available, including **tembleque** (a local version of jello with a sweet, creamy texture) and the bite-sized **majarete** (a sweet made with rice flour).

A little further along, you can stop and listen to music, whether a stage performance or as part of an impromptu **descarga** (jam session) where someone takes a bongo, others pull out güeros, maracas or tambourines and everybody sings. Behind them, a sign advertises **chicharrón de dieta**, which is puzzling, given that chicharrón is normally made by frying the pork rinds in lard. This chicharrón, however, is made of puffed wheat. It is still fried in oil, but is infinitely better for you than the real thing. All of it can be washed down with a cup of **mavi** (cider extracted from the bark of the ironwood tree), which is very refreshing when served ice cold from giant wooden barrels.

At the end of the walk you hit the Raíces Fountain where a spectacular sculpture celebrates the founding peoples of Puerto Rico, the African, Taino and Spanish. You've now hit the end of the Paseo and there is only one option: go back and do it all over again.

Fillete de Res (beef steak) with mushrooms & strips of sweet pepper,
Mira de Linda restaurant near Cayey, Puerto Rico

Street Food

The line between street-food stalls and permanent fast-food eateries is blurry to say the least. This is due in part to stalls that look temporary, but stay in the same place serving the same food to the same clientele day after day. The islands are littered with thousands of such stalls, either concentrated in designated areas or standing in isolation on highways. The food sold is simple, prepared in the proprietor's house or on the spot in purpose-built kitchens. In the Bahamas, for example, the stalls at Potter's Cay in Nassau are equipped with a charcoal-fired grill for the fish and a couple of burners for cooking the accompanying sauce.

Impromptu street food often requires no structure at all. In San Juan, Puerto Rico, we discovered a man selling chilled seafood salad from the shelter of an apartment garage. The man, who wore pants patterned with the houndstooth print favored by chefs around the world, had prepared a bucket of his signature dish (a mixture of conch and whitefish with onions, peppers, tomatoes and lime juice) in his nearby home. His set-up consisted of nothing more than a large cooler for the seafood salad and a small table for the plastic bowls, serviettes and condiments. In 10 minutes he served no fewer than three groups as cars stopped, ordered, then drove off.

In Martinique, street food is a more mobile affair. At the south end of Le Savanne (Fort-de-France's beautiful central park) a number of trucks with in-built kitchens move in around 8pm, fire up their grills and wait for the eating onslaught. All feature the word 'express' on wide awnings that cover the attached dining areas. Each has its own sound system, creating a cacophony of rhythm that's initially painful but somehow becomes harmonious as

A Rasta stand selling corn, drinks and snacks on the streets of Kingston, Jamaica

the evening progresses. The food is broiled by brave souls who get as smoked as the food they cook. Their discomfort is our gain. Beef, lamb and chicken is cooked over coals on long skewers and served on rice or with fries or in a bun with a hot, salty sauce of sauteed onions and thyme. Be sure to ask for hot pepper to enhance the flavor, because if you're not local, they will simply assume you won't want it.

The best Jamaican street stalls serve pan chicken from smoky road-side barbecues (see the boxed text Friday Night, Red Hill Rd, Kingston, Jamaica later in this chapter). But there are plenty of other things to get on the street in Jamaica: cold beers, soft drinks, salty snacks and chocolate (buyer beware: chocolate bought anywhere that isn't air-conditioned is a mess waiting to happen). Many of these stalls are run by dreadlocked Rastafarians who painstakingly decorate the walls with slogans of peace and love and Haile Selasse (see the boxed text What Did Marley Eat for Breakfast? in the Regional Variations chapter). Peanuts are an especially popular street snack, either roasted on portable stoves as in Jamaica and Trinidad, or served in small white cones sold by a **manisero** (peanut seller) as in Cuba.

ARAWAK CAY, NASSAU

If you've only got a few days in the Bahamas and you're looking for a true Bahamian dining experience, be sure to visit Arawak Cay. Located on the east end of Nassau opposite Fort Charlotte and the Nassau Cricket Club, this collection of independent eateries offers diners the most typical of Bahamian dishes: conch and every sort of fish dish. It is also a fine place to hang out and have a few drinks under the shade of the patios lining the street.

Upon arrival at Arawak Cay, you're greeted by a sign that prohibits entering with glass bottles in tow. Next to the sign is a small building housing a branch of the Nassau constabulary. Their proximity is no coincidence and indicates that this area has been the site of more than one violent exchange – the strip is known to get a bit wild at night.

But during the day it is a perfectly safe lunch spot. We recommend a visit to Goldie's at the eastern end of the strip. Be sure to sit at the bar for a perfect view of the chef preparing your conch salad. Wielding a large knife, he goes through an onion, green pepper and tomato in a matter of seconds. The conch itself is scored but not tenderized and takes a little more time. When the all the chopping is over, he mixes the ingredients with salt, piles them into a bowl and adds the juice of a whole lime and orange to finish the dish. The result is a refreshing and tangy seafood salad – the perfect meal for a hot day.

Barbecue

If the wind is favorable, you should easily be able to find a barbecue restaurant, as the smell of smoke seasoned with dripping and the sweet caramelized sugar of the sauce should be more than enough to direct your nostrils.

Barbecue restaurants aren't common in the Caribbean, but are definitely worthy of mention for the simple fact they originated here (see Amerindians in the Culture of Caribbean Cuisine chapter). The Amerindians barbecued all sorts of meats, but chicken and pork are favored by today's cooks. Sauces may be used, but the emphasis is on adding spice, as opposed to the sweet, tomato-based sauces that you may be used to (see the boxed text).

FRIDAY NIGHT – Red Hill Road, Kingston, Jamaica

You might not have come to Jamaica for the food. In fact why you're here has more to do with not having seen the sun in 12 or more weeks. But because the sun goes down at 7pm you might be looking for something to do later in the evening, like a trip to a nightclub or a dance hall. And once you've danced until your clothes are soaked through, you've had your fill of Red Stripe beer and the loud music is making you feel as if a swarm of hornets just landed inside your ears, it's time for a little something to eat. So why not head out to Red Hill Rd in Kingston and get yourself some real Jamaican pan chicken. Now you no doubt know what chicken is, because they do have that in your country too, but you might not know that real Jamaican pan chicken is made in barbecues fashioned out of old oil drums. They call those drums 'pans' in the Caribbean and they are what Trinis use to make musical instruments.

But back to the food. On Red Hill Rd you will find a row of chefs, all imbibing the smoke of their pans, tending to their chicken. They start up about 6pm, catering to home-bound and hungry workers. Instead they decide to see Shorty for their evening meal.

Now Shorty is the name of the man you want to see because – according to the good people of Kingston – he's got the best pan chicken on Red Hill Rd. And despite the fact there's plenty of chicken ready to be eaten at the other guys' places, locals wait for Shorty to cook up his offerings.

Later on, people who are coming home from a night out will also stop by to see Shorty, looking for something to cure those late night munchies. He knows you're coming, so he'll stay open until 5am cooking the chicken legs and breasts over a charcoal-fired pan. You still might have to wait a bit, but that's all right, just chat with other diners. They won't bite! And neither will the stray dogs who wander around, looking hopeful at you as you pick chicken from the bones and lick sauce from your fingers. Eat it all up and soak up the juices with a piece of bread. Now you're done. Now you're ready for a sleep. Go home. Shorty will be there tomorrow.

MRS SCATLIFFE'S RESTAURANT

While the US Virgin Islands (St Thomas, St John, Buck Island and St Croix) are a bit cruise-shippy and hard sell, the British Virgin Islands are low-key and lazy, with impossibly lovely beaches and killer sunsets. It's the kind of place you can tire yourself out snorkeling and then get a cocktail delivered to your hammock strung between palm trees on the sand. The eatery that best sums up the easygoing atmosphere and fresh tropical tastes of the BVI is Mrs Scatliffe's Restaurant (tel 284-495-4556) in Carrot Bay on Tortola's north shore.

The restaurant is the Scatliffe home, set back from the street on stilts in a garden of rampant greenery. Guests are restricted to a friendly four or five tables on the breezy screened verandah. When you ring up to make a booking, you'll be given a choice of whatever's cooking for your main course – it might be fresh fish served with an onion sauce, curried goat cooked in a shell or coconutty chicken curry.

Strung-up in the British Virgin Islands

For starters, you get what you're given: it could be a milky breadfruit soup, cooked up with sweet peppers and herbs (some fresh from the garden) or conch fritters. All of it comes with Mrs Scatliffe's home-baked bread. For dessert, offerings skip from vanilla-tinged soursop sorbet to cookies hot from the oven.

The service can be a bit haphazard, ranging from gawky youngsters to grumpy old-timers but the food seems to be prepared with heapings of love. The family only caters to the number of bookings, so you can enjoy your food in the knowledge that it was made just for you.

After dinner, there's usually a bit of a sing-along – it might be Mrs Scatliffe herself, letting loose with a few prayerful tunes, sometimes with a couple of younger family members holding the harmonies. Other nights a local fungi band does the honors. All in all the atmosphere is homely and cosy, the food is what the locals eat and you'll leave full and satisfied.

Dani Valent is a well-travelled writer living in Melbourne, Australia

WHERE TO EAT & DRINK

Where to Drink

Drinking is done with gusto in the Caribbean, by visitors and residents alike. Places to drink range from elegant bars in five-star hotels to flights of stairs outside private homes. If you really want to go local on the English islands, find yourself a stool at a local rum shop. Slightly more than a hole in the wall, these places serve a limited menu of drinks – mostly hard liquors and beers. Decor depends on how recently the beer or rum rep visited bearing posters. Food in rum shops are usually as basic as a pack of chips. But it's the atmosphere that can be a real treat as you try and keep up with the talk on local politics, the Reggae Boyz upcoming soccer match and other local gossip.

A COFFEE CRUSADE

John Hackett sits in a throne-like chair behind the counter of Syps, the coffee and wine bar he owns in Port of Spain, Trinidad. It is an unlikely place from which to orchestrate a crusade, but Mr Hackett has chosen to wage a war from this very spot. His goal is nothing short of revolutionary: to change the coffee drinking habits of his fellow Trinis and turn the Republic from a 'Nescafé culture' to one that appreciates a fine cup of coffee.

This is an uphill battle. Trinidad used to be an important coffee-growing country, and its people appreciated a quality brew. However, the convenience and modern appeal of freeze-dried coffee slowly pushed the quality coffees aside. "As a people, we not only lost good coffee, but the joy of knowing a good cup from an ordinary one," says Mr Hackett.

A large man with slow, deliberate speech, Mr Hackett rediscovered good coffee for himself while living in North America. In early 1999, he opened Syps cafe on Cipriani Boulevard near Tragarete Rd and equipped it with espresso machines and other coffee culture accoutrements as part of his strategy to convert the masses.

When interviewed, Mr Hackett's demeanor suggested that his mission was yet to find success. But he anticipated as much. The menu at Syps is full of items you would not normally expect in a Caribbean cafe, including pancakes, omelets and hamburgers. There is even a short wine list – another rarity in a country where imbibing most often means beer or rum.

But there is something about the place – the cozy atmosphere, the big window that looks out onto the street – that makes you think that Syps is on the right track. After all, the thousands of Trini expats exposed to the elaborate gourmet brews offered around the world will come back with a taste for a quality espresso, or a café au lait made with slow-roasted Arabica beans.

Mr Hackett will be waiting.

Hotel Nacional, Havana, Cuba

FABRICATING A LEGEND

The American writer Ernest Hemingway was passionate about Cuba; one of his best loved works *The Old Man and the Sea* was set here, as was *To Have and to Have Not*. And Cuba loves Hemingway. His house, the Finca Vigia, has been turned into a museum. His books are sold on the street next to the works of José Marti and *Guerrilla Warfare* by Ché Guevara. His Nobel Prize medal is on display and the places he slept, ate and drank have become shrines.

Two of his favorite drinking spots were the bars at El Floridita and La Bodeguita del Medio. Both are compulsory stops on any city tour and both are filled with tourists blighted by Papamania. El Floridita makes one of the finest daiquiris known to humanity, where it's made with any number of fruit juices. Ernest preferred grapefruit, a fact reflected in the drink named for him, the Hemingway Daiquiri. The bar, which was renovated extensively in the early 1990s, is still a classic from an era when drinking was a much more serious pastime: leather chairs, waiters in waistcoats and plates of salty **mariquitas** (fried plantains) to help keep your thirst from getting too quenched.

La Bodeguita del Medio is famous for its **mojito**, a popular Cuban cocktail made with white rum, sugar, lime juice and a sprig of mint. In stark contrast to the pristine surroundings of El Floridita, La Bodeguita's walls are blackened with thousands of signatures of those who have imbibed there before.

In Cuba, drinking is best accompanied by music and fittingly, most bars in tourist areas (including most of Havana) feature live bands. A friend who grew up in Havana described these bar musicians as third-rate, but his frame of reference is Cuba, where music is an integral part of the national identity. This is a country where children learn to play an instrument, dance or sing in the same way that other kids learn to walk. In Havana you can barely walk a block without hearing someone playing a traditional Cuban **son**, the music made popular in the 30s and 40s then revived by the Buena Vista Social Club and its many spin-offs. These bars offer an accessible way into Cuban music. Very few places will charge a cover, but during a particularly long **descarga** (jam session) expect a hat to be passed around.

Both Floridita's daiquiri and Bodeguita's mojito owe much of their reputation to Hemingway's legendary drinking habits. The writer AE Hotchner reports that the first time he met Hemingway in the 1950s, he was drunk and bragging about how he had downed 13 double daiquiris in a single sitting. One wall of El Floridita is covered with framed photographs of the aging Hemingway with a number of celebrities and friends. On another wall, hanging in solemn tribute, is the famous Yosef Karsh photograph, where the bearded Hemingway, dressed in a thick wool turtleneck, looks into the distance.

A handwritten sign hangs above the bar at La Bodeguita del Medio. It reads:

My Mojito in La Bodeguita
My Daiquiri in El Floridita

And it is dated and signed by Ernest Hemingway. Drinking under it gives you a true sense of history, of all that Hemingway and his books represent: dignity, simplicity, hard boozing.

Trouble is, it's a fake.

The American writer Tom Miller discovered this and told the world in *Trading with the Enemy,* a travelogue written in the early 1990s. The Bodeguita del Medio was initially just a neighborhood grocery store. The owners then added a bar and began serving the mojitos that attracted writers and artists who lived in the area. After the revolution, they wanted to expand and to capitalize on its connection to the artistic community and so a graphic artist was hired to forge Hemingway's handwriting. The sign was hung up and the legend was born.

Not that the exposed lie will do anything to hurt business at either bar. After all, as they say, any publicity is good publicity. And in fact, it gives the patrons just one more story to tell.

On the smaller islands, where tourism is vital to the economy, drinking establishments either resemble any conventional western bar or pub, or simply conform to the image of drinking spots presented by tourism brochures: palm-thatch roofs, brightly colored drinks with cheesy paper umbrellas served by locals in brightly colored shirts.

It's important to remember to keep your fluid levels up while under the Caribbean sun. Fortunately there are a wide variety of flavorsome drinks available, so it should never be hard to quench your thirst. Chilled coconut water is particularly good for quenching thirst and in comparison to fresh juices is the least expensive alternative. You'll find people selling drinks such as sno-cones, soft drinks and juices at markets, from stalls and on the streets (see Soft Drinks, Fruit Juices & Sno-Cones in the Drinks chapter).

The Menu

When it comes to menus in the Caribbean you won't need a translator as most places print their menu in both English and the native language. In fact, on more than one occasion in Puerto Rico, we encountered menus written deliberately in Spanglish, the local word for a mixture of both Spanish and English. These menus advertised such dishes as 'churrasco a la parrilla con papaya sauce served with Mexican rice y guacamole' and 'flour tortillas llenitas de queso con tu choice de chorizo chicken or beef'.

If there is no menu, one of the staff will tell you your options. One word of warning with oral menus: be sure to get the price. At one restaurant in Cuba, we learned that the choices on the written menu (which all ranged around US$5) were not available. The server then gave us a number of options and we made our selections accordingly. Everything was fine until the bill came. Each entree was over US$15!

In simple places where choice is limited, dishes are advertised on a sandwich board outside the restaurant or on handmade signs posted inside. The price should be listed right next to the dish in question. Sometimes, what you see is what you get. For example, if you wander into a joint in Jamaica and ask for a serve of jerk chicken, that's what you'll get. If you want a festival (small oblong piece of fried bread) or some macaroni and cheese to go with it, you'll have to order that separately. In Martinique, however, the kebab we ordered came with a pile of French fries and coleslaw, much to our surprise.

The soup from La Tasca restaurant in San Juan is advertised as an aphrodisiac, Puerto Rico

Prix Fixe & A La Carte

The prix fixe (fixed-price meal) is alive and well on the French islands, whether you're ordering Parisian-style food or Creole cuisine. Your meal will generally include a soup and/or a salad, a main of meat or fish, a side dish and possibly a glass of wine. The menu of the day will be posted outside the restaurant, along with the price.

Almost everywhere else, menus are a la carte. Most are neatly divided in the traditional way: starters (soups, salads) and then main courses (divided into meat, chicken, seafood and vegetable dishes). Desserts come at the end as do drinks.

Lunch and dinner menus can vary greatly, but in many local eateries the lunch and dinner menus are the same. This is certainly the case on the Spanish islands where the midday meal has traditionally been the largest, although this is changing as the long lunch gives way to work commitments.

A nice spread at the Rystafel Indonesian Restaurant in Willemstad, Curaçao

Vegetarians

While there are fewer vegetarian-only restaurants in the Caribbean, vegetarians shouldn't have any trouble finding meat-free dishes throughout the Caribbean. Trinidad, with its strong East Indian heritage perhaps offers the most options (and among the most interesting). Channa (chick pea) stews, callaloo, and coo-coo are all vegetarian mainstays, as are most of the side dishes. In fact, one simple option for a vegetarian is to order a full meal and simply ask them to leave the meat dish out. You will get heaps of food (much of it starchy) including peas & rice, plantains and yucca.

Mashed plantain with garlic and butter, served with mixed stewed vegetables, tomatoes, lettuce and avocado, garnished with a slice of sweet pepper, Puerto Rico

a caribbean
banquet

Given the immense regional variety across the islands, there are two approaches to throwing a party with real Caribbean flair: either focus on one specific region or try and get a sampling from across the islands. Can't decide? Don't know what to do? Throw caution to the wind and hold two parties!

First, start with the drink: rum. This is a fine opportunity to introduce your friends to some of the world's finest rums. Buy a couple of bottles of Havana Club Añejo (which is available everywhere but the US), one of the higher end Appleton rums or Bacardí 8. Serve them straight up, with a wedge of lime or with a few cubes of ice but under no circumstances allow your guests to mix these rums with cola, juice or anything else. You may get protests, but ignore them, be insistent and you will win them over to the wonders of a truly well-made rum.

In fact, you might want to do a rum tasting. Get yourself a collection of comparable rums (all dark, all light or all aged) and several glasses. To ensure objectivity, obscure the labels, cover them with paper. Have each guest take a small amount and comment on the quality before rating it.

If straight rum is still not your ideal tipple, pull out the blender and start mixing. We are yet to discover a fruit juice that does not go well with rum, although any of the citrus family are fail-safe options.

In terms of food, think seafood, but only if the fish available is fresh. Any fish appropriate for grilling will do though it must be served whole for authenticity such as with Baked Grouper (see the recipe later in this chapter). Also prepare a variety of side dishes such as **fried plantains** (see the recipe in the Staples & Specialties chapter), **moros y cristianos** (peas & rice; see the recipe in the Home Cooking & Traditions chapter) coleslaw and baked macaroni and cheese. **Jerk pork** is another must (see the boxed text The Jerk and the recipe in the Regional Variations chapter). Be sure to marinade the meat for at least a full day before cooking and consider the spice tolerance of your guests. You also have to have pepper sauce available, preferably something homemade. If that's a problem, get a bottle of the stuff and dump it into a bowl to at least give the appearance!

Baked Grouper

When your fish is fresh, keeping it simple is the best way to go. Dunking a fish in some fancy butter sauce is no way to show respect for this fine creature. This recipe calls for grouper but you can substitute red snapper if you prefer. It even works with dried cod (just be sure to soak it first).

Take a few grouper filets (one per person should do) and season them with salt, freshly ground pepper and just a sprinkle of red pepper flakes. Then drizzle on enough lime juice to give the filets a nice shiny coat. Place them all in a baking dish and chop up some onion, pepper and tomato (not too much, just enough add a little flavor and texture). Add them to the dish, then bake it at 300°F (150°C) for about 20 minutes. Serve the fish on a bed of steamed rice.

Boris enjoys a meal of jerk chicken, ackee & saltfish, goat and fried plantains, the Native Restaurant, Montego Bay, Jamaica

CARIBBEAN BANQUET

Enjoying a meal including roasted pork and peas & rice, Cuba

Now if your party is going to have a Latin angle, you have to have salsa. No, not the kind for dipping nachos, we're talking about the music. There are several good compilations out there, but true aficionados will look for the Fania label, which was founded in the 1960s in New York and which launched the careers of some of salsa's greatest names: Richie Ray, Hector Lavoie, Ruben Blades and the incomparable Pete 'El Conde' Rodriguez.

If you're going Cuban, the plethora of recent releases from the Buena Vista Social Club will keep you chan chaning into the night. Cuban Jazz also offers hours and hours of great listening, from Gonzalo Rubacalba to Chucho Valdés.

Jamaica-themed parties will have to include **jerk** (meat marinated with a mixture of spices; see the boxed text The Jerk and the recipe in the Regional Variations chapter). This is best accompanied by Red Stripe beer (or some other type of light lager if Red Stripe is not available). Jamaican music begins with Bob Marley but it is also worth exploring the sounds of some of the early pioneers of ska, including Tommy McCook and the Skatalites.

Moving south, consider having a party with a Trini theme. The dish should be **roti** (see the recipe later in this chapter), which is easy to serve to big crowds. Make up the bread (also available at specialty shops in most larger cities), meat, curried potatoes and vegetables separately and have your guests construct their own roti wraps. You might want to add some peas & rice but if the roti is well stuffed, it should be more than enough. And don't forget the pepper! The music in this case should be classic calypso with its tin pan drumming; look for some David Rudder or The Mighty Sparrow.

Roti

This Indian-style bread is easy to make but, to be honest, not as easy as buying it.

Ingredients

2 cups	flour
1/4 cup	water
1	pinch of salt
	oil

Start with two cups of all-purpose flour in a bowl. Add a pinch of salt and about 1/4 cup of water. Begin to mix the dough, adding more water until you get a semi-soft consistency. Knead it for at least 15 minutes and then cover it with a damp cloth and let it sit for 20 minutes. Then knead it some more (about 5 minutes). Break off golf-ball sized pieces of dough and roll them as flat as you can without breaking them. Cook them on a lightly oiled griddle until brown. Flip them to do both sides. Serve immediately as roti goes stale quickly.

Decor is a wide open question. Our favorite places were those that never seemed to have a plan. These are the houses that are peppered with assorted trinkets, religious icons and souvenirs from all over the world. In the arts and crafts fairs that every island boasts, you might be able to pick up a generic painting with that certain Caribbean kitsch: brightly colored nature portraits of a tropical bird, scenes from the sugarcane fields or vintage cars on a narrow street. Its not high art, but it is cheap and will definitely generate lots of conversation.

Otherwise, go nuts with every cliche you can think of: umbrellas and cut fruits in the drinks, torches on the patio, Bermuda shorts and coral jewelry – your party should have all of that.

Relaxing in Havana, Cuba

In the Caribbean, parties tend to start late and end early – the next morning, that is. Depending on the crowd, the dancing and drinking could go on until dawn, which is usually taken as a sign that it's time to go home. But don't let that stop you. Just make sure you plan ahead and be prepared to spend the next day catching up on sleep.

fit & healthy

Getting sick on the road is only too easy and sometimes even a slight adjustment in the diet will disrupt your system. Nevertheless there are a few ways to lower the possibility of illness and heighten the enjoyment of the fine food of the Caribbean.

The first defense is common sense. Avoid places that do not measure up to your standards. If the dining room is a sty, you can be sure that the kitchen is not much better. Be especially careful when ordering shellfish. In general, you should avoid shellfish at places that are far inland or that simply don't pass judgment based on your own instinct.

Cruising the streets of Cuba

Water

While tap water is generally safe throughout the islands, you are better off sticking to the bottled stuff if only in the Caribbean for a short period. Tap water, however, is fine when it comes to washing fruit and vegetables or brushing your teeth.

Heat

Even if you feel perfectly healthy, be sure to drink plenty of fluids in the Caribbean heat. The best choice is water or fruit juice. You can help prevent problems like dehydration and sun stroke by avoiding the sun during the midday hours when it is strongest. Have lunch indoors or at least on a shaded patio. Maybe take a nap.

Hanging-out on the streets of Havana, Cuba

Allergies

Cooking with rum is common in the Caribbean (rum cake included) and so those with an alcohol allergy should be wary. In restaurants, rum recipes are usually spelled out on the menu or in the name of the dish, but always ask if you have any doubts. Note that **souse** (stew) does not include alcohol. Peanuts are not common in cooking but they are a common snack and people with an allergy should take the usual precautions. Those allergic to shellfish should watch for it in casseroles or rice dishes, but again, it is normally the main ingredient and will be identified on the menu.

Diabetics

Caribbean food, and in particular the breads, will generally contain sugar. Moreover, with the heavy emphasis on carbohydrate-rich foods, Caribbean diets tend to be high in calories that may affect insulin levels. On the other hand, Caribbean beers tend to be lower in alcohol. Those planning long-term stays should consult their physicians before departure.

Diarrhea

Although disturbing and certainly not a great way to spend valuable holiday time, experiencing diarrhea may be nothing more than your body adjusting to a new climate and cuisine. To prevent it, stick to bottled water and eat well, but not to excess. Even in establishments that seem to be clean it's always wise to prevent potential discomfort by sprinkling lime juice on the salad or by eating raw garlic.

If and when diarrhea does strike, be sure to replace the fluids you're losing by drinking plenty of bottled water, black tea with a little sugar, or soft drinks that have gone flat. It's also wise to completely avoid spicy foods while in recovery mode, which will take considerable discipline in such a spice-crazed region.

Rehydration is extremely important for complete recovery. The World Health Organization recommends the following solution to help you maintain fluid levels and electrolyte balance: Mix one liter of bottled water with ¾ teaspoon of salt, 1 teaspoon of baking soda, 1 cup of orange juice and 4 tablespoons of sugar.

You can look for relief from Lomotil or Imodium, available at most pharmacies. Both will plug you up effectively, but they do not cure the problem and should only be taken when absolutely necessary.

If diarrhea includes blood or mucus, is accompanied by fever or lethargy, or persists for more than five days, it is an indication that what you have picked up requires more urgent attention. Don't take Imodium or Lomotil in these cases and consult a doctor as soon as possible.

A sugarcane worker makes his way home through the Pinar del Río area, Cuba

Good friends, Havana, Cuba

Children

Children can be especially susceptible to the heat and so make sure they get plenty of fluids. Also, the spiciness of certain cuisines (namely Jamaica's jerk) can cause stomach problems.

eat your words
language guide

A

ABC Islands thus called not only because their initials represent Aruba, Bonaire and Curaçao but also because they are situated close together in the Caribbean Sea. Dutch is the official language with English and Papiamento commonly spoken.

aceitunas alinadas olives are enjoyed in Cuba, and this marinated olive dish is no exception. Made with pitted Spanish olives with cumin, hot peppers, lemon, garlic and vinegar, this marinade is traditionally refrigerated for a couple days then served as an appetizer at room temperature.

ackee the national fruit of Jamaica. Eaten at breakfast or enjoyed in ackee & saltfish. Due to its amino acid content, this pear-shaped fruit can cause illness if eaten while unripe. The fruit is ready to be used once it splits open (due to exposure to the sun).

adobo a Puerto Rican dry-rub seasoning for meat that combines garlic, oregano, salt and pepper

aguacate salsa Cuban avocado sauce. Main ingredients include avocado, tomato, bell pepper, onion, cucumber and white rum.

aguadiente raw sugar spirit

ají Spanish term for hot peppers

akkra though sometimes referring to bean fritters, the term akkra most commonly refers to saltfish cakes. Rinsed and heated codfish is mixed with flour, sugar, onions, garlic, peppers, chives, salt and generous amounts of pepper to form a mixture that is then fried in tablespoon-sized portions until golden brown. Akkra are served hot as appetizers with drinks. **Phulouri** Trinidad's version is a similar yet less spicy fritter.

albondigas Cuban meatballs made with minced pork or beef, garlic, breadcrumbs, egg, **allspice**, rosemary, ginger, gold rum, corn flour and corn oil. Similar to Mexican meatballs known as *albondiguitas*.

alcapurrias a Puerto Rican snack of **yucca** dough wrapped around beef or seafood and fried until golden

algodón Puerto Rican sweet confection made from cotton candy

alioli *see* **garlic**

allspice also known as pimento berries or pimento seed. A native of Cuba, the Spanish named it *pimentia*. **Allspice** is similar in flavour to a blend of cinnamon, cloves, black pepper and nutmeg.

ananas *see* **pineapple**

angostura bitters a product of Trinidad, this flavoring agent is used in popular Caribbean cocktails such as **sevilla**. Although the mixture is a closely guarded secret, it is thought that tamarind pulp is one of the primary elements.

annatto red seeds, also known as *achiote*. Used by Caribbeans to color cooking oil a bright yellow-orange. An inexpensive substitute for saffron, annatto also imparts its own flavor. In the US, butter and cheddar cheeses are colored using annatto seeds.

arabica coffee species grown in high altitudes that accounts for roughly 70 percent of the world's coffee. Arabica beans contain less caffeine and produce a more delicate and slightly more acidic brew than **robusta** beans.

arañitas a Puerto Rican specialty of shredded **plantain** deep fried in clumps. Direct translation means 'little spiders'.

Arawak these native peoples of the Antilles were agriculturists who lived in villages and practised slash-and-burn cultivation of **cassava** and corn. They were driven out of the Lesser Antilles by the **Carib** shortly before the appearance of the Spanish.

arrowroot starchy, white powder obtained from the plant of the same name. It is used as a flavorless thickening agent in soups, stews, sauces and glazes.

arroz the Spanish term for rice

arroz con leche the dessert rice pudding. Rice and water is mixed with lemon rind, cinnamon, milk, salt and sugar and is then boiled.

arroz con pollo a Latin American classic of rice and chicken that is a hearty staple in many Latin Caribbean countries. The rice is colored yellow with saffron and the chicken is sauteed.

asado a style of cooking where food is roasted, either in the oven or in the ground

asopao a combination of chicken, rice and approximately twenty other ingredients, depending on the whim of the cook. The dish has clear antecedents in Spain's *paella*, and could be called Puerto Rico's national dish. Also refers to a soup-like dish from the Dominican Republic made on a base of rice with several types of meat and beer added.

atun con ron the Cuban dish, tuna with rum sauce

avocado *see* **peer**

B

bacalaitos Puerto Rican cod fritters

bacalao the Spanish term for cod

bacchanal popularly used to refer to any situation that is enjoyably chaotic from rowdy behavior to extravagant parties. Carnival is often known as bacchanal.

bahama mama rum-based cocktail made from a mixture of dark rum, coconut liqueur, 151-proof rum, coffee liqueur, lemon and pure pineapple juice

Bajan of or from Barbados

bakes **Bajan** fried bread

bakijow Dutch term for cod when marinated in vinaigrette with a little pepper

balchi di pisca fish balls as referred to on the **ABC Islands**

bambooshay nuts dry-roasted peanuts cooked and coated in sugar, cumin and hot red pepper flakes. During Carnival revelers are likely to yell out 'Bambooshay', which means 'enjoy yourself, have a great time'.

bammy Jamaican bread made from the **cassava** root. Cassava is grated, pressed, sifted and grilled to make round cakes 10cm in diameter and 1cm thick. Cassava contains a natural cyanide-based toxin so it is critical that all the juice is carefully squeezed out during.

banana particularly high in potassium, low in protein and fat, and a good source of vitamins C and A. Ripe bananas are 75% water. Though most commonly eaten fresh in the islands, bananas are also used as vegetables in dishes. Unripe banana is boiled or stewed with meat and can be fried or mashed and used in pies, puddings, cakes and breads.

banane pesé a hot snack of deep-fried **plantain** slices sprinkled with salt. Served on the French islands.

bandera dominicana a dish from the Dominican Republic made with chicken, white rice, beans, **plantain**, **yucca** and avocado

bara East Indian in origin, small discs of fried bread popular in Trinidad and Tobago

baracoa special Cuban cocktail made from a mixture of Santiago White Label rum, coconut cream, grapefruit juice, Marinero dark rum and lime juice. Poured over cracked ice and served in a champagne glass.

barbecue the Amerindians supposedly dried and preserved their food by cooking it on a *brabacot* (wooden frame over a pit of coals). The Spanish adopted this and named it *barbacoa*, from which the word 'barbecue' was adapted.

barritas de mango mango bars that are extremely tasty but very rich. Sometimes rolled in powdered sugar. Raspberry is a popular variation during the festive season.

basil although there are over fifty types of this aromatic herb, two varieties are predominantly used in cooking: sweet basil and bush basil. On the Spanish islands basil is used with tomato dishes and in turtle soup.

batabano banana bread Cuban country-style banana bread

batata Spanish term for sweet potatoes. *Batatas* is an **Arawak** word from which the word potato is derived. Batatas are used in both sweet and savoury dishes.

bay leaf shiny, leathery leaves from the bay-rum tree. Used in pickles, stews and soups. When added to a dish, the leaves should be removed before serving.

bay rum a multi-purpose aromatic lotion made from the bay leaf. Its uses include men's cologne, after-shave or after-shower refresher. In the Caribbean, bay rum is traditionally used as a rub for muscular pain or minor skin irritations. Bay rum is for external use only.

beans several varieties are grown across the islands, including red and black kidney beans, haricot or *blanco* beans, French beans, **pigeon peas**, congo peas, pinto, flageolet, black-eyed beans and white beans. Beans were a substantial part of the diet of indigenous Caribbeans.

berehein na forno aubergine in coconut milk. Popular on the island of Sint Maarten.

bifteck à la créole rump steak marinated in a mixture of olive oil, red wine, garlic, rump steak, dark rum, salt and pepper. Popular on the French islands of Martinique and Guadeloupe.

bistec on rollo Cuban rolled beef

bitter orange *see* **sour orange**

black cake fruitcakes made for the Christmas season. Flavored with rum and vanilla essence, the high consistency of diced preserved fruit is held together with a very moist mixture, with the main ingredient, molasses, providing the color. One's black cake is a source of great pride among islanders.

black pudding made from animal blood, this large black sausage is a delicacy in the region – each village producer has his or her own secret recipe. Made from either rice or bread soaked in the steamed blood of pigs or cows. Garlic, onions, herbs and peppers are added to the blood mixture and then stuffed into animal intestines. Used in typical breakfast 'fry-ups' or served as a first course.

blue marlin found in the waters around Jamaica, blue marlin is a great substitute for salmon

bocadillo Cuban sandwich filled with ham or cheese

bocaditos Cuban term for snacks. Often substantial enough to be served as small meals, pizza is the most popular Cuban bocadito.

bocadito jamon this traditional ham spread is served on crackers as an appetizer at Cuban parties. It also serves as a filling in Cuban meat pastries or in **croquetas**.

bois bande a local aphrodisiac of St Lucia, used in alcoholic drinks such as ginger liqueur

bois d'inde similar to **allspice** and bay rum berries, this spice is popular throughout the Caribbean

bolita di keshi batata Puerto Rican term for sweet potato. Refers to cheese balls in the Dutch islands.

bombas de camarones y papas prawn and potato balls popular in the Dominican Republic

boniatillo a rich Cuban dessert made from **boniato** (sweet potato). Other key ingredients include sugar, cinnamon, lime, egg yolks and dry sherry.

boniato Cuban variety of sweet potato with brown skin and white flesh. Used for a paste-like dessert known as **boniatillo**.

bonito a tropical fish larger than a kingfish and smaller than a tuna. Schools of bonito are plentiful but not easily caught. Salted, smoked or dried in the sun, a catch of bonito is said to secure the fish needs of a village for several weeks at a time.

bora very similar to runner beans. Also known as bodi beans, snake beans or yard long beans.

borinquen a cocktail that includes passionfruit syrup, lime juice, orange juice and rum

boulangerie bakery

bounty rum known as the 'Spirit of St Lucia'. Distilled and blended fine golden rum, purported to be St Lucia's most popular.

braata means a little extra; like the thirteenth cookie in a baker's dozen; or an extra helping of food. In Caribbean musical shows it has come to mean the encore.

braff also referred to as boil-up, braff is a sort of fish soup or stew made from kingfish, mackerel and various root vegetables including **cassava**, **plantain**, yams, **pigeon peas**, **dasheen** and green bananas. This revered meal is enjoyed all year round. However, it is eaten with gusto on **Jouvay** morning. Carnival is as big as Christmas in the Caribbean, and **braff** is equivalent to turkey.

breadfruit native to the Pacific, breadfruit is large (20-24cm in diameter), has a bumpy green skin and rather bland-tasting cream-colored flesh. It is picked and eaten before ripening, when it becomes sickly sweet. Breadfruit can be baked, grilled, fried or boiled and served as a sweet or savory dish.

breadnut a yellow fruit that is generally boiled or roasted. Can also be made into flour.

bread pudding this imported dessert from England features crumbled slices of white bread soaked in milk and egg, and flavored with sugar, cinnamon, butter, vanilla, raisins and slivered almonds. It is baked and served at room temperature.

bulla cakes popular Jamaican cookies or small round cakes made with brown sugar, flour, molasses, ginger and nutmeg

bunuelos a Cuban Christmas pastry of fried **yucca**, **taro** and anise, drenched in a vanilla, cinnamon and sugar syrup

bush tea made from herbs and leaves, bush teas are very popular in the Caribbean. Recipes are handed from generation to generation. Ingredients like lemongrass, lime and **soursop** are said to release curative properties when steeped in hot water.

C

Cacao Creole a brand of chocolate liqueur made from cocoa beans blended with rum. A main ingredient in the drink Cacao L'amour, that is mixed with Bounty Rum, fresh coconut cream and nutmeg.

cafetales coffee plantations near Santiago de Cuba built by French coffee and sugar planters in the early 1800s

café carib a rum-based cocktail including Tia Maria liqueur, dark rum, coffee and whipped cream

café con leche translated from the Spanish, meaning coffee with milk. Similar to *café au lait*. Café con leche is made from boiled milk, sugar and espresso coffee.

café cubano simple Cuban coffee preparation requiring cold water, a Cuban blend and around eight teaspoons of sugar

calabaza term for pumpkin in the Spanish islands

calamares Cuban squid tapas

calas a popular fritter in Curaçao with black-eyed **phulouri** peas and onions. Similar to **akkra**.

caldillo cubano Cuban hotpot made with braised steak, onions, tomatoes, potatoes, hot peppers, garlic, brown sugar, cumin seeds and corn oil

callaloo spelled a multitude of ways including *callaloo*, *calaloo*, *calalou* or *callalou* it also has several meanings. In the eastern Caribbean the term refers to the leaves of the **dasheen**. In Jamaica it is a leafy, spinach-like green also known as Indian kale or Chinese spinach. It also refers to the savory soup for which it is the main ingredient accompanying pumpkin, **pigeon peas**, crabs, beans, dumplings, pepper sauce and a nourishing yellow broth. Popularly used to refer to Trinidad's eclectic cultural mix.

calypso native to Trinidad, this music and rhythm is derived from the *caiso*, singing of West Africa. Early calypsonians were mouthpieces for the community. They spun actual incidents into social and political commentary. Stick-fighting chants also became a part of calypso, endowing it with rhythm, melody and a unique combative style.

camarones shrimp appetizer popular in Cuba

campo colloquial Cuban term for the countryside

cantiques religious and festive songs sung at Christmas

carambola also known as star fruit this yellow fruit is most often used in fruit salads or simply eaten raw

Carib American Indian people who inhabited the Lesser Antilles and parts of the neighboring South American coast at the time of the Spanish conquest, to which they responded with mass suicides rather than suffer enslavement. The Island Carib were warlike and allegedly cannibalistic. The last remaining Carib reserve is located in Dominica.

Caribbean guacamole this green dip differs from the avocado-based guacamole of Latin cultures with papaya being the main ingredient and peppers and local hot sauce added for seasoning

Caribbean lobster although the spiny lobster lacks meaty claws its tail meat is delicious. Due to over-fishing in the Caribbean, lobster is growing scarce. However, enforced lobster seasons have been adopted to preserve numbers.

Caribbean seasoning this spice mixture includes cayenne, salt, white pepper, black pepper, dried basil, dried thyme and paprika, but is modified to the taste of each cook throughout the Caribbean

carnicero Cuban meat loaf. A combination of minced pork, onion, salsa, breadcrumbs, egg, mustard powder, tomato puree, vinegar, brown sugar, pineapple juice, rosemary and anejo rum.

carrucho the term used for **conch** in the Spanish islands, especially in Puerto Rico

cascadura also known as *hassar*, when stewed in a pot with broth, this local fish of Trinidad and Tobago is said to guarantee that those who consume it will return to Trinidad

cashew the popular name for this native nut of the Americas is derived from the Amerindian word *acaju*. Preserves are made from the red cashew apple – the stalk of the flower which produces the nut. Care must be taken when harvesting cashews, to drain off a poisonous liquid found in the shell. Cashews can be eaten raw but are generally roasted and eaten as snacks.

cassava a staple root vegetable in the Caribbean diet. Cassava has been processed into a vast range of products in South America and the Caribbean since pre-Columbian times. It contains hydrocynanic acid, a toxin which must be boiled or baked out of the vegetable before use. In Jamaica *bam bam* is the collective term used for food made from cassava such as bread, pancakes and muffins.

cassia Until the 19th century when cinnamon became available in the Caribbean, the cinnamon-like bark of the cassia tree was used as a substitute.

cerasee the slightly bitter leaf from the cerasee plant is well known for its medicinal properties. It has traditionally been prepared as tea for the treatment of diabetes mellitus in the Caribbean because it helps to build glucose tolerance.

chalice also *chillum* or *chalewa*. A pipe for smoking during Rasta ritual. It is usually made from coconut shell and rubber tubing or some form of natural tubing.

channa generic term referring to chick-pea dishes eaten by East Indians from Trinidad

chayote *see* **christophene**

cherimya *see* **sweetsop**

chicharrón deep-fried pork rinds popular in Puerto Rico

chicharrón de dieta literally, 'diet' deep-fried pork rinds, popular in Puerto Rico

chicharrón de pollo chicharrón with chicken skin. Flour batter is used to add volume and texture to this Puerto Rican specialty.

chicken pelau a chicken and rice dish from the islands of Trinidad and St Vincent

chile *see* **hot pepper**

chilled cucumber soup a light summer soup from Barbados

chispa tren literally means 'train sparks' and is an apt name for this rum-based Cuban firewater

chorizo originally a Spanish staple that varies according to local spice recipes. Typically seen hanging in butcher shop windows, these meat marvels actually crumble when added to a dish instead of staying intact. This characteristic causes the flavor to spread throughout any dish. Mix chorizo with eggs to create a classic fiesta meal.

christophene this popular Caribbean vegetable has many names, including *mirliton*, *chocho*, *xuxu*, *vegetable pear*, or *chayote*. Green and pear shaped, it grows on a tropical vine that is related to the cucumber and can be used in almost all recipes that call for zucchini.

churros a Puerto Rican treat of donut-like ribbed strips stuffed with chocolate, vanilla or strawberry filling

chutney mango, sorrel or tamarind chutneys are served with many curry dishes, and with meats, salads and sandwiches. Chutney is also used as a spread or dip on cheese and crackers. Musically, chutney refers to bawdy folk music brought from India by indentured laborers.

cilantro (coriander) this wild spice belonging to the chervil, cumin and dill family is common across the islands. Referred to as *culantro* on the Spanish islands and *shadow bennie* in Trinidad.

cinnamon this popular spice is thought to be an aphrodisiac. The Spanish islands made do with bark from the cassia (a similarly flavoured spice) until cinnamon was available for import.

coco see **taro**

coco bread also known as *toto*, *coconut bread* or *buns* in Jamaica. Refers to coconut cake shaped into loaves, served as desserts or snacks. Ingredients include whole-wheat flour, freshly grated coconut and, occasionally, raisins.

coco quemado coconut pudding. The literal translation of this Cuban dish is 'burnt coconut', however, the finished pudding – a combination of sugar, water, grated coconut, egg yolks, cinnamon and white rum – simply needs to be browned under a griller.

cloves a pungent, fragrant spice well known world-wide and cultivated in the Caribbean by the French and Dutch. Cloves are dry, unopened buds that look like nails. The word clove is derived from the Latin word for nail, *clavus*. On the Spanish islands cloves are known as *clavo*. Cloves appear in numerous Caribbean dishes.

coconut cream the thickened cream scooped off the top of **coconut milk** once it has been allowed to sit until it separates

coconut milk to make, pour 2 cups boiling water over 4 cups grated fresh coconut, and allow the mixture to stand for 30 minutes. It is then squeezed to extract the milk.

coconut water a young coconut between six and nine months contains about 750ml of water. It is from this water or juice that the flesh of the nut forms. Although a sports drink has recently been developed from coconut water, locals prefer to take a machete to the base of a fresh coconut, pour in a little local rum, and enjoy a great Caribbean drink in its 'unlabeled' form.

codfish This cold-water, deepwater fish is not native to the Caribbean, but is a Caribbean staple used in dishes such as ackee & saltfish as well as **akkra**. Also eaten for breakfast. The fish is soaked in water to remove the salt, roasted on a coal fire, shredded and then seasoned with spices. It is served with cucumber and tomatoes.

colombo generic term for curry. The Indian community introduced curries to the Caribbean. Colombo de porc, a combination of pork, black pepper, garlic, hot pepper, lemon juice, peanut oil, green onions, curry powder, allspice, cloves, parsley, thyme, eggplant, zucchini and christophene is one popular curry.

colombo de poisson curry made with white fish or shark, poached in a broth with onions, coconut cream, lime juice and dark rum. This dish can also be made with lamb and chicken, but the fish version is most popular.

comedor a cafeteria, dining room or eatery

conch pronounced 'conk' and called *lambis* on French islands, this large marine snail with an attractive ornamental shell is often souvenired by tourists. Tough, meaty conch flesh can be broiled, used in salads or in conch chowder, or as 'cracked' conch seasoned with spices.

congo peas *see* **gungo peas** and **pigeon peas**

congri santiago Creole stew popular in Cuba

consommé à l'orange a Haitian summer soup made with chicken stock, orange juice, ground **allspice**, salt and white pepper

coo-coo from Trinidad and Tobago, a dish of steamed **breadfruit** and cornmeal pudding topped with steamed fish

Corilla also known as bitter melon, *carailla*, *caraili* or bitter gourd, this dark green vegetable-like fruit is extremely bitter when ripe. Conversely, its bright red seeds are sweet. Corilla is used in curries and pepper sauces. The leaves of the Corilla bush are also thought to have curative properties.

cotta a roll of cloth used to cushion the skull from the weight of a load carried on the head. Also known as *kata*.

crab backs also known as *siri* in Brazil, crab meat is mixed with seasonings and breadcrumbs to form a pâté that is served in the crab shell

crabes farcies a delicacy in the French islands these land crabs are stuffed with French herbs and breadcrumbs

crème de vie this Cuban eggnog is a favorite at Christmas. A syrupy mixture is combined with milk, vanilla and egg yolks, and served cold in a decorative bottle.

croquetas Cuban ham croquettes are very popular at restaurants, walk-up counters and bakeries all over Miami, a reflection of their popularity in Cuba itself. Chicken croquetas are also extremely popular. Though croquetas can be baked it is argued that they are best fried and eaten fresh and hot.

Cuba bella Cuban cocktail that includes light dry rum, extra aged dry rum, lime juice, crème de menthe, cracked ice, sliced orange and **hierbabuena** mint

Cuba libre rum-based Cuban cocktail that also includes lime juice, lime peel, ice and cola

Cuba linda a Cuban cocktail made with French dry vermouth and light dry rum garnished with a single olive and a scraping of lemon peel

Cuban pound cake drenched in sweet wine or rum syrup and requiring numerous eggs, this cake is an incredibly rich but popular Cuban specialty

cubanito a Cuban cocktail made from light dry rum, lime juice, Worcestershire sauce, tomato juice, salt, pepper and ice cubes

Cubita Cuba's national coffee label

culantro *see* **cilantro**

cumin aromatic seeds most commonly used to flavor meat or fish

Curaçao liqueur the Spanish introduced Valencia oranges to the Caribbean but the species never thrived, producing sour, inedible fruit. The rinds, however, were found to yield an aromatic oil ideal for flavoring drinks. The Curaçao factory is situated at Chobola, one of Curaçao's Dutch farmhouses.

curry Caribbean curry is a mixture of spices used to flavor chicken, goat, beef or oxtail. Drawing inspiration from India, Asia and America, common ingredients include **cilantro**, hot chile powder, **garam masala**, poppyseed, green cardamom, cumin seed, black mustard and ground ginger. Caribbean curry dishes are served with either rice & peas or in roti.

custard apple also known as the sugar apple, custard apple is from the same family as the **soursop** and is used similarly to both the soursop and the **sweetsop**.

cutchie communal smoking pipe

D

daal split peas usually cooked as a thick soup, introduced by Indian indentured servants

daiquiri named after Daiquiri a small town in Cuba, this classic cocktail contains rum, lime juice and syrup or sugar. Fresh fruit can also be added.

dasheen also known as taro root, dasheen was brought to the Caribbean from the South Pacific. A starchy, potato-like tuber with brown, fibrous skin and gray-white (sometimes purple-tinged) flesh. Though acrid-tasting in its raw state, the root has a somewhat nutlike flavor when cooked. Some varieties are highly toxic unless thoroughly cooked. Dasheen's large edible leaves are called **callaloo**. *See* **tannia chips**.

deaders Rasta dialect for meat or meat by-products

djon-djon mushrooms from north Haiti. The djon-djons used in *riz djon-djon* (rice with mushrooms) are small black mushrooms with an inedible stem that lend this dish an exquisite color, taste and aroma. Riz djon-djon is a side dish typically served with **griots**, fish or other meats during the main course of a meal.

dreadlocks hair that is neither combed nor cut. A person with dreadlocks is known as a dread or dready.

dready a friendly, warm fellow; a person with dreadlocks

drumfish *see* **kingfish**

dub electronic music featuring poetic verse with music created by re-engineering previously recorded tracks

dukunu Jamaicans refer to this delicious snack made of **plantain**, green banana, **cassava** or cornmeal, in myriad ways, including *dokono, dokunu, blue drawers* and *tie-a-leaf*. A common version is sweetcorn dumplings wrapped and steamed in banana leaves.

dumplings made from flour, water and eggs, dumplings range in size and preparation from island to island. Dumplings are moulded into oblong-shaped portions and either baked or fried. Small dumplings are found in soups such as the famous red beans, dumplings & pigs' feet.

dutchie a heavy, round-bottomed pot used for general cooking as well as roasting coffee

E

eddo *see* **coco**

enchilados meanings vary in both Latin America and the Caribbean. However, on the islands the word generally refers to stuffed tortilla snacks. Although fillings vary, a variety of fish or meat are always the main ingredients.

empanas Cuban meat and vegetable patties

ensalada Cuban term for salad

ensalada Cubana tipica a simple, Cuban salad made with tomatoes, iceberg lettuce, radishes and white onion dressed with garlic, olive oil, vinegar and lemon juice

ensalada de pepinos y col salad of finely sliced cucumber, chopped cabbage and olive oil

ensalata mixta Cuban term for a mixed salad or, more specifically, diced vegetable salad

escargot calypso garlic butter is the classic sauce for escargots and this rum-enhanced preparation is a slightly different but equally appealing approach

escovitch *escobeche, escoveitch* and *caveach* all mean 'pickled' and refer to a method of marinating seafood in lime and seasonings.

Eskabaycheh is a soup made with pickled onions and chicken or fish **escovitch**

everything cook and curry an expression used throughout the English-speaking Caribbean that means 'everything is well and taken care of'

F

fajitas means 'small thin belts' and refers to marinated strips of steak

Fanta imported from North America and sold in glass bottles, this orange soda has long been a favorite soft drink on the islands

farine grated **cassava** that has been roasted in a giant wok, often eaten with avocado or gravy. It is also used as a side dish like potato or rice. Farine is often eaten in villages with **codfish** on rainy days when the fishermen cannot sail.

feroce a dip from Martinique made of avocado, **cassava** flour and hot peppers, similar to guacamole but made with cassava meal for a stiffer consistency. Can also include shredded cod. Also called *féroce*, *ferace* and *féroce d'avocat*.

festival small oblong piece of fried bread eaten with **jerk** in Jamaica

fete from the French word festival. Fete refers to parties with music, dance and food.

finger pepper an extremely hot variety of chile

fit Jamaican word referring to fruit and vegetables that are fully grown and ready to be picked though not necessarily ripe

fizzy coconut a favorite drink in St Lucia, made from Coco Cristal, orange juice, vodka, coconut jelly and lemonade.

flan the original baked custard flan is rich in evaporated and condensed milk and packed with eggs. This fluffy traditional dessert is topped with a glaze of thick rich caramel browned during baking.

flan de coco 'coconut flan' is a cold dessert made with condensed and evaporated milk, coconut cream and egg. It is a regional variation of the classic caramel **flan**.

flanked fish cooked with local seasonings, and most often served with cornmeal and flour **pan bati**. This specialty dish is popular in Aruba and marries Dutch and African culinary influences.

floating islands Although eaten throughout the islands, both Jamaica and Barbados claim this dessert as their own. Known as *isla flotante* in the Spanish islands, its origin lies in the French dessert *oeufs à la Neige*.

fly fish commonly found in tropical waters, particularly throughout the Caribbean. Its name is derived from its ability to soar through the air for great distances. The flying fish builds up speed in the water, and then leaps into the air, extending its large, stiff pectoral fins, which act like wings. Flying fish have a firm texture and a pleasant, savory flavor. They are best battered in flour and fried. Extremely popular in Barbados.

fowl down-in-rice a Barbadian dish of chicken with rice, lime juice and mustard

fried wontons pork wrapped in light pastry. Served either baked or fried with a ginger sauce, or floating in a broth or soup.

frijoles the generic Spanish term for beans

frijoles bayos cilantro a simple Cuban dish of black beans and cilantro

frijoles negros con ron y miel al horno honey-rum-baked black beans is the Cuban version of the American classic Boston baked beans. It takes nearly an entire day to bake but it is worth the wait.

frogs referred to as mountain chicken in Dominica, frogs' legs are a national delicacy. Stewed or fried they taste like chicken and are used much like chicken. Cooks have to hunt for their own frogs since they are not available from markets.

fronta Jamaican referring to the tobacco used to roll marijuana

fruta bomba a Cuban expression for papaya

fry bake a circular flatbread that is fried just enough to make the outer dough crispy while the inside remains soft and chewy

fufu a hot dish of mashed **plantains** similar to mashed potatoes. It is flavored with garlic and lime, and pieces of roast pork are added to the mash.

G

ganja patois for marijuana. Also known as herb.

garam masala an aromatic spice mix of cardamom, **cilantro**, peppercorn, caraway seed, cumin, mustard seed, cloves, fenugreek and cinnamon that enhances the flavor and fragrance of curries

garlic known as *ajo* on the Spanish islands. Cubans love **alioli**, or garlic mayonnaise made from olive oil, lemon juice, salt, pounded garlic and sometimes egg yolk.

gelleticas de guayaba y mantequilla de mani these guava and peanut butter cookies are a variation on American peanut butter and jelly. Mango peanut butter cookies are a tasty version.

ginger globally popular, this eminently useful knotty rhizome is a favorite across the islands

ginger ale ginger-flavored drink, which is used for mixing spirits

ginger beer made in both non-alcoholic and alcoholic forms, the carbonated version of this brew tastes like ginger ale but stronger. This traditional drink has many health benefits such as protection from stroke and heart attack because of its ability to help prevent blood-clotting, reduction of inflammations and/or pain as an alternative to aspirin, a tonic for digestion, cholesterol reduction, relief from motion sickness, coughs, colds, colon and stomach spasms, constipation, indigestion, gas, headaches, morning sickness and sinus congestion. Ginger beer sooths sore throats and has been proven to relieve menstrual cramps and upset stomach.

goat East Indians use goat extensively and historically it took the place of lamb in most diets

gombay refers to one of two fruit-based bottled drinks drunk by Bahamian kids

grapefruit many experts believe grapefruit originated in Jamaica. It was a well-established staple long before other islands or countries had heard of it. The name is said to reflect the perceived taste similarity between the grapefruit and grapes.

green banana *see* **banana**

green herb sauce an extremely versatile sauce made from watercress leaves, tarragon, onions and spices. It can accompany any fish, be used as a dip for crudités,

spread on sandwiches or tossed into a salad of vegetables and cooked pasta.

grenadine made from pomegranate juice and used to sweeten and color drinks such as **sevilla**, a Cuban cocktail.

griots tasty Haitian treat made by boiling then frying cubes of pork. Usually presented in the main course of a meal and accompanied by peas & rice or **riz djon-djon** and **bananes pesees**. Most Haitians eat their griots with fiery hot **ti-malice** sauce.

groundnut soup in the Caribbean peanuts are also known as groundnuts. This soup, popular on St Kitts includes either groundnut or corn oil, onion, green or red pepper, chicken stock, cream, chives, salt and pepper.

guanabana *see* **soursop**

guarana high in caffeine, this nut was used by the Amerindians for medicinal purposes. It is now used in many energy drinks.

guava native to the Americas it is used to flavor many preparations including juice, jelly, ice cream and cheese. Round with green to yellow-pink skin, the flesh is dotted with little seeds and is deliciously aromatic. In Cuba, guava is also known as *guayabillo*. In the Cuban province of Pinar del Río a slightly tart variety called *guayabita*, is used for the liqueur *Guayabita del Pinar*.

guava gelatima guama guava jelly. The Cuban recipe calls for guava, water, granulated sugar, lime juice and **allspice**.

guava guayaba in Spanish, this term refers to any fruit eaten raw, turned into juice, candy jam or jelly. Guava jelly is rich and smooth. It is an excellent accompaniment to roast lamb and **jerk** shrimp.

güero a musical instrument made from a hollowed-out gourd that is tapped with a stick to produce a hollow sound

guinep small green stone fruit with apricot-colored flesh. Guineps grow in abundance in St John where they are relished as after-school snacks. They also make lovely jelly.

guisos Cuban stews and sauces

gungo peas green and brown peas common in many dishes. Also known as **pigeon** or **congo peas**.

H

habanos Cuban term for cigars that is an adaptation of Habana, the Cuban spelling for Havana, Cuba's capital. This term is slowly replacing the established Havanas used in the English-speaking world to refer to cigars made in Cuba.

harddo bread a typically thick Caribbean white bread similar to, but drier than, sourdough bread

hassar see **cascadura**

Havana comodoro popular Cuban cocktail made with extra–aged rum, pineapple juice, a dash of **maraschino**, a dash of **Curaçao** and ice cubes

Havana libre rum-based Cuban cocktail made with gold rum, extra aged rum, **grenadine**, lime juice, mint and ice cubes

helado Cuban ice cream

hibiscus this beautiful tropical plant is a favorite in the tropics since it blooms so profusely and all parts of the plant are edible. The leaves are used to adorn plates, the flowers to decorate the table and the petals to make a gorgeous, vibrantly colored tea that's drunk either hot or cold.

higglers primarily women who buy and sell imported goods in the Jamaican markets.

hierbabuena a variety of Cuban mint. The Spanish word means 'good grass' and is believed to have medicinal properties. Used in the popular Cuban drink **mojito**.

hojas de plátano Cuban term for banana leaves. These are used across the islands instead of plates or as a wrapping for food such as **tamales**.

hurricane leah a rum-based cocktail with a mind-blowing combination of ingredients: gin, vodka, tequila, cherry brandy, lime juice, orange juice and Blue **Curaçao**

I

iguana soup dish popular in the **ABC Islands**. Curaçao iguanas are now endangered but efforts are being made to establish iguana farms rather than plunder already depleted numbers.

irie a typical Caribbean greeting that can also mean 'excellent', 'cool' or 'outstanding'

Irish Moss Irish Moss is made from seaweed that grows among submerged rocks off coastal areas. It is widely used for its medicinal and nutritional value, and is proven to provide strength to those recovering from illness. Irish Moss is thought to be a stimulating aphrodisiac. Irish Moss is administered for tuberculosis, coughs, bronchitis and intestinal problems. It is popular as a rich creamy health drink.

island coconut lobsters local lobsters simmered in coconut cream sauce and spiked with a shot of coconut rum

isoba di bestia chiquitis a hearty stew of kid goat and vegetables popular in Aruba that has clearly been influenced by Dutch and African cuisine

ital cooking a form of cooking in keeping with the Rastafarian faith. The Rasta diet eschews meat and salt and avoids canned goods or processed foods

J

jack generic name for a family of fish including over two hundred different varieties such as amber jack, yellowtail and greenback

jackass rope homegrown tobacco that is twisted into strong multi-purpose rope

jackfruit a fleshy yellow fruit, the seed of which is eaten roasted or boiled. This huge relative of the **breadfruit** and fig can weigh up to 100 pounds. Spiny and oval or oblong-shaped, the tropical jackfruit grows in parts of Africa, Brazil and South-East Asia. When green, both its flesh and edible seeds are included in curried dishes. Ripe jackfruit has a bland, sweet flavor and is generally used for desserts.

Jamaican cigars made from Jamaican tobacco. The brand Jamaica Platinum is known for its popular rum-dipped cigars as well as vanilla-flavored cigars.

Jamaican crawler rum-based cocktail consisting of light rum, melon liqueur, fresh pineapple juice and **grenadine** a popular sweetener

jamón ham

janga Jamaican term for crayfish

jankunu also spelled *junkanoo* or *jonkonnu*. Different versions of this costumed dance are found in Jamaica and Bahamas; in Belize the costume and dance originate from a comical ridicule of slave masters. In the Bahamas the term refers to the Christmas and New Year Carnival. Also refers to one of two fruit-based bottled drinks drunk by Bahamian kids.

jelly nut refers to coconut once it is past water-bearing stage. The base is cut with a machete, the remaining water drained and the jelly nut is sliced in half. Coconut water is best drunk while the coconut is maturing. Once mature (when outer shell is brown and hairy) the remaining coconut water is thought to be rancid, however, the flesh is at its peak.

jerk a spicy marinade and method of preparing pork, chicken and occasionally fish. By no means a new technique, Jamaica's **Arawak** Indians prepared fish and meat by 'jerking'. Later the Maroons (run away slaves) adopted the method; smoking heavily seasoned wild pork over bark from the **allspice** tree. Today, for ease of preparation, many store-bought **jerk** sauces or seasonings are used to recreate the hot, spicy taste of jerk.

joints small, independent eateries

johnnycake sometimes *janny kake*. Fried or baked balls or flat discs of bread eaten at breakfast. Also used in the dish boiled fish & johnnycakes. May have derived its name from the English 'journey cake'.

Jouvay sometimes *joovay*. Derived from the French *jour ouvert*, the opening day of Carnival. Jouvay originates from the celebration of slave freedom. Jouvay begins in the wee hours of the Monday morning before Ash Wednesday. Thousands of revelers take to the streets dressed as blue or red devils or in costumes covered with mud or black oil. Witnessing sunrise after dancing all night is a transcendental experience – considered the essence of Carnival.

jub jub sugar-coated, fruit-flavored gelatin squares, also known as gummy squares. A traditional fruit candy of the Caribbean.

jump up the most common meaning refers to participants in Carnival. It's also informally used to describe gate-crashing a band, dancing at Carnival without a costume or playing in street clothes.

jump-and-wave an exuberant dance that involves jumping and waving the arms simultaneously. It looks and feels fantastic when performed by large groups of masqueraders, creating an elating sense of movement en masse.

K

kachourie East Indian split-pea fritters

kari kari a specialty dish popular in Aruba that marries Dutch and African culinary influences

karni term used for meat on the Dutch islands. Similar to the Spanish word *carne*.

kata *see* **cotta**

keshi also keshy, the term for cheese on the Dutch islands. Similar to the Spanish word *queso*.

keshi yena an unusual dish from the **ABC Islands**, for which whole Edam cheese is skinned, hollowed-out, filled with spiced chicken or seafood, and baked whole

khurma East Indian sweet snack made from flour and sugar. Shaped into long, thin pieces that are deep-fried and rolled in sugar.

kidney beans also known as red kidney beans or red peas in Jamaica. Cubans refer to them as *colorado* beans. Commonly used on the Spanish islands in rice dishes. The stewed bean dish *haricot rouges* is popular in the French Caribbean and is usually served as an accompaniment to boiled rice and vegetable dishes.

kingfish two different types of fish are referred to as kingfish. The first is actually the regional name for king mackerel. The second type, found along the Atlantic coast, applies to any of several species of drum. Kingfish can be coated with flour and fried and then steamed with lemon juice, or stewed in a **braff**. Kingfish is often served with boiled root vegetables and peas & rice.

kola is another Caribbean standard made by several different firms. Similar to cola in name only, it is copper-colored, intensely sweet and fruity. In the Bahamas, locals enjoy two fruit-based bottled drinks: **junkanoo** and **gombay**. Kids love this stuff but it might curl more mature palates.

kreng-kreng an old-fashioned meat rack, hung high over a fire to infuse the meat with smoke

krokechi term for croquettes on the Dutch islands

L

lab porridge made with any of a number of ingredients, including **cassava**, flour and **plantain**.

lambis *see* **conch**

langoustine a large prawn or small lobster

lapo cabway a single skin drum, the playing of which ushers in the beginning of Carnival

lechónerias outdoor mountainside barbecue stalls in Puerto Rico serving **lechón asado**. In Puerto Rico people travel miles to taste this meat on-site.

lechón asado small pig or pork leg roasted in an oven or earth oven and served with a light gravy and starchy side dishes

limes brought over on Columbus's second voyage to the Caribbean, limes are an essential component of the local cuisine. Integral to rum punch, the juice of this fruit is used as a meat tenderizer and marinade, as an astringent for the skin and as a mosquito repellent. Cuba is the biggest lime producer in the Caribbean. The Spanish word for lime is *limon*.

M

macho asado large pig roasted in a conventional oven or earth oven

mahi mahi *dolphin fish*, *dolphin* or *dorado*. No relation to the porpoise, these brilliantly colored fish are the most delicious available in the Caribbean.

mahi mahi niçoise salad filet of dolphin fish, pan-fried and served with niçoise salad

maize also known as Indian corn, this staple food of the **Arawak** was known as *mahis* or *elote*. All three varieties of maize are used across the Caribbean including sweet corn, dent corn and popcorn.

mai tai rum-based cocktail invented in California and commonly associated with Hawaii. Aficionados will demand pure Jamaican rum. Components include lime juice, orange **Curaçao**, rock candy syrup, French **orgeat** and mint.

majarete a Puerto Rican sweet made with rice flour

malta a non-alcoholic, beer-like soft drink that is a primary ingredient in the popular health drink **Irish Moss**

mammee apple the pink-orange flesh of the mammee apple is good either raw or stewed, and makes excellent chutney.

mango eaten raw and whole or used in fruit salads, mangoes are high in vitamins A, C and D. Brought to the Caribbean by Indian indentured servants, mangoes are now used fresh in various vegetable and lentil dishes. Also used to tenderize meat (just like papaya, green mango contains enzymes that will break down connective tissue).

mannish water a goat curry popular in Jamaica. Often, the goat's head will be used.

manzanas candy apples

maraschino a liqueur made from marasca cherries. Maraschino tastes like bitter almonds.

marché de legumes the term for vegetable market on the French islands

mariquitas Cuban term for deep-fried **plantain**

Maroons bands of African people in Jamaica who were able to escape their English captors by living in the rugged mountainside. During the British occupation, Maroon numbers escalated as escapees headed to the hills.

Maroon societies have been an important element in the preservation of African culture in the Caribbean and the continuing existence of which are a symbol of pride in a history of oppression.

matapie hanging sack used for the critical stage during the making of **cassava** bread when grated cassava pulp is separated from its highly poisonous juice

mauby bark a bitter tonic made by boiling the bark of the mauby with water and rosemary. A favorite in the Eastern Caribbean. Useful in cleansing the body of excess salt.

mavi Puerto Rican cidar extracted from the bark of the ironwood

mint commonly referred to as *menta* on the Spanish islands. However, its Spanish botanical name is *herbabuena* or *herbabuena,* which is also the term for the mint variety used in **mojito** a Cuban cocktail.

mobbie according to a travel writer of the 1600s, this malty beverage was made from sweet potatoes, which resulted in an alcoholic beverage of reddish hue

mofongo a Puerto Rican dish for which mashed **plantains** are fried and either added to or wrapped around a **sofrito**-based stew

mojito rum-based cocktail that includes lime juice, soda water, sugar and a sprig of **hierbabuena** or *herbabuena* mint. Made famous by Ernest Hemingway who favored this tipple when dining at Cuba's well-known restaurant, *La Bodeguita del Medio.*

molondrones *see* **okra**

montell a man who befriends women in the pursuit of financial gain; a gold-digger

moros y cristianos literally 'Moors and Christians', referring to a dish of black beans & rice. The Diaspora have been eating black beans since the Moors invaded Spain in the late 8th century. Traditionally black beans are served on top of cooked white rice, however, in this dish the beans & rice are cooked together.

mulata invented by Cuban barman Jose Maria Vazquez in the 1940s this cocktail is a blend of aged rum, crème de cacao, lime juice and ice. It is served in a cocktail glass, sprinkled with chocolate.

N

nacional Cuban cocktail made from a mixture of gold rum, apricot brandy, pineapple juice, lime juice and cracked ice

nanny an infusion of dried anise leaves and stems in rum. The rum extracts and absorbs the flavour and greenish color of the anise. To be drunk as a shot and chased with water.

nasi goreng spicy fried rice with chicken and chopped vegetables. An Indonesian dish popular on the Dutch islands.

natural still water

Noche Buena Christmas Eve

nutmeg a popular spice throughout the islands. Nutmeg is grown for commercial export on the island of Grenada.

nyam Jamaican for 'to eat'

O

obeah traditional African science and religious practice, relating to matters of the spirit, spells, divination, omens and extra-sensory knowledge. Popular throughout the Caribbean, the most powerful obeah is said to be practised by the African Diaspora, in Haiti.

okra green pods also known in the Spanish islands as *quimbombó* and in the Dominican Republic as *molondbrones*. Okra have ridged skin and a tapered, oblong shape. They can be prepared in a variety of ways such as braising, baking and frying. When cooked, okra gives off a rather viscous substance that serves to thicken any liquid in which it is cooked. It is best in okra soup and **yambo**. Fresh okra contains fair amounts of vitamins B and C.

olives both olive oil and olives are commonly used in Cuban cooking. However, in pioneering times Cubans were banned from cultivating olives or olive oil, lest their efforts affect the income of Spanish traders.

one love a parting phase or expression of unity in Jamaica

opstayz hous the traditional style of Creole house with the living areas built at least 8 or 10ft off the ground on posts. This construction provides an outside shaded area underneath for daytime activities, greater security upstairs and escape from low-flying insects, as well as snakes and high water.

orgeat an almond-flavored, non-alcoholic flavoring syrup

oregano an aromatic herb generally used in meat and tomato sauces but is also for medicinal purposes

ostiones a Cuban delicacy that is both a drink and an appetizer. Made with half a dozen sweet mussels or oysters, white rum, lime juice, salt and pepper, Tabasco sauce and tomato juice.

otaheite apples also called *ambarella* these are native to the Pacific islands and grown in tropical and subtropical regions, the yellow, egg-shaped fruit is eaten fresh or pickled

oxtail in times past the oxtail referred exclusively to oxtail meat. But nowadays the term generally refers to beef or veal tail. Bony but

CARIBBEAN CULINARY DICTIONARY

flavorful depending on the age of the animal, oxtail requires slow braising. Often served in roti or featured in stews and soups such as the hearty English classic oxtail soup, which includes vegetables, barley and herbs and is often flavored with sherry or Madeira.

oxtail & butter beans traditional Caribbean stew; old fashioned, economical and full of goodness

oysters near Caroni Swamp in Trinidad, mangrove oysters thrive amid the tropical vegetation. On other islands mangrove oysters can be found but numbers are dwindling as mangroves are cleared.

oysters caribe a delectable combination of bacon, garlic, roasted pepper, mango and breadcrumbs on oysters

P

paladares Cuban house-based restaurants that offer some of the best food in Cuba including the hearty home-style dish *pollo asado* (roast chicken)

palm chestnut once a staple in the diet of the Amerindians, these oil-rich nuts must be boiled in salt water for a couple of hours before they're ready to eat

palm oil palm oil is extracted from the boiled, crushed flesh of the palm fruit or palm nut and used instead of olive oil or corn oil

paloon wooden bowl that **mofongo** is served in

pan bati a relatively sweet, thick, pancake-shaped, Aruban griddle bread made with cornmeal

pan Cubano typical Cuban bread made from flour similar to tortilla

panaades minced fish wrapped in a fried soft tortilla. Known as *empañada* in Spanish.

panetela a cigar shape or model usually around 5 inches in length and 37/64ths of an inch in girth (cigar length is measured in inches, while girth is measured in 64ths of an inch). Many brands offer their own version of this shape, and in each case the dimensions may differ slightly, as well as the name of the cigar. Some of these include the Cohiba Panetela, Le Hoyo du Gourmet and the Gloria Cubana Médaille d'Or #3.

papas brava a traditional Spanish potato dish. Served with eggs for breakfast or as an accompaniment to meat dishes.

papaya also known as pawpaw, this fruit grows widely throughout the Caribbean. The flesh and leaves contain a tenderizing enzyme, which softens the toughest meat. Unripened green papaya is often used in chutneys and salads. The fully ripened, bright orange papaya is eaten fresh and included in drinks.

Papiamento/Papimiento Language spoken in the Dutch Islands of Aruba, Bonaire and Curaçao. Papiamento is a blend of Dutch, Portuguese, Spanish, English, French and African.

parang Christmas music sung in Trinidad and involving carolling from house to house. In recent times private and public performances have been organised during the parang season from early October to 6 January.

parrillada Cuban poolside 'grills' that serve a range of hot snacks

passionfruit grows on a vine and resembles a thick-skinned plum, has yellow or orange translucent flesh with a tart, citrus-like flavor that is wonderful in sorbets, jams and tropical drinks

patchoi a bastardization of *bok choi*, the cabbage-like vegetable essential in Chinese cooking

pate en pot tripe soup

Patois spoken throughout the Caribbean, patois refers to a dialect that combines the diverse linguistic influences of the Caribbean. In Jamaica, patois is predominantly rooted in the English language, whereas some of the smaller islands speak a Creole patois that draws heavily from French.

pattie similar to the Latin American *empanada*, Jamaican patties are flaky pastry filled with spiced sea-soning. This popular snack food is filled with chicken, vegetable, beef, shrimp, **callaloo** or soya. The beef pattie, or turnover, is Jamaica's number one fast-food.

peanut punch smooth, creamy punch made from oven-roasted peanuts, peanut butter spices, cream and rum. Served on ice.

peer on some islands in the Caribbean an avocado is referred to as *peer* or pear. In Cuba avocado is known as *aguacate*.

pelau refers to a mash-up or mix of meat or fish with rice and vegetables. Similar to the Spanish paella.

pepper called **ají** in the Spanish islands, the word refers mostly to the small, spicy peppers, chopped up and used fresh or in **pepper sauce**. Some are extremely hot, but flavorful.

pepper sauce a blend of hot peppers, garlic and spices. The Scotch bonnet pepper reigns hottest among peppers and is the most commonly used in this condiment.

pepper wine made from small hot peppers that are soaked for several days in dry sherry. The sherry picks up heat from the peppers, and serves as a lively addition to soups, stews and other dishes.

perino an ancient Amerindian drink. Perino was originally made by toothless Amerindian women who chewed **cassava** roots into mush before spitting them into containers filled with fresh water. Saliva enzymes started fermentation that resulted in a crude brew.

petit punch an aperitif, similar to **punch vieux** that is extremely popular on the French islands. Made from a mixture of syrup, white rum, ice and a small piece of lime rind or peel. Also known as *punch au petit citron vert* (punch with green lime) or *punch blanc* (white punch).

phulouri a sort of fritter made with black-eyed peas and onions and popular in Trinidad. Similar to the Curaçao dish **calas**, its origins can be traced back to West Africa. *see* **akkra**.

picadillo a ground beef hash with bell peppers, raisins, ham, spices, olives and rice. The rice, meat mixture and eggs are layered and served hot. Although popular in Latin America, in the Caribbean, picadillo is undisputably Cuban.

pickapeppa a pepper sauce made and bottled in Jamaica

pickled pigs' ears served as an appetizer, this delicacy is popular in Aruba, Curaçao and Bonaire

pigeon peas native to Africa, these tiny legumes are also called **congo peas** and no-eyed peas. They are particularly popular in the southern states of the US where they grow in long, twisted fuzzy pods.

Pigeon peas are cooked like dried beans.

pimentón Spanish for pepper – both the spice and capsicum

pina *see* **pineapple**

pina colada refreshing rum-based cocktail made from a mixture of light rum, coconut milk and crushed pineapple. In fact, pina colada means 'strained pineapple'.

pineapple *ananas* or *pina* in Spanish, the flesh of this native Caribbean fruit takes about fifteen months to reach maturity. When Columbus clamped his eyes on the sweet fruit's prickly exterior (resembling pine cones) he called them *piñas*. The **Caribs** called them *ananas*, the name by which they are known in France. Used in myriad ways, some of the more inventive uses include as a meat tenderizer or as a vessel for the refreshing rum-based cocktail **pina colada**.

pizza al momento Cuban pizzas. 'Al momento' shouldn't be taken literally. In Cuba pizzas are not pre-made; queuing is the norm.

plantain a very large, firm banana variety, also referred to as 'cooking banana'. It has a mild, almost squash-like flavor and is used as potatoes are in much of the western world. Served boiled, sliced and fried, or in stews or boil-ups. Its leaves are used to wrap foods for steaming.

plantain chips Caribbean version of potato chips made from sliced, deep-fried **plantain**

planter's punch also known as milk punch, an alcoholic drink made from a mixture of liquor (typically rum, whisky or brandy), milk, sugar and vanilla. The mixture is usually blended with crushed ice and strained into a tall glass.

plantos dulce fritos fried **plantain**, cooked in such a way as to release its sweetness

play mass to put on a costume, masquerade and participate in a *mas* (Carnival) band or as an individual. The expression 'to play mas' has found its way into Trinidadian vernacular and means to enjoy yourself to the fullest or express yourself to the extreme, as only you are able to do.

poisson en blaff made with red snapper or kingfish, poisson en blaff requires marinating the fish in lime, pepper, garlic and salt, then boiling it in a sauce. Often prepared right on the beach.

pollo en salsa chicken in sauce. with onions, sweet peppers and a pinch of oregano.

poulet au lait de coco a Haitian dish that is a combination of French, Spanish and Indian influences. Ingredients include peanut oil, chicken, curry powder, onions, saffron, paprika, hot peppers, coconut milk, salt and black or white pepper.

prickly pear also known as Indian fig or *higo jumbo*, its tasty red flesh can be eaten raw or used to make jam. The young leaves of the prickly pear are used in stews and salads.

pudin de Pan *see* **bread pudding**

puerco asado pig roasted in a conventional oven or earth oven. Roast pig is the customary way to for Cubans to celebrate **Noche Buena** (Christmas Eve). The roasting of a pig is an all-day process.

pumpkin known as **calabaza** in the Spanish islands Caribbean pumpkins are renowned for being firm succulent and sweetly flavored.

punch in the French islands, punch is the word used to describe mixed drinks or fruit- or spice-flavored liquor such as **ti-punch**

punch vieux (old punch) a simple, elegant aperitif similar to **petit punch** and popular on the French islands. Made from a mixture of cane juice, rum, water and ice.

Q

quebrahacha from Curaçao this drink is made from a mixture of white rum, orange **Curaçao**, lime juice and ice.

queso fruta bomba Cuban appetizer of warm papaya and cheese

quimbombós *see* for **okra**

R

Rastafarian (Rasta) a member of the politico-religious movement practised among members of the black population. Rastafarians worship Haile Selassi, the former emperor of Ethiopia, under his pre-coronation name, Ras (prince) Tafari. Rastafarian lifestyle may include dietary strictures like opting for uncombed locks and beards; vegetarianism; or smoking marijuana.

red snapper by far the best known and most popular fish in the Caribbean is the red snapper, so named because of its reddish-pink skin and red eyes. Its flesh is firm-textured and contains very little fat. Red snapper grows to 35lbs but is most commonly sold in the 2–8lb range. The smaller ones are often sold whole, while larger snappers can be purchased in steaks and fillets. Red snapper can be fried, broiled or boiled, but it is best broiled with spices, onions and tomatoes.

rijsttafel banquets old-style Dutch-Indonesian ceremonial banquets that feature up to thirty dishes. Common in the **ABC Islands.**

riz djon-djon Haitian dish of rice with mushrooms

robusta also known as canephora. Unlike delicately flavored arabica beans, robusta beans produce a strong, crudely-flavored brew. Consequently the beans are generally used in coffee blends rather than on their own. Robusta plants are hardy, with a strong resistance to pests and diseases.

rolos de primavera spring rolls

ropa vieja a shredded beef dish from Cuba

rosemary brought to the Caribbean by early Spanish settlers, the Spanish term for this popular culinary herb is *romero*

roti flour pancake traditionally wrapped around meat and potato curry. Though East Indian in origin, like many Caribbean dishes, roti has been localized. Sold in rustic roadside roti stands as well as comfortable seated restaurants, they're filling and cheap. Roti refers to both the tortilla-like wrapping and the meal itself. The most popular fillings are curried chicken, goat, shrimp or **conch** with potato chunks and **channa** (chick peas).

royal palm indigenous to Cuba, the royal palm is also known as *palma real* or *roystonea regia*. The pulp surrounding the royal palm seed can be used in fruit salads.

rum fermented from molasses, rum is inextricably linked to the Caribbean. Dished out by village vendors, local rum is purchased and poured from large barrels into every type of container imaginable. An important ingredient for punch and **nanny**, rum is drunk as 1-2 ounce shots chased with a glass of water. However, if seeking a more refined spirit, the Caribbean boasts countles reputable distilleries with labels such as Havana Club and Mont Gay.

rum cream a smooth blend of cream, custard, spices and rum served chilled. Rum cream is a popular Christmas drink.

rundown Jamaican fish stew made by reducing coconut then adding fish (mackerel, snapper or swordfish), chopped onions, thyme and other seasonings

run dung Jamaican term used to describe food cooked in coconut milk

S

saheena East Indian spinach fritters

salmorejo de jueyes Puerto Rican crab stew with a sauce made of vinegar, oil, salt and pepper and sometimes **annatto** oil

Salpicón a traditional Cuban salad made from cold roast beef, cold roast chicken, cold boiled potatoes, stuffed green olives, capers, olive oil, spring onions, lettuce, pineapple, red and green peppers and white wine vinegar

salsa the Cuban term for sauce and for Cuba's popular form of music. Peppers are the primary ingredient along with herbs and spices.

salsa de arandano agrio con ron a holiday favorite made with cranberries, dried sour cherries, sugar, redcurrant jelly, water and rum.

saltfish a popular ingredient in Caribbean cuisine, saltfish is simply that: salted, dried fish, usually cod, though other fish (such as mackerel) is also used. A primary ingredient in Jamaica's national dish, ackee & saltfish.

sancocho Spanish term for a hearty stew with loads of vegetables and meat

saoco Cuban cocktail made from a mixture of light dry rum, fresh coconut milk and ice cubes

sate spicy grilled pieces of meat and poultry on skewers served with peanut sauce. An Indonesian-influenced dish extremely popular in the **ABC Islands**.

sazon a seasoning mixture containing ground **annatto** seeds, **cilantro** and other seasonings

scallion sometimes spelled *escallion* in Jamaican verse. It is a main ingredient in **jerk** sauce and has an intense flavour.

schaubb a Martinique Christmas drink made by immersing orange peel in a bottle of white rum and leaving it for several months

seasoned-up Caribbean dishes are full of flavor. Seasoned-up refers to the process of adding more spices and peppers to an already flavorsome dish.

sesame brought to the Caribbean by West African slaves, sesame seeds are used in a multitude of recipes from baked breads and pastries to soups and stews

sevilla Cuban cocktail named after the Sevilla Biltmore Bar. Ingredients include light dry rum, **grenadine**, lime juice, sugar syrup, **angostura bitters**, a slice of lime and cracked ice.

seville *see* **sour orange**

shadow bennie *see* **cilantro**

sidra a Spanish hard-apple cider

sky juice cocktail consisting of one part gin, one part coconut juice and a splash of sweet condensed milk. Popular in the Bahamas.

snak eateries on the islands surrounding Curaçao that offer smaller, lighter fare compared to standard restaurants

sno-cone a refreshing drink of shaved ice and sweet cherry-flavored syrup

soca a fusion of East Indian rhythms with the African musical structure of calypso. Also influenced by North American soul music. Today soca is a generic term used for the new music from Trinidad and Tobago.

sofrito this Spanish word means lightly fried or sauteed and is a potent combination of onion, green pepper, garlic, tomato, cilantro, thyme and oil. It's the backbone of many popular Puerto Rican preparations. The Cuban version usually includes peanut, corn or olive oil and sometimes peanuts and hard-boiled eggs.

solomon gundy the name is a corruption of *salmigondis*, a French salad popular in the 16th century. Jamaica's version is far from a salad but rather, is a mash of pickled fish (herring, mackerel, shad) and various spices. Eaten as a snack with johnnycakes or bread, or as an ingredient in salads, sauces and entrees, this mash is unmistakably pungent.

sopa de plátano verde a traditional green **plantain** soup for which the fresh fruit is cooked, mashed-up and then added to steaming chicken or beef broth

sopi di banana Dutch term for banana soup. Popular on Aruba, Bonaire and Curaçao.

sopi di binja wine soup as referred to on the Dutch islands

sopi di yuwana Dutch term for iguana soup.

soup jomou Haitian term for pumpkin soup

sopito fish chowder made with coconut milk, popular in Aruba

sorrel sometimes called sour grass or silver leaf, this bushy red-stemmed shrub is traditionally brewed to make sorrel drink for the Christmas season. Its spinach-like leaf are used to flavor cream soups, pureed to accompany meat or added to breads. Younger and milder versions of the leaf are used in salads or cooked as a vegetable.

sour orange also know as Seville or bitter oranges, these deep-orange fruits have thick, rough peels. In the Caribbean they are used in cooked entrees and desserts.

soursop the taste of the soursop is sweet and musky. This large, oblong fruit has a tough, green exterior with a creamy-white interior and black pumpkin-like seeds. It is eaten raw or made into juice or desserts. Rich in vitamins, the soursop acts as a mild tranquilizer. Known as *guanabana* on the Spanish islands.

souse a stew with a gravy-like texture. Can be made with fish, conch, chicken or pork.

spiny lobster also known as the Caribbean lobster it is the very same crustacean as the *langouste* in France and the Italian *aragosta*

star fruit *see* **carambola**

steel band musical ensemble whose members play on instruments constructed from steel drums. Before the onset of mobile sound trucks, steel bands provided the music for *mas* (Carnival) bands.

steel drum a drum made from a metal container. Steel drum music has an African aesthetic: repetitive, syncopated, with a strong beat and dense polyrhythms.

stobá di concomber lamb and cucumber stew from Curaçao

stout strong, dark beer that originated in the British Isles. Stout is more redolent of hops than regular beer and because the process involves dark-roasted barley it has a dark color and bittersweet flavor

sugar apple *see* **custard apple**

sunflower the seeds of the sunflower are extremely nutritious and can also be pressed and ground for oil. The Spanish term for sunflower oil is *aceite de girasol*.

surullitos Puerto Rican corn and cheese sticks

sweetsop also called *cherimoya*, or *anon* this Cuban fruit is similar in flavor to the pineapple but resembles a pine cone.

sweetbreads animal thymus glands or pancreas, collectively referred to as 'variety meats'. Perishable, sweetbreads must be precooked then cubed for salads or dipped into an egg wash and breadcrumbs and sauteed.

sweet potato this Caribbean staple is yellowish in color and has a tough consistency

T

tablette tablayta a slab of candy made with dried coconut, cashews or peanuts. A Christmas season treat, tablette is sweet, crunchy and caramelized.

tamales a food made of chicken and cornmeal wrapped in a **plantain** leaf and boiled. Latin American Spanish refer to this dish as tamales or *tamalii*, meaning a cornflour dough mixed with meat and sweet peppers wrapped in corn leaves.

tamales de carne de cerdo pork **tamales** cooked in banana leaves or cornhusks and served as appetizers. The Mexican version of tamales are filled with meat; in this Cuban rendition the meat is mixed in with the dough.

tamarind a brown colored, sour-tasting fruit used to flavor many dishes of East Indian origin

tannia chips tannia, also known as **dasheen**, **taro** or *yautia*, is sliced and deep-fried to create a local Caribbean version of potato chips

tapioca

taro a potato-like root, with hairy, brown skin known also as *coco* or *eddo*. When cooked, taro has a nut-like flavor. The flesh can be eaten hot, cold and pickled in soups or mashed.

taro root *see* **dasheen**

tassot a traditional Haitian dish for which pork, beef or poultry is dried in the sun on a hot tin roof before being marinated in spiced lime juice and then grilled

thyme one of the most popular herbs in the Caribbean. Fresh parsley, celery and thyme grown locally are simply known as 'seasonings'. The tiny oval leaves of thyme release an earthy, pungent aroma that permeates many Caribbean dishes. It is this flavor that bridges the gap between sweet and hot, spicy and delicate, making island spices such as **allspice** and nutmeg compatible with assertive flavors such as that of Scotch bonnet peppers.

Ting an export of Jamaica, Ting is a refreshing grapefruit carbonated drink. Sold in green glass single-serving bottles, it is a favorite with **roti** or **patties**.

ti-malice an important ingredient in most Haitian meals. This extra-hot sauce brings out the flavor of meat and fish dishes but can also bring tears to the eyes. Use with **griots** and with extreme caution. Components include hot yellow pepper, onion, shallots, garlic, clove, lemon juice, olive oil, salt and pepper.

ti-punch national drink of Martinique, made from a mixture of rum, sugar and lime juice. Similar to Brazilian *cipiria*, the term ti-punch is from the French *un petit* or small punch.

titiwi tiny, transparent freshwater fish. Usually battered and fried as **akkra** because they're not substantial enough to serve solo.

tuberose a tall slender plant with large very fragrant white flowers

tofu *see* **coco**

tomaton a red-skinned cherry-like fruit that can be eaten raw or made into jam

torcedores cigar factory workers in Cuba who twist loose tabacco leaves into cigars

torticas de navidad authentic Christmas cookie studded with walnuts, raisins and bright maraschino cherries

tortillas Cuban egg omelets that bear little resemblance to Mexico's famous tortillas

tostones green **plantain** cut into 1-inch slices, fried and seasoned with salt

tuna pear *see* **prickly pear**

turrones originally imported from Spain as an almond candy, turrones are now found throughout the Caribbean in flavors of chocolate, nougat, cream-walnut, honey and fruit, and egg

turtle from the earliest days of the Amerindians the people of the Caribbean have enjoyed turtle meat (particularly that of the green turtle), which is said to taste similar to veal. The Grand Cayman Green

Turtle Farm supplies much of the Caribbean with commercially farmed turtles. Other turtle species in the Caribbean include: the hawksbill, the leatherback, loggerhead and olive ridley all of which are currently endangered.

V

vanilla a product of the vanilla orchid, native to Mexico. Although the flower can only be pollinated in the wild by one type of bee and one type of hummingbird, however, an alternative method of pollination was discovered in 1841. The bean or pod has to be cured to release its beautiful flavor.

vanilla rum on some Caribbean islands, vanilla flavoring was once a rare treat. When a lucky cook got hold of a vanilla bean, it was immediately soaked in a bottle of rum to preserve the bean and to flavor the rum.

vieux agricole aged, dark rum

W

wine a dance form involving fluid pelvis rotations, either alone or in full physical contact front or back with another person. The expression comes from winding the hips in a circle. The erotic movement can be traced to various African dances. 'Jam and wine' has approximately the same meaning. Also known as win or wining.

Y

yambo the national dish of Curaçao, also known as *gumbo*. Yambo means **okra** in patois.

yams one of the world's largest crops and most important staples. In the US, yams and sweet potatoes are often confused, although the true yam is no relation to the sweet potato. In the Caribbean, yams are scruffy, hairy brown tubers the size of footballs. They make fantastic chips and, when boiled, provide a starchy counterpoint to saltfish.

yautia *see* **tannia chips**

yucca in the countries of the Latin Caribbean this root vegetable is boiled and sauteed, or sometimes cut into strips, fried and served as French fries

yucca con mojo **yucca** that is boiled and then sauteed with a garlic sauce.

Z

zapote also known as *naseberry*, *sapodilla*, *sapote* or *nispero*. Brown with a rough skin, the pulp is dotted with small, black seeds and can be eaten raw or made into delicious jam. The flesh has a strong aroma but subtle taste and is often used as a cake filler, for ice cream and for making custard.

zouq 'party' in Creole, zouq has come to refer to a fusion of calypso, merengue and French African music. It is sung in French or patois and is danced as a Caribbean version of Brazil's lambada. Most popular in the French islands.

Recommended Reading

Austin Clarke *Pig Tails 'n Breadfruit* The New Press (2000)

Bastrya, Judy *Caribbean Cooking* West Indies Publishing (1994)

Grant, Rosamund *Caribbean and African Cooking* Interlink Books (1998)

Gravette, Andy *Classic Cuban Cookery* Fusion Press (1999)

Hafner, Dorinda *Dorinda's Taste of the Caribbean* Ten Speed Press (1996)

Hamelecourt, Juliette *Caribbean Cookbook* Culinary Arts Institute (1980)

Harris, Dunstan *Island Barbecue* Chronicle Books (1995)

Hawkes, Alex *The Flavors of the Caribbean & Latin America* Viking (1978)

Lalbachan, Pamela *The Complete Caribbean Cookbook* Landsdowne (1994)

Mackie, Cristine *Life and Food in the Caribbean* New Amsterdam (1991)

Ortiz, Elisabeth *A Taste of Puerto Rico* Plume (1997)

Ortiz, Elisabeth *The Cooking of the Caribbean* Sainsbury (1991)

Quinn, Lucinda *Jamaican Cooking* MacMillan (1997)

Randelman, Mary *Memories of a Cuban Kitchen* MacMillan (1992)

Photo Credits

Jerry Alexander Front cover, p1, p5, p8, p9, p10, p11, p12, p13, p14, p15, p16, p17, p18, p20, p22, p24, p25, p26, p27, p28, p29, p30, p32, p33, p34, p36, p37, p38, p41, p43, p44, p45, p47, p48, p50, p51, p52, p54, p55, p56, p57, p58, p59, p60, p61, p62, p63, p65, p66, p67, p68, p70, p71, p72, p73, p74, p76, p77, p78, p79, p81, p82, p84, p85, p86, p88, p89, p90, p91, p92, p93, p94, p96, p97, p98, p99, p101, p103, p104, p106, p108, p109, p112, p114, p115, p116, p117, p118, p119, p120, p121, p124, p128, p129, p130, p131, p134, p136, p138, p144, p146, p151, p152, p153, p154, p155, p157, p158, p159, p161, p165, p168, p170, p171, p172, p173, p174, p175, p177, p178, p180, p183, p184, p187, p188, p189, p191, p192, p193, p194, p195, p196, p197, p198, p200, p201, p202, p203, p204, p205, p206, p210, p212, p214, p215, p216, p217, p218, p220, p222, p223, p224, p225, p226, p228, p229, back cover.

Jean-Bernard Carillet p142, p164.

Aaron McCoy p126.

Christina Lease p209.

Eric L. Wheater p162.

Lee Foster p40.

Michael Lawrence p139.

Veronica Garbutt p141.

A

achiote 63
ackee 21, 55
    ackee & saltfish 21, 42, 55, 131
agouti 13
ají, *see* peppers
alcoholic drinks 72-88, *see also* beer,
    rum, cocktails
    chispa tren 81
    magnum 81
    mavi 205
    schaubb 81, 127
    sky juice 81
    ti punch 81
    wine 20, 88, 164
alligator 13
allspice 63
Amerindians 11-6, 20, 23, 39, 46, 49,
    63-4, 118, 173
Anguilla 14, *see also* English islands
    under regions
ants 13
Antigua & Barbuda 14, 140, *see also*
    English islands under regions
aphrodisiacs 175
apples 21
    manzanas 205
Aruba 15, 165-76, *see also* Dutch
    islands under regions
avocado 54
    feroce 54, 164

B

Bacardí, Facundo 79, *see also* rum
Bahamas 11, 14, 27, 60, 72-3, 76, 79,
    82, 95, 122, 140-1, 179-83, 195,
    203, 206-7, *see also* English islands
    under regions
bananas 17, 20-1, 57-61
    arañitas 57
    banane pesé 57

fried plantains 58
mariquitas 57
mofongo 57, 159
tostones 57
banquets 217-22
Barbados 14, 32-3, 49, 79, 80, 110-
    11, 128, 140, *see also* English
    islands under regions
Barbuda, *see* Antigua & Barbuda
barbecue 13, 208
beans 17, 47, 109, 143-5
    moros y cristianos 47, 109, 143-5
beef 17, 21-2, 45-6, 64-7, 131-3, 147,
    182, 207
    patty 64-7, 131-3
    picadillo 147
beer 20, 31, 73-6
    Amstel 76
    Bucanero 76
    Budweiser 73
    Carib 73
    Corona 76
    Cristal 76
    Curaçao 76
    Dragon Stout 73
    Guinness 72-3
    Heineken 73-6
    Kalik 73-6
    Medalla Light 76
    Red Stripe 73
Bermuda 14, *see also* English islands
    under regions
Bonaire 15, 165-76, *see also* Dutch
    islands under regions
breadfruit 55
    coo-coo 64, 139
breads & pastries 10, 21, 29, 64-70,
    160, 170-1, 187
    alcapurrias 205
    arepas 170
    cassava bread 64
    churros 205

coco bread 133
cornbread 64
doubles 139
empanas 170-1, 176, 195
festival 64
fry bake 64
johnnycake 29, 31, 64
patty 64-7, 131-3
roti 23, 65, 139, 221
breakfast 10, 29, 64, 160
British Virgin Islands 14, 209, *see also*
    English islands under regions
butter 21

C

Caicos Islands, *see* Turks & Caicos
    Islands
cashews 17
cassava 17, 21, 49, 64
    cassava bread 64
Castro, Fidel 143, 150
caterpillar 13
Cayman Islands 14, 128, 140, *see also*
    English islands under regions
celebrating 119-28, *see also* festivals
    birthdays 121-3
    carnival 122-3
    Christmas 127
    family day 126
    new year's 114-7
Chanca, Diego Alvarez 60
chayote 55
cheese 170-1, 176, 187
    bolita di keshi 171, 176
    keshi yená 170, 176
    macaroni and cheese 130
chicken 26, 45-6, 130, 145, 207-8
    arroz con pollo 46
    fowl down-in-rice 46
    fried 130
    pan 130, 207-8
    pelau 46

pollo en salsa 145
tamales 59
chile, *see* peppers
Chinese influence 25-6, 47, 126, 139
chives 63
christophenes 55
cigars 148-50, 152-5, 200-1
    etiquette 200-1
    production 152-5
    types 148-50
    varieties 200-1
cinnamon 17
Clarke, Austin 110-1
cocktails 81-8, 212-3
    Bahama Mama 82
    Norinquen 85
    Café Carib 83
    Cuba Libre 82
    Daiquiri 82, 213
    Hurricane Leah 83
    Jamaican Crawler 83
    Mai Tai 84
    Mojito 83, 212-3
    Pina Colada 85
    Planter's Punch 84
    Ti Punch 84
coconuts 17, 142
    coconut water 90
cod 21, 39, 42-3, 176
coffee 93-102, 211
    Blue Mountain coffee 95-9
    brewing 100-2
    history 93
    regions 94-5
Columbus, Christopher 17, 54, 150
conch 27, 39-41, 141, 183
cooking 30-1, 103-18, 107, 217-22
    home cooking 103-18
corn 17
cotton 20-1
crab 39, 41
craupad 46

Creole cuisine and culture 23, 29, 164
crocodile 46
Cuba 15, 17, 21, 23, 25-7, 30, 45-6,
     49, 51, 57, 63, 70, 76, 79-80, 82-
     3, 90, 94, 105-7, 109, 114-7, 122,
     143-59, 185, 193, 195-7, 200-1,
     212-3, *see also* Spanish islands
     under regions
culture 9-36, 110-1
Curaçao 83, 165-76, 182, 203, *see also*
     Dutch islands under regions
curry 26, 49, 133
customs 29-36

D

dancing 121-3
dasheens 49
     callalloo 49, 139
deer 13
dessert 70
dinner 30
dishes, *see also* breads & pastries
     ackee & saltfish 21, 42, 55, 131
     alcapurrias 205
     arañitas 57
     arepas 170
     arroz con pollo 46
     balchi di pisca 176
     banane pesé 57
     bandera dominicana 159
     bolita di keshi 171, 176
     callalloo 49, 139
     cassava bread 64
     chicharrón 159
     chicken pelau 46
     chicken, fried 130
     chicken, pan 130, 207-8
     churros 205
     coco bread 133
     coo-coo 64, 139
     cornbread 64
     doubles 139

empanas 170-1, 176, 195
feroce 54, 164
festival 64
fried chicken 130
fowl down-in-rice 46
fry bake 64
jerk 10, 45, 63, 128, 136-7
johnnycake 29, 31, 64
keshi yená 170, 176
krokechi 176
lechón asado 114-7, 145
macaroni and cheese 130
majarete 205
mannish water 46, 121
manzanas 205
mariquitas 57
mofongo 57, 159
moros y cristianos 47, 109, 143-5
nasi goreng 171
pan chicken 130, 207-8
pate en pot 164
patty 64-7, 131-3
peas & rice 47
pelau chicken 46
phulouri 139
picadillo 147
pollo en salsa 145
roti 23, 65, 139, 221
rundown 31, 133
sancocho 159
sofrito 61, 156-7
sopa de plátano verde 57
souse 130
tamales 59
tembleque 205
ti-malice 164
tortillas 145
tostones 57
yambo 166-7, 195
dolphin fish 39
Dominica 14, 20, 46, 140, 142, *see
     also* English islands under regions

268

Dominican Republic 15, 80, 94, 159, *see also* Spanish islands under regions
Dutch influence 15, 20, 21, *see also* Dutch islands under regions
drinks 31, 71-102, 211-6, *see also* alcoholic drinks, non-alcoholic drinks, coffee, beer, rum, cocktails

E

East Indian influence 23, 26, 47, 49, 65, 126, 133, 139
eddoes 49
El Floridita bar 79, 212-3
emigration 24
English influence 14, 20, 42, 195, *see also* English islands under regions
etiquette 36

F

fast food 27, 203
festivals 128
    carnival 122-3
    Cook Off 128
    Festival of Native Dishes 128
    Fish Festival 128
    Jamaica Spice Festival 128
    yam festival 128
fish 21, 31, 39, 42-3, 55, 64, 133, 176, 179-83, 219, *see also* seafood
    ackee & saltfish 21, 42, 55, 131
    balchi di pisca 176
    cod 21, 39, 42-3, 176
    coo-coo 64, 139
    dolphin fish 39
    flying fish 39
    grouper 39, 219
    kingfish 39
    marlin 39
    rundown 31, 133
    shark 39
    snapper 39
    tuna 39
flavorings 63
flying fish 39
Fort-de-France 160-4, 179, 195
French influence 16, 20, 23, 42, 160-4, *see also* French islands under regions
frog 13
    craupad 46
fruit 51-61
    ackee 21, 55, 131
    apples 21
    avocado 54
    bananas 17, 20-1, 57-61
    breadfruit 55
    christophenes 55
    coconuts 17, 142
    grapefruit 51
    grapes 17
    guava 17, 55
    guinep 51, 186
    limes 17, 51
    mangoes 51, 70
    naseberry 55, 70
    oranges 17
    papaya 54
    peppers 21, 60-1, 156-7
    pineapple 17, 21, 54
    plantains 57-61
    soursop 55, 70
    watermelon 54

G

game 45-6
garlic 63
Georgetown (market, Grenada) 182
ginger 63
goat 17, 26, 46, 121
    mannish water 46, 121
Goldie's restaurant 207
Golding, William 41
grapefruit 51
grapes 17

Grenada 14, 182
Grenadines, *see* St Vincent & the Grenadines
grocery stores 186
grouper 39, 219
grubs 17
Guadeloupe 16, 84, 94, 160-4, 182, *see also* French islands under regions
guava 17, 55
Guevara, Ché 107
guinea pigs 13
guinep 51, 186

H

Hackett, John 211
Haiti 16, 95, 164, 182, *see also* French islands under regions
Hamilton, Edward 80
Havana 26, 30, 79-81, 114-7, 122, 143-50, 185, 193, 195-7, 212-3
health 223-8
    allergies 227
    children 228
    diabetics 227
    diarrhea 227
    heat 225
    water 225
Hemingway, Ernest 212-3
herbs 63
    herbal medicine 173-5
history 11-24, 105-6
    coffee 93
    rum 77-80
home cooking 103-18
Hotchner, AE 213

I

ice cream 70
Iceland 43
iguana 13, 167
indentured servants 23

influences
    African 21-3, 131, 139
    Amerindian 11-6, 20, 23, 39, 46, 49, 63-4, 118, 173
    Chinese 25-6, 47, 126, 139
    Dutch 15, 20, 21
    East Indian 23, 26, 47, 49, 65, 126, 133, 139
    English 14, 20, 42, 195
    French 16, 20, 23, 42, 160-4
    Indonesian 171
    Mexican 27
    Portuguese 42
    Rastafarian 133
    Spanish 13, 15, 17, 23, 45, 47, 143-59
    US 27, 156, 159
    Venezuelan 170
Island Grill restaurant 136
Ital cuisine 133

J

Jaanchi's restaurant 167
Jamaica 10-1, 14, 21, 23, 25-7, 39, 42, 45-7, 51, 55, 59, 60, 63, 70, 73, 79, 80-1, 83-4, 95, 97-9, 121, 128, 131-8, 182, 194, 207-8, *see also* English islands under regions
jerk 10, 45, 63, 128, 136-7

K

Kennedy, President John F 148
kingfish 39
Kingston 131-3, 194, 207-8
Kurlansky, Mark 42

L

La Bodeguita del Medio bar 212-3
lamb 46
language 176, 229-64
    Papiamento 176

INDEX

limes 17, 51
lobster 39, 41
lunch 30

M

malanga 49
mangoes 51, 70
marijuana 133
markets 179-85
    floating market, Curaçao 182
    Georgetown market, Grenada 182
    marché de legumes, Martinique
        179
    Montego market, Jamaica 182
    Pétionville market, Haiti 182
    Plaza del Mercado, Puerto Rico
        182
    Potter's Cay Market, Bahamas
        179-83, 206
    Rio Piedras Market, Puerto Rico
        185
Marley, Bob 133
marlin 39
Martí, José 150
Martinique 10, 16, 29, 43, 46, 64,
    80-1, 84, 93-4, 127, 160-4, 179,
    182, 195, 206, see also French
    islands under regions
Mathieu de Clieu, Captain 93
meat 20, 31, 45-6, 176
    agouti 13
    alligator 13
    beef 17, 21-2, 45-6, 147
    craupad 46
    crocodile 46
    deer 13
    frog 13
    game 45-6
    guinea pigs 13
    iguana 13, 167
    jerk 10, 45, 63, 128, 136-7
    goat 17, 26, 46, 121

lamb 46
mutton 17
opossum 46
rabbit 13
pork 17, 22, 45-6, 114-7, 145,
    159, 164
turtle 13, 46
menus 214-5
Miller, Tom 213
Montego (market, Jamaica) 182
Montserrat 14, 140, see also English
    islands under regions
Mrs Scatliffe's Restaurant 209
music 10, 24, 121-3, 220-1
mutton 17

N

naseberry 55, 70
Nassau 82, 140-1, 179, 183, 195,
    203, 206-7
Nevis, see St Kitts & Nevis
non-alcoholic drinks 89-102, see also
    coffee
    coconut water 90
    cola 90
    fruit juices 90, 213
    health drinks 90
    malta 81
    sno-cones 90-1
    soft drinks 90, 213
    tea 93
    water 89, 225
Norma's 136, 194
nouvelle cuisine 194
nutmeg 63

O

okra 21, 50
olives 17
opossum 46
oranges 17
oregano 63

P

papaya 54
Papiamento culture and language 176
pastries, *see* breads & pastries
peas 47
peas & rice 47
Pétionville (market, Haiti) 182
pepper, black 63
peppers 21, 60-1, 156-7
    pepper sauce 61
picnic 187-9
pineapple 17, 21, 54
pizza 145-7, 195
places to eat & drink 29-31, 72, 164-6,
        191-216, *see also* restaurants
    El Floridita bar 79, 212-3
    Goldie's restaurant 207
    Island Grill restaurant 136
    Jaanchi's restaurant167
    La Bodeguita del Medio bar 212-3
    Mrs Scatliffe's Restaurant 209
    Norma's restaurant 136, 194
    Queen of Sheeba restaurant 133
    Syps cafe 211
    Tasty Patty restaurant 131
plantains 57-61
    arañitas 57
    banane pesé 57
    fried plantains 58
    mariquitas 57
    mofongo 57, 159
    tostones 57
pork 17, 22, 45-6, 114-7, 137, 145,
        159, 164
    chicharrón 159
    lechón asado 114-7, 145
    jerk pork 137
Port of Spain 122-3, 126, 211
potatoes 49
Potter's Cay (market, Bahamas) 179-
        83, 206

poultry 45-6, *see also* chicken
pubs 195
Puerto Rico 15, 17, 27, 41, 43, 61,
        76, 79, 80, 85, 95, 128, 143, 156-
        9, 182, 185, 193-5, 205-6, *see also*
        Spanish islands under regions
pumpkin 50

Q

Queen of Sheeba restaurant 133

R

rabbit 13
Rastafarianism 133
regional variations 129-76
regions 129-76
    Dutch islands 15, 43, 165-76
    English islands 14, 29, 31, 46, 49,
        130-42
    French islands 16, 29, 39, 43,
        160-4
    Spanish islands 15, 39, 41, 43, 46,
        122, 143-59
restaurants 193-203, *see also* places to
        eat & drink
    cheap eateries 203
    joints 203
    mid-range 195
    paladares 197
    pubs 195
    shacks 203
    snak 203
    street food 206-7
    street stalls 186
    upscale 193-4
    vendors 186
rice 21, 47, 159
    arroz con pollo 46
    fowl down-in-rice 46
    moros y cristianos 47, 109, 143-5
    nasi goreng 171

peas & rice 47
rum 20, 63, 70, 77-85, 219
  añejo 79
  Appleton 79
  Appleton Twelve Year Old 80
  Bacardí 79-80
  Bacardí Ocho Años 80
  Barbancourt Five Star 80
  Bermudez Anniversario 80
  Havana Club 79
  history 77-80
  LaFavorite Eight Year Old 80
  Mount Gay 79
  Mount Gay Extra Old 80
  tasting 219
  Wray & Nephew 77-9

S

San Juan 143, 156, 182, 185, 193-4,
  205-6
Santamaria, Mongo 156-7
seafood 11, 26, 39-43, 176, 219, see
  also fish
  conch 27, 39, 40-1, 141, 183
  crab 39, 41
  shellfish 41
  shrimp 39, 41
shellfish 41
shopping 51, 177-90
shark 39
shrimp 39, 41
Sint Maarten 15, see also Dutch
  islands under regions
slavery 21-2
snacks 70
snapper 39
sno-cones 213
sofrito 61, 156-7
soup 46, 50, 57, 121, 159, 164, 167
  mannish water 46, 121
  sancocho 159

sopa de plátano verde 57
soursop 55, 70
space food 157
Spanish influence 13, 15, 17, 23, 45,
  47, 143-59, see also Spanish islands
  under regions
spices 63
squash 21
St Barthélemy 16, see also French
  islands under regions
St Kitts & Nevis 14, 140, see also
  English islands under regions
St Lucia 14, 140, see also English
  islands under regions
St Martin 16, see also French islands
  under regions
St Vincent & the Grenadines 14, 140,
  see also English islands under
  regions
staples 37-70
street food 206-7
street stalls 186
sugarcane 20-1
supermarkets 186
sweet potatoes 49
Syps cafe 211

T

Tasty Patty restaurant 131
tea 93
termites 13
thyme 63
tobacco 20
Trinidad & Tobago 14, 25-6, 65, 73,
  90, 95, 122-3, 126, 139, 211, see
  also English islands under regions
tubers 49
tuna 39
Turks & Caicos Islands 14, 140, see
  also English islands under regions
turtle 13, 46

U

utensils 105, 118

V

Veeris, Dinah 173-5
vegetables
    asparagus 37
    cassava 17, 21, 49, 64
    chives 63
    dasheens 49
    eddoes 49
    malanga 49
    peas 47
    potatoes 49
    pumpkin 50
    squash 21
    sweet potatoes 49
    tubers 49
vegetarians 47, 216
vendors 186
Villapol, Nitza 106-7

W

water 89, 225
watermelon 54
wheat 64
Willemstad 165-70
wine 20, 88, 164

Boxed Text

Arawak Cay, Nassau 207
A Caribbean Love Story 32-3
A Codfish Story 42-3
A Coffee Crusade 211
A RUMble Through the Islands 82
Captain Coffee 93
Caribbean Coffee Tour 94
Carnival 122-3
Celebracion! 114-7
Cigar Etiquette 200-1
Cigars: From Bench to Box 152-5
Creole in Context 23
Don't Miss – The Dutch Islands 172
Don't Miss – The English Islands 138
Don't Miss – The French Islands 161
Don't Miss – The Spanish Islands 151
Eating out in Cuba 196-7
Fabricating a Legend 212-3
Family Day, St Ann's Church, Trinidad 126
Foreign Influences 25-7
Friday Night: Red Hill Road, Kingston, Jamaica 208
Austin Clarke – Guest Interview 110-1
Lunch of the Iguana 167
Markets of the Caribbean 182
Mi Ta Tuma Pida Keshi ... 176
Mrs Scatliffe's Restaurant 209
Okonorote & the Land of Walking Animals 13
Origin & Influence 14-6
Paradise Has a Well-Stocked Humidor 148-50
Pass the Dutchie 100-2
Promenade in Puerto Rico 205
Puerto Rico Space Food 157
Roots by the Sea 142
Seafood Alfresco 40
Sunday Afternoon, Coffee Country 97-9
The Bold Palate 46
The Herbalist: Dinah Veeris 173-5
The Inimitable Nitza Villapol 107
The Jerk 136
What Did Marley Eat for Breakfast 133

Recipes
Bahama Mama 82
Baked Grouper 219
Borinquen 85
Café Carib 83
Cuba Libre 82
Daiquiri 82
Fried Plantains 58
Hurricane Leah 83
Jamaican Crawler 83
Jerk Pork 137
Johnnycake 31

Mai Tai 84
Mojito 83
Moros y Cristianos 109
Patties 67
Picadillo 147
Pina Colada 85
Planter's Punch 84
Roti 221
Sofrito 156
Ti Punch 84

Maps
Caribbean 6
Dutch Islands 172
English Islands 138
Fort-de-France 160
French Islands 161
Havana 145

Kingston 132
Map Key 2
Nassau 140
Spanish Islands 151
Willemstad 166

ESSENTIALS

Read This First books help new travellers to hit the road with confidence. These invaluable predeparture guides give step-by-step advice on preparing for a trip, budgeting, arranging a visa, planning an itinerary and staying safe while still getting off the beaten track.

Healthy Travel pocket guides offer a regional rundown on disease hot spots and practical advice on predeparture health measures, staying well on the road and what to do in emergencies. The guides come with a user-friendly design and helpful diagrams and tables.

Lonely Planet's **Phrasebooks** cover the essential words and phrases travellers need when they're strangers in a strange land. They come in a pocket-sized format with colour tabs for quick reference, extensive vocabulary lists, easy-to-follow pronunciation keys and two-way dictionaries.

Miffed by blurry photos of the Taj Mahal? Tired of the classic 'top of the head cut off' shot? **Travel Photography: A Guide to Taking Better Pictures** will help you turn ordinary holiday snaps into striking images and give you the know-how to capture every scene, from frenetic festivals to peaceful beach sunrises.

Lonely Planet's **Travel Journal** is a lightweight but sturdy travel diary for jotting down all those on-the-road observations and significant travel moments. It comes with a handy time-zone wheel, a world map and useful travel information.

Lonely Planet's eKno is an all-in-one communication service developed especially for travellers. It offers low-cost international calls and free email and voicemail so that you can keep in touch while on the road.
Check it out on **www.ekno.lonelyplanet.com**

ON THE ROAD

Travel Guides explore cities, regions and countries, and supply information on transport, restaurants and accommodation, covering all budgets. They come with reliable, easy-to-use maps, practical advice, cultural and historical facts and a rundown on attractions both on and off the beaten track. There are over 200 titles in this classic series, covering nearly every country in the world.

 Lonely Planet Upgrades extend the shelf life of existing travel guides by detailing any changes that may affect travel in a region since a book has been published. Upgrades can be downloaded for free from **www.lonelyplanet.com/upgrades**

For travellers with more time than money, **Shoestring** guides offer dependable, first-hand information with hundreds of detailed maps, plus insider tips for stretching money as far as possible. Covering entire continents in most cases, the six-volume shoestring guides are known around the world as 'backpackers bibles'.

For the discerning short-term visitor, **Condensed** guides highlight the best a destination has to offer in a full-colour, pocket-sized format designed for quick access. They include everything from top sights and walking tours to opinionated reviews of where to eat, stay, shop and have fun.

CitySync lets travellers use their PalmTM or VisorTM hand-held computers to guide them through a city with handy tips on transport, history, cultural life, major sights, and shopping and entertainment options. It can also quickly search and sort hundreds of reviews of hotels, restaurants and attractions, and pinpoint their location on scrollable street maps. CitySync can be downloaded from **www.citysync.com**

Guides by Region

Lonely Planet is known worldwide for publishing practical, reliable and no-nonsense travel information in our guides and on our Web site. The Lonely Planet list covers just about every accessible part of the world. Currently there are 16 series: Travel guides, Shoestring guides, Condensed guides, Phrasebooks, Read This First, Healthy Travel, Walking guides, Cycling guides, Watching Wildlife guides, Pisces Diving & Snorkeling guides, City Maps, Road Atlases, Out to Eat, World Food, Journeys travel literature and Pictorials.

AFRICA Africa on a shoestring • Cairo • Cairo City Map • Cape Town • Cape Town City Map • East Africa • Egypt • Egyptian Arabic phrasebook • Ethiopia, Eritrea & Djibouti • Ethiopian Amharic phrasebook • The Gambia & Senegal • Healthy Travel Africa • Kenya • Malawi • Morocco • Moroccan Arabic phrasebook • Mozambique • Read This First: Africa • South Africa, Lesotho & Swaziland • Southern Africa • Southern Africa Road Atlas • Swahili phrasebook • Tanzania, Zanzibar & Pemba • Trekking in East Africa • Tunisia • Watching Wildlife East Africa • Watching Wildlife Southern Africa • West Africa • World Food Morocco • Zimbabwe, Botswana & Namibia • **Travel Literature:** Mali Blues: Traveling to an African Beat • The Rainbird: A Central African Journey • Songs to an African Sunset: A Zimbabwean Story

AUSTRALIA & THE PACIFIC Auckland • Australia • Australian phrasebook • Australia Road Atlas • Cycling Australia • Cycling New Zealand • Fiji • Fijian phrasebook • Healthy Travel Australia, NZ & the Pacific • Islands of Australia's Great Barrier Reef • Melbourne • Melbourne City Map • Micronesia • New Caledonia • New South Wales • New Zealand • Northern Territory • Outback Australia • Out to Eat – Melbourne • Out to Eat – Sydney • Papua New Guinea • Pidgin phrasebook • Queensland • Rarotonga & the Cook Islands • Samoa • Solomon Islands • South Australia • South Pacific • South Pacific phrasebook • Sydney • Sydney City Map • Sydney Condensed • Tahiti & French Polynesia • Tasmania • Tonga • Tramping in New Zealand • Vanuatu • Victoria • Walking in Australia • Watching Wildlife Australia • Western Australia • **Travel Literature:** Islands in the Clouds: Travels in the Highlands of New Guinea • Kiwi Tracks: A New Zealand Journey • Sean & David's Long Drive

CENTRAL AMERICA & THE CARIBBEAN Bahamas, Turks & Caicos • Baja California • Belize, Guatemala & Yucatán • Bermuda • Central America on a shoestring • Costa Rica • Costa Rica Spanish phrasebook • Cuba • Dominican Republic & Haiti • Eastern Caribbean • Guatemala • Havana • Healthy Travel Central & South America • Jamaica • Mexico • Mexico City • Panama • Puerto Rico • Read This First: Central & South America • World Food Mexico • Yucatán • **Travel Literature:** Green Dreams: Travels in Central America

Guides by Region

EUROPE Amsterdam • Amsterdam City Map • Amsterdam Condensed • Andalucía • Austria • Baltic States phrasebook • Barcelona • Barcelona City Map • Belgium & Luxembourg • Berlin • Berlin City Map • Britain • British phrasebook • Brussels, Bruges & Antwerp • Brussels City Map • Budapest • Budapest City Map • Canary Islands • Central Europe • Central Europe phrasebook • Copenhagen • Corfu & the Ionians • Corsica • Crete • Crete Condensed • Croatia • Cycling Britain • Cycling France • Cyprus • Czech & Slovak Republics • Denmark • Dublin • Dublin City Map • Eastern Europe • Eastern Europe phrasebook • Edinburgh • England • Estonia, Latvia & Lithuania • Europe on a shoestring • Europe phrasebook • Finland • Florence • France • Frankfurt Condensed • French phrasebook • Georgia, Armenia & Azerbaijan • Germany • German phrasebook • Greece • Greek Islands • Greek phrasebook • Hungary • Iceland, Greenland & the Faroe Islands • Ireland • Italian phrasebook • Italy • Krakow • Lisbon • The Loire • London • London City Map • London Condensed • Madrid • Malta • Mediterranean Europe • Mediterranean Europe phrasebook • Moscow • Munich • Netherlands • Normandy • Norway • Out to Eat – London • Out to Eat – Paris • Paris • Paris City Map • Paris Condensed • Poland • Polish phrasebook • Portugal • Portuguese phrasebook • Prague • Prague City Map • Provence & the Côte d'Azur • Read This First: Europe • Rhodes & the Dodecanese • Romania & Moldova • Rome • Rome City Map • Russia, Ukraine & Belarus • Russian phrasebook • Scandinavian & Baltic Europe • Scandinavian phrasebook • Scotland • Sicily • Slovenia • South-West France • Spain • Spanish phrasebook • St Petersburg • St Petersburg City Map • Sweden • Switzerland • Tuscany • Ukrainian phrasebook • Venice • Vienna • Walking in Britain • Walking in France • Walking in Ireland • Walking in Italy • Walking in Spain • Walking in Switzerland • Western Europe • World Food France • World Food Ireland • World Food Italy • World Food Spain • **Travel Literature:** After Yugoslavia • Love and War in the Apennines • The Olive Grove: Travels in Greece • On the Shores of the Mediterranean • Round Ireland in Low Gear • A Small Place in Italy

INDIAN SUBCONTINENT & THE INDIAN OCEAN Bangladesh • Bengali phrasebook • Bhutan • Delhi • Goa • Healthy Travel Asia & India • Hindi & Urdu phrasebook • India • Indian Himalaya • Karakoram Highway • Kerala • Madagascar • Maldives • Mauritius, Réunion & Seychelles • Mumbai (Bombay) • Nepal • Nepali phrasebook • Pakistan • Rajasthan • Read This First: Asia & India • South India • Sri Lanka • Sri Lanka phrasebook • Tibet • Tibetan phrasebook • Trekking in the Indian Himalaya • Trekking in the Karakoram & Hindukush • Trekking in the Nepal Himalaya • **Travel Literature:** The Age of Kali: Indian Travels and Encounters • Hello Goodnight: A Life of Goa • In Rajasthan • Maverick in Madagascar • A Season in Heaven: True Tales from the Road to Kathmandu • Shopping for Buddhas • A Short Walk in the Hindu Kush • Slowly Down the Ganges

Guides by Region

MIDDLE EAST & CENTRAL ASIA Bahrain, Kuwait & Qatar • Central Asia • Central Asia phrasebook • Dubai • Farsi (Persian) phrasebook • Hebrew phrasebook • Iran • Israel & the Palestinian Territories • Istanbul • Istanbul City Map • Istanbul to Cairo • Istanbul to Kathmandu • Jerusalem • Jerusalem City Map • Jordan • Lebanon • Middle East • Oman & the United Arab Emirates • Syria • Turkey • Turkish phrasebook • World Food Turkey • Yemen • **Travel Literature:** Black on Black: Iran Revisited • The Gates of Damascus • Kingdom of the Film Stars: Journey into Jordan

NORTH AMERICA Alaska • Boston • Boston City Map • Boston Condensed • British Columbia • California & Nevada • California Condensed • Canada • Chicago • Chicago City Map • Florida • Great Lakes • Hawaii • Hiking in Alaska • Hiking in the USA • Las Vegas • Los Angeles • Los Angeles City Map • Louisiana & the Deep South • Miami • Miami City Map • Montreal • New England • New Orleans • New York City • New York City City Map • New York City Condensed • New York, New Jersey & Pennsylvania • Oahu • Out to Eat – San Francisco • Pacific Northwest • Rocky Mountains • San Francisco • San Francisco City Map • Seattle • Southwest • Texas • Toronto • USA • USA phrasebook • Vancouver • Virginia & the Capital Region • Washington, DC • Washington, DC City Map • World Food New Orleans • **Travel Literature**: Caught Inside: A Surfer's Year on the California Coast • Drive Thru America

NORTH-EAST ASIA Beijing • Beijing City Map • Cantonese phrasebook • China • Hiking in Japan • Hong Kong • Hong Kong City Map • Hong Kong Condensed • Hong Kong, Macau & Guangzhou • Japan • Japanese phrasebook • Korea • Korean phrasebook • Kyoto • Mandarin phrasebook • Mongolia • Mongolian phrasebook • Seoul • Shanghai • South-West China • Taiwan • Tokyo • World Food Hong Kong • **Travel Literature:** In Xanadu: A Quest • Lost Japan

SOUTH-EAST ASIA Bali & Lombok • Bangkok • Bangkok City Map • Burmese phrasebook • Cambodia • Hanoi • Healthy Travel Asia & India • Hill Tribes phrasebook • Ho Chi Minh City • Indonesia • Indonesian phrasebook • Indonesia's Eastern Islands • Java • Lao phrasebook • Laos • Malay phrasebook • Malaysia, Singapore & Brunei • Myanmar (Burma) • Philippines • Pilipino (Tagalog) phrasebook • Read This First: Asia & India • Singapore • Singapore City Map • South-East Asia on a shoestring • South-East Asia phrasebook • Thailand • Thailand's Islands & Beaches • Thailand, Vietnam, Laos & Cambodia Road Atlas • Thai phrasebook • Vietnam • Vietnamese phrasebook • World Food Thailand • World Food Vietnam

Mail Order

Lonely Planet products are distributed worldwide. They are also available by mail order from Lonely Planet, so if you have difficulty finding a title please write to us. North and South American residents should write to 150 Linden St, Oakland, CA 94607, USA; European and African residents should write to 10a Spring Place, London NW5 3BH, UK; and residents of other countries to Locked Bag 1, Footscray, Victoria 3011, Australia.

SOUTH AMERICA Argentina, Uruguay & Paraguay • Bolivia • Brazil • Brazilian phrasebook • Buenos Aires • Chile & Easter Island • Colombia • Ecuador & the Galapagos Islands • Healthy Travel Central & South America • Latin American Spanish phrasebook • Peru • Quechua phrasebook • Read This First: Central & South America • Rio de Janeiro • Rio de Janeiro City Map • Santiago de Chile • South America on a shoestring • Trekking in the Patagonian Andes • Venezuela • **Travel Literature**: Full Circle: A South American Journey

ALSO AVAILABLE: Antarctica • The Arctic • The Blue Man: Tales of Travel, Love and Coffee • Brief Encounters: Stories of Love, Sex & Travel • Chasing Rickshaws • The Last Grain Race • Lonely Planet ... On the Edge: Adventurous Escapades from Around the World • Lonely Planet Unpacked • Not the Only Planet: Science Fiction Travel Stories • Sacred India • Travel Photography: A Guide to Taking Better Pictures • Travel with Children

OUT TO EAT SERIES

Packed with independent, unstuffy opinion on hundreds of hand-picked restaurants, bars and cafes in each city, Lonely Planet's Out to Eat guides take food seriously but offer a fresh approach. Along with reviews, each Out to Eat identifies the best culinary cul-de-sacs, explores favourite ethnic cuisines, and the food trends that define each city. They also serve up the nitty-gritty on dish prices, wheelchair access and other useful facts with each review, and all include useful quick-scan indexes.

Updated annually, Out to Eat titles cover:
Melbourne, Sydney, London, Paris & San Francisco

MAPS & ATLASES

Lonely Planet's **City Maps** feature downtown and metropolitan maps, as well as transit routes and walking tours. The maps come complete with an index of streets, a listing of sights and a plastic coat for extra durability.

Road Atlases are an essential navigation tool for serious travellers. Cross-referenced with the guidebooks, they also feature distance and climate charts and a complete site index.

PLANET TALK

Our FREE quarterly printed newsletter is full of tips from travellers and anecdotes from Lonely Planet guidebook authors. Every issue is packed with up-to-date travel news and advice, and includes:

* a postcard from Lonely Planet co-founder Tony Wheeler
* a swag of mail from travellers
* a look at life on the road through the eyes of a Lonely Planet author
* topical health advice
* prizes for the best travel yarn
* news about forthcoming Lonely Planet events
* a complete list of Lonely Planet books and other titles

To join our mailing list, residents of the UK, Europe and Africa can email us at go@lonelyplanet.co.uk; residents of North and South America can do so at info@lonelyplanet.com; the rest of the world can email talk2us@lonelyplanet.com.au, or contact any Lonely Planet office.

MORE WORLD FOOD TITLES

Brimming with cultural insight, the World Food series takes the guesswork out of new cuisines and provides the ideal guide to your own culinary adventures. These books cover the full spectrum of food and drink in each country - the history and evolution of the cuisine, its staples & specialities, and the kitchen philosophy of the people. You'll find definitive two-way dictionaries, menu readers , useful phrases for shopping , drunken apologies, and much more.

The World Food series is the essential guide for travelling and non-travelling food lovers across the globe.

The Lonely Planet Story

Lonely Planet published its first book in 1973 in response to the numerous 'How did you do it?' questions Maureen and Tony Wheeler were asked after driving, bussing, hitching, sailing and railing their way from England to Australia. Written at a kitchen table and hand collated, trimmed and stapled, Across Asia on the Cheap became an instant local bestseller.

Eighteen months in South-East Asia resulted in their second guide, South-East Asia on a Shoestring, which they put together in a backstreet Chinese hotel in Singapore in 1975. The 'yellow bible', as it quickly became known to backpackers around the world, soon became the guide to the region. It has sold well over ¾ million copies and is now in its 10th edition, still retaining its familiar yellow cover.

Today there are over 400 titles, including travel guides, walking guides, language kits & phrasebooks, travel atlases & maps, diving guides, restaurant guides, first time travel guides, condensed guides, illustrated pictorials and travel literature. The company is the largest independent travel publisher in the world.

The emphasis continues to be on travel for independent travellers. Tony and Maureen still travel for several months of each year and play an active part in the writing, updating and quality control of Lonely Planet's guides.

They have been joined by over 120 authors and over 400 staff at our offices in Melbourne (Australia), Oakland (USA), London (UK) and Paris (France). Travellers themselves also make a valuable contribution to the guides through the feedback we receive in thousands of letters each year and on our web site.

The people at Lonely Planet strongly believe that travellers can make a positive contribution to the countries they visit, both through their appreciation of the countries' culture, wildlife and natural features, and through the money they spend. In addition, the company makes a direct contribution to the countries and regions it covers. Since 1986 a percentage of the income from each book has been donated to ventures such as famine relief in Africa; aid projects in India; agricultural projects in Central America; Greenpeace's efforts to halt French nuclear testing in the Pacific.

Lonely Planet Offices

Australia
90 Maribyrnong Street Footscray, Victoria, 3011
☎ 03 8379 8000
fax 03 8379 8111
email: talk2us@lonelyplanet.com.au

USA
150 Linden St, Oakland, CA 94607
☎ 510 893 8555 TOLL FREE: 800 275 8555
fax 510 893 8572
email: info@lonelyplanet.com

UK
10a Spring Place, London NW5 3BH
☎ 020 7428 4800
fax 020 7428 4828
email: go@lonelyplanet.co.uk

France
1 rue du Dahomey, 75011 Paris
☎ 01 55 25 33 00
fax 01 55 25 33 01
email: bip@lonelyplanet.fr